PRIVACY IN THE INFORMATION AGE

LIBRARY IN A BOOK

PRIVACY IN THE INFORMATION AGE

Harry Henderson

☑®

Facts On File, Inc.

PRIVACY IN THE INFORMATION AGE

Facts On File, Inc.
11 Penn Plaza
New York NY 10001

Library of Congress Cataloging-in-Publication Data

Henderson, Harry, 1951–.
   Privacy in the information age / Harry Henderson.
     p. cm.—(Library in a book)
   Includes bibliographical references (p.) and index.
   ISBN 0-8160-3870-8 (alk. paper)
   1. Privacy, Right of—United States. 2. Data protection—Law and legislation—United States. I. Title. II. Series.
   KF1263.C65H46 1999
   323.44'8'072073—dc 21   99-21572

Facts On File books are available at special discounts when purchased in bulk quantities for businesses, associations, institutions, or sales promotions. Please call our Special Sales Department in New York at 212/967-8800 or 800/322-8755.

You can find Facts On File on the World Wide Web at http://www.factsonfile.com

Text design by Ron Monteleone

Printed in the United States of America

MP FOF 10 9 8 7 6 5 4 3 2 1

This book is printed on acid-free paper.

To my brother, Bruce Henderson, 1953–1997,

Computer pioneer, techie supreme, and all-around family person

CONTENTS

———————————

PRIVACY IN THE INFORMATION AGE

PART I

OVERVIEW OF THE TOPIC

CHAPTER 1

INTRODUCTION TO PRIVACY IN THE INFORMATION AGE

Privacy has been described as "the claim of individuals, groups, or institutions to determine for themselves when, how, and to what extent information about themselves is communicated to others."[1]

The right to privacy has not always been very important. In the Middle Ages (and indeed, in many tribal societies around the world), people generally lived together as extended families under one roof (often in one room). The idea of a person having a private bedroom was virtually unknown. Under such circumstances, there was little that one individual didn't learn about another. On the other hand, there was little need to keep track of details about individuals outside of the immediate group. Written records were not generally kept, except perhaps for the church's records of birth, marriage, and death, and the charters of nobles' holdings. Rulers generally had little interest in the details of the lives of ordinary people.

However, the Industrial Revolution that began in the late 18th century created a tidal wave of change in living conditions for people in Britain and Western Europe. It brought thousands of people together to work in factories and offices in huge, teeming cities. As increasing numbers of people began to change from a rural, subsistent, agricultural way of life to urban wage labor, families tended to break from extended families into smaller units. A young person who left a rural home in search of work in the city, or even a couple that married and raised a "nuclear" family, was likely to fall out of touch with the extended family.

This more mobile but in some ways more isolated life created new social needs. The medieval world had imposed rigid social classes but offered some security in providing everyone with a well-defined status, a "place in life." The industrial world and the growth of the middle class broke down rigid barriers and offered new opportunities for upward mobility, but it also created

3

insecurity as people from different backgrounds and with different customs were thrown together and had to find ways to live comfortably with one another. The need to enable individuals and families to establish boundaries of personal space found expression in the idea of a right to privacy. For example, the act of visiting another person's home became more ritualized, and wealthier people started to devote a special guest room in their house for such visits.

At the same time people were starting to define new social customs that protected privacy, the political philosophy of thinkers such as John Locke was starting to emphasize the rights and even the sovereignty of the individual in interaction with the government. Eighteenth century British statesman William Pitt declared in a speech before Parliament that

> *The poorest man may, in his cottage, bid defiance to all the forces of the Crown. It may be frail, its roof may shake; the wind may blow through it; the storm may enter; the rain may enter; but the King of England may not enter; all his force dares not cross the threshold of the ruined tenement.*[2]

In the medieval world, rights were attached to social status (most of the rights in the British Magna Carta of 1215, for example, referred to the nobility, not the common people). In the emerging new nation-states of the industrial world, however, rights were attached to a universal citizenship and (theoretically at least) did not depend on social class.

The modern nation-states that emerged in Europe by the mid-19th century began to develop central governments that concerned themselves with many matters that were formerly considered private and local. Germany under Bismarck, for example, developed a national social welfare system. The drafting of large citizen armies also required the registration, training, and tracking of millions of citizens as potential soldiers. The science of statistics began to be used to evaluate economic conditions and to plan national policies. By 1890, the U.S. census was using electromechanical tabulating machines and punch cards not merely to count the populace, but to keep track of the number of people in dozens of categories such as occupation, income, and ethnicity. The growing amount of information-gathering was still largely invisible to the ordinary citizen, however, and so did not arouse much concern about threats to privacy.

A CULTURAL PERSPECTIVE

This chapter began with a rather legalistic definition of privacy. But while privacy issues may ultimately be decided by politics and law, understanding why privacy is important to people—and how they think about it—requires an exploration of culture and psychology. From the point of view of the individual, "The right to privacy includes a sense of autonomy, a right to develop a unique personality and living space, and a right to distinguish one's own persona from everyone else's."[3] But this is a sentence that would have made little sense more than a couple hundred years ago.

Just as lines in a geometric polygon define an inside and an outside, the existence of a sense of self is what gives rise to the idea that some things are interior, personal, and private, while others are public, belonging to the world as a whole. To modern society, it seems quite obvious that people have an inside and an outside—and that protecting and nurturing what's inside is of special concern. But when one looks at the literature and art our ancestors have left for us, it seems that the emergence of the modern sense of self was a gradual process. As one literary scholar has noted:

> . . . *Medieval literature knew almost nothing of individual personality: its introspection proceeded along rigidly casuistic [formally logical] lines. During the Renaissance subjectivity began to stir, particularly in dramatic literature, where the feelings associated with decisions were displayed, and in sonnets, which did much to explore one range of private emotions. The 17th century epigram did more. And the inquiries of Burton and Browne (in their very different ways) enlarged the possibility of self-consciousness. But it was only in the 18th century that literature made a sustained attempt to express the individual feelings of those with the leisure to discover themselves.*[4]

As art and literature began to depict the world in more realistic detail, the textures of individual personalities became a major focus of novels such as those of Jane Austen. Turning toward the 19th century, the Romantic poets, such as Wordsworth, Coleridge, and Blake, looked at universal ideas through the bright, sharply focused light of the individual imagination.

While few people in the early 1800s had the leisure or talent to become popular poets or novelists, the new focus on the self in high culture reached middle-class readers who could participate through the fashionable new practice of keeping a diary, a private space in which one could assess one's daily experience, and express one's hopes and fears.

SCIENTIFIC REVOLUTIONS: REDEFINING THE INDIVIDUAL

The assertion of the importance of the individual personality took place against a background that would become familiar for the next two centuries:

the seemingly inexorable Industrial Revolution and the impact of technological change on society. Technology and industrialization threatened to turn emerging selves into interchangeable parts of some great machine.

In America, a land that celebrated both limitless growth and individual freedom, Henry Thoreau retreated to the woods, and Ralph Waldo Emerson protested that "Society everywhere is in conspiracy against the manhood of every one of its members. . . . The virtue in most request [demand] is conformity. Self-reliance is its aversion. It loves not realities and creators, but names and customs."[5] This restated the Romantic vision: the creative power of the individual versus the deadening power of conformity and "custom." In America, the apparent boundlessness of the land could postpone the regimentation that would characterize emerging European states such as Prussia in the latter part of the 19th century.

But the autonomy of the self was also being challenged by new developments in science. The Newtonian explanation of the mechanics of the universe had already led to the suggestion that if the paths of planets could be predicted by exact mathematics, perhaps nature and human life itself were equally determined by a clockwork-like interaction of forces. (And thus, the Romantic poet William Blake turned Isaac Newton into a demonic figure of fearful power.)

At first, the incredible complexity of biology seemed to resist mechanistic explanations. It took Louis Pasteur to demonstrate that even microscopic life always came from preceding life, rather than being generated from some mysterious "vital force." Later, Charles Darwin introduced his elegant and powerful explanation of evolution by natural selection. When Darwin examined the "human animal" and its position in the scheme of all things, he concluded that

> *The great difference in mind between men and the higher animals . . . is certainly one of degree and not of kind. The senses and institutions, the various emotions and faculties, such as love, memory, attention, curiosity, imitation, reason, etc., of which man boasts, may be found in an incipient, or sometimes in a well-developed condition, in the lower animals.[6]*

In the 20th century, thoughtful people would find ways to see evolution in less simplistic terms, and to suggest that human consciousness, far from being an unimportant add-on to the human animal, instead might begin to drive evolution itself. But in its early years, Darwinism seemed to be undermining the possibilities of human uniqueness, and thus the importance of an inner self.

The other two great explainers of the 19th century scientific revolution were Karl Marx and Sigmund Freud. Marx attempted to demonstrate that the conditions of human life and culture arise not from the individual will, but from inexorable historical forces: One might say that at least in the things that mattered, people did not make history, history made people. In this view, the inner self was peripheral, not primary.

Freud, on the one hand, made the private self more, not less important. He made dream interpretation, free association, and the systematic examination of memories and feelings the key to freeing the individual from mental illness. But on the other hand, Freud, like Darwin and Marx, was a determinist: He said that human behavior was determined by forces of which the individual was usually unconscious—forces that acted according to laws not unlike the hydraulic behavior of fluids. While exploring the private self was given new importance, its privacy, its harmful secrecy, would be seen as a barrier that was to be pierced by the light of analysis. (Later, 20th-century behavioral psychology would attempt to dispense with the inner world entirely, working directly on observable behavior through stimulus, response, and reinforcement.)

The Victorian individual lived in a world of rapidly growing complexity. Science and technology offered explanations and new capabilities—even new leisure for some people to explore their private selves. But science and technology also threatened to make the self obsolete or irrelevant—and perhaps to annihilate privacy.

THE ALL-SEEING EYE

Around the turn of the 19th century, a British social critic and philosopher named Jeremy Bentham developed a theory of utilitarianism, which viewed life as a kind of balance sheet of pleasure and pain. For Bentham, the object of a scientific, rational society was to maximize the former and minimize the latter, crafting social policies that would create "the greatest happiness for the greatest number."

For the reformation of individuals who broke the laws designed to secure their happiness, Bentham designed a new kind of prison that he called the "Panopticon." This circular prison would carefully be designed so that its inmates could be watched everywhere and at every moment by guards who themselves could not be seen. Apparently Bentham thought that a prisoner who *could* always be seen and thus, at any time, *might* be under observation, would have no choice but to behave "rationally" and gradually be reformed into being a productive, happy citizen.

No Panopticons were ever built, but just as 19th century science began to put the self into troubling new perspectives, 19th and early 20th century technology would change what it would mean to hear and be heard, see and be seen. The telephone, introduced in 1876, seemed magical at first, but soon became indispensable. The ability to talk to people without meeting them made it possible to sustain a much larger web of business and social relationships at a much faster pace then the daily rounds of the mail carrier.

But besides being disembodied, phone conversations were not necessarily under the sole control of their participants. "The mere *possibility* that unknown and unseen agents are bugging your line is enough to puncture the psychological intimacy afforded by a phone call, transforming your humble handset into an insidious tentacle of unwanted and invisible powers."[7] And as early as the late 1870s, Bell's assistant, Thomas Watson, was confronted by a man who was convinced that enemies had connected his brain to a telephone circuit so they could implant fiendish suggestions. (Each new technology seems to offer an image to be seized by paranoids: later, they would wear tin foil hats to block mind-control radio waves; recently, some have claimed that they are under the control of implanted computer chips.)

Until the 1930s, though, most people who were not spies or gangsters—or paranoids—didn't spend much time worrying about phone tapping. But the powerful new totalitarian systems of fascism and communism used the telephone to pierce privacy and coordinate oppression, and used the invention of broadcasting—the radio—to try to mold opinion on a vast scale. World War II demonstrated weapons of unparalleled physical destructiveness, but it also demonstrated the effectiveness of technology of social control.

In 1948, George Orwell wrote the famous novel *1984*, which seemed to be the summation of all that people had learned to fear about the use of technology to destroy liberty. In Orwell's world, a still newer technology, television, would realize the Panoptic vision. No citizen would escape the eye of Big Brother. Even the idea of having a self separate from Big Brother becomes "thoughtcrime."

Indeed, this ultimate dictatorship aimed not merely to punish such crime, but to make it impossible. As *1984*'s protagonist Winston Smith is informed, the medium of television would be used to mold minds through a specially designed language, Newspeak:

> *Don't you see that the whole aim of Newspeak is to narrow the range of thought? In the end we shall make thoughtcrime literally impossible, because there will be no words in which to express it. Every concept that can ever be needed, will be expressed in exactly one word, with its meaning rigidly defined and all its subsidiary meanings rubbed out and forgotten. . . . The whole climate of thought will be different. In fact there will be not thought, as we understand it now. Orthodoxy means not thinking—not needing to think. Orthodoxy is unconsciousness.*[8]

And in the world of Big Brother, privacy cannot exist because without consciousness, there is no sense of self.

MEDIA, MAINFRAMES, AND POPULAR CULTURE

Today, with the year well past 1984, Orwell's totalitarianism seems to be as primitive and simplistic as the huge public works beloved by the leaders of the defunct Soviet Union. The "telescreen" indeed became ubiquitous, but it showed not Big Brother, but *I Love Lucy* and the resplendent wonders of modern kitchen appliances.

Social critics of the 1950s and 1960s began to see the threat to the individual as coming, not from the focused propaganda of a Big Brother, but from the pressures for conformity in the corporate workplace and at home, in the relentless display of TV commercials. Privacy can be threatened overtly by police raids, covertly by phone taps and hidden cameras. Now came a warning that privacy could be threatened more insidiously, by homogenizing the individual, masking the unique inner self with a bland construct of images and desires. If privacy depends on identity, loss of any unique identity would make privacy irrelevant. (The 1998 movie *Pleasantville* uses the metaphor of color versus black-and-white to portray a rebellion against the conformist 1950s world.)

"The Big Brother Society that was imagined in 1970," one critic notes, "depended on coercion and fear. The society we are developing now appears to be more [Aldous] Huxley-like than Orwellian. It is a Brave New World dominated not so much by tyranny as by a deadening political and cultural phenomenon that Ralph Nader calls 'harmony ideology.' "[9] Linguist and radical critic Noam Chomsky refers to this phenomenon as "the manufacture of consent." In other words, people are given a superficial individuality (defined mainly by possessions and lifestyle), and an illusion of having an inner self.

Many TV viewers came to internalize the lives portrayed on the screen, thinking of characters like Dharma and Greg much in the way one would think of an interesting couple that lived next door. Critics argue that TV creates an enticing substitute for real community:

> *The TV audience may be, today, the most pervasive type of social community, but if this is so then it is a very special type of community:* an anticommunity or a *social antimatter—electronically composed, rhetorically constituted, an electronic mall which privileges the psychological position of the voyeur (a society of the disembodied eye) and the cultural position of* us *as tourists in the society of the spectacle.*[10]

Perhaps the Teletubbies, alternately charming and disturbing, represent the ultimate absorption of the viewer/consumer into the television screen. After all, these strange beings have literally assimilated TV, with sets in their tummies and antennae coming out of their heads. What's more, they exist in a strange hybrid landscape of merged natural and artificial elements, where protruding electronic devices emerge from the ground and emit programming.

The media, and TV in particular, have come under intense public criticism in recent years. Whether it was the O.J. Simpson spectacle, the endless coverage of Princess Diana's death and funeral, or the Clinton sex and impeachment story, people seem to increasingly see the media as an out of control threat to privacy rather than as a platform for crusading journalists to hold secretive governments and corporations accountable. Perhaps people who identify with beleaguered celebrities are vicariously experiencing their own concern about their privacy as they worry about personal information being stolen by criminals or diverted, sold, or abused by institutions such as insurance companies, stores, and government agencies.

Accompanying television as postwar high tech, the mainframe computer was also seen as an ominous threat to individuality. Science-fiction writers began to visualize Big Brother in a new guise as the ultimate computer. (As the joke went: when the huge room-filling computer was asked "Is there a God?," it blinked and whirred a while and then announced, "There is one *now*.")

Computers of the 1950s and early 1960s had several characteristics that encouraged such a perception: they were large, their method of operation was unknown to most people, they were tended by a white-garbed "priesthood" of operators, and they were too expensive for anyone except big corporations and the government. The punch card became a symbol of an individual life reduced to a pattern of holes.

The three big TV networks and IBM thus became emblems of a power that dazzled and disturbed, promised and threatened, seeming to point at the same time to the ultimate in modern lifestyle and an emptying out of the inner self. TV seemed to replace the stuff of life with manufactured images. The computer might steal privacy by turning the uniqueness of life into mere data. But the technology would prove to be much more fertile than the doomsayers could imagine.

POSTMODERNISM, CYBERSPACE, AND VIRTUAL COMMUNITIES

The 1960s (now fading into the realm of nostalgia) brought a new rebellion against the idea of the machine society. As the British Romantic poets and Thoreau had rejected the "dark, Satanic mills" of incipient industry, the counterculture rejected both the computerized, managerial State and the blandishments of consumerism on TV. But the rebellion did not reject technology entirely: indeed, it was fueled by electric guitars, a growing sophistication in electronic sound and visual effects, and hallucinogenic chemistry.

As 1960s activism seemed to hit a political dead end by the early 1970s, exploration of spiritual disciplines or alternative lifestyles appealed to many young people. But one loosely knit group of explorers and activists were more technological than most of their countercultural cousins. They were seeking not to destroy the computer, but to reinvent it. Their name for themselves, "hackers," today has come to mean people who break into computer systems to destroy them or to steal valuable information.

Originally, though, the hackers were brilliant, albeit obsessive programmers who took the new generation of smaller "minicomputers" like the PDP series and taught them amazing new tricks such as playing space war games or creating electronic music. By the early 1970s, they began to play with the newly invented microprocessor, building primitive desktop computers—and thinking about their revolutionary possibilities.

In 1974, when the microprocessor was still just something for electronic hobbyists to play with, the visionary Ted Nelson proposed ". . . a screen in your home from which you can see into the world's hypertext libraries . . . offer high-performance computer graphics and text services at a price anyone can afford . . . allow you to send and receive written messages . . . [and] make you a part of a new electronic literature and art, where you can get all your questions answered . . ."[11] Today it's called the World Wide Web. Hypertext, the universal organization system of the World Wide Web, links words, images, and other resources into a document that has no single linear path for readers to follow. A hypertext is as many texts as there are readers: it is a postmodern artifact.

Around the same time that the personal computer was being created, a new sort of game entitled Dungeons & Dragons started to become popular. The game had no board, no fixed object, and a set of rules that seemed to combine craps and method acting. The rules told prospective players that

> As [the Dungeon Master or DM] describes your surroundings, try to picture them mentally. Close your eyes and construct the walls of the maze around yourself. Imagine the hobgoblin as [the DM] describes it whooping and gamboling down the corridor toward you. Now imagine how you would react in that situation and tell [the DM] what you are going to do.[12]

While most young people have taken part in a school play or two, Dungeons & Dragons and its competitors offered a way to create an immersive fantasy world that could continue week after week. It was virtual reality, paper and pencil style. Like hypertext, it held an endless number of paths.

Bringing hypertext and role-playing to the computer required more powerful hardware and a way to link computers together. By the 1980s, computer networking was moving from being the province of government and military bureaucrats to a widespread system linking college campuses as well as

11

stand-alone, dial-up "bulletin board systems." Besides offering the ability to post messages to discussion groups and to send private e-mails, programmers began to create online versions of role-playing games such as MUDs (multi-user dungeons).

Soon, according to psychologist and cyberculture student Sherry Turkle, "Thousands of players spend up to eighty hours a week participating in intergalactic exploration and wars. Through typed descriptions and typed commands, they create characters who have casual and romantic sexual encounters, hold jobs and collect paychecks, attend rituals and celebrations, fall in love and get married."[13]

If privacy is about identity and preserving the inner self, what can one make of D&D, MUDs, and computer chat rooms? Online, a person can have many identities. One can represent the ordinary, relatively straightforward daily self. Another can be a fantasy hero in a D&D world, an army general, a business tycoon, or for that matter, a talking, leather-wearing, lady rabbit. What information is "private" to each of these characters? If one person's character discloses a secret to another person's character, do the people have the right to use or act on that information outside of their *persona*?

While these might seem to be idle or abstruse questions, the carrying out of seduction, consensual sex, and even a kind of rape-by-proxy have raised real questions in virtual communities. After all, "The commands you type in the computer [in a MUD] are a kind of speech that doesn't so much communicate as *make things happen*, directly and ineluctably."[14]

In the *real* year of 1984, science fiction writer William Gibson, in his book *Neuromancer*, described "Cyberspace: A consensual hallucination . . . A graphic representation of data abstracted from the banks of every computer in the human system. . . . Lines of light ranged in the non space of the mind.[15]" This future cyberspace extrapolated the primitive, text-only computer networks of the time into an era where brain implants, sensors, and super powerful graphics computers would create a fully immersive "virtual reality."

Cyberspace is a far cry from the Panopticon or the world of Big Brother's dictatorship. Big Brother projects his wishes into minds that have been so formed that they can hold nothing but his wishes. Television had been accused of being an instrument for imprinting conformity on millions of passive eyeballs. But in *Neuromancer*, "The sky above the port was the color of television, tuned to a dead channel.[16]" Cyberspace is "inside" the TV set, and there are no watchers, only characters. The choice of whether to be active or passive lies, as in "real life," with each individual.

For Gibson and the other "cyberpunk" authors who created postmodern science fiction, none of this meant that cyberspace was necessarily a healthful or beneficent place. Indeed, for cyberpunks, cyberspace is filled with violent conflict, techno-gangsters, and the exploitation of the slow or unlucky by the fast and efficient. The world of cyberpunk, while not monochromatic like that of Orwell, is still a place where privacy and identity are very precarious.

PRIVACY ISSUES AND THE AMBIVALENCE OF TECHNOLOGY

Today, virtual reality is still a relatively expensive technology used for some games and specialized applications. The Internet and the World Wide Web, today's less ambitious cyberspace, have both modern (TV-like advertising, passive content) and postmodern (interactive, many-pathed content) aspects. Most people who are used to the passive role of TV viewer are now coming to the Internet, particularly as parents and consumers. They have been told that the Internet is the information superhighway of the future, a convenience but also a necessity for tomorrow's citizens. At the same time, they have seen lurid accounts of computer crime, identity theft, and pornography. Thus the same technology that intrigues them also makes them feel vulnerable.

The public reaction to the Internet is part of a larger ambivalence about technology that is expressed in much of popular culture. Years of *Star Trek* series have testified to the belief in an optimistic future, but TV's later hit *X-Files* portrays a world where nothing is as it seems and the explanation for life's problems is to be found by uncovering a web of alien conspiracies. The *X-Files* resonates in a world where the media seems to constantly tell people that neither government nor business can be trusted.

There are thus two competing visions: in one, the Internet and the new media are sources of endless possibilities, whether for artistic expression, business success, or new forms of human relationships. In the other, the technology is out of control, threatening privacy and even identity itself. Most people probably partake of both visions in varying degrees.

How do people decide how to respond to the challenge of a technology that is as ripe with unforseeable consequences as the invention of writing itself? People look to the models that their culture has provided. One model is the taming of technology through regulation. After all, the telephone, the automobile, TV—all have been integrated into society through a combination of regulation and social custom.

Another model is technocratic. It seeks to find the solution to technological problems through the technology itself. It argues that the new technology is developing far too quickly to be enclosed in a web of regulations. From this point of view the answer to identity thieves or government or private snooping is encryption: using technology to protect secrets.

Science-fiction writer and futurist David Brin offers a different kind of technocratic solution—one could say, a postmodern one. His solution is to create what he calls "the transparent society." He notes that

---

Each time government acquired new powers of sight, citizens seized another tool for enforcing transparency and accountability from government. From open-meeting laws, to special prosecutors and conflict-of-interest prosecutions, to whistleblower protections, to financial disclosure codes and the vaunted FOIA [Freedom of Information Act], we have (so far) successfully used such tools to thwart the potential of tyranny . . . not by blinding our officials but by granting them the vision they claimed to need, and then insisting that they walk around (metaphorically) naked, observed, supervised, and forced to account for each marginal abuse of power. [17]

Techno-futurist Esther Dyson seems to agree: "Our best defense [against government spying] is offense. Spy back! We need the ability to follow more closely what governments are doing." [18]

Brin and Dyson seem to be saying that the Panopticon cannot be dismantled, but it can be made to work both ways. The watched can watch the watchers, and thus hold them accountable. Critics have replied, however, that it is unrealistic to think that governments or big corporations can really be made to play by the same rules as ordinary individuals.

The cultural background to privacy issues is thus multi-textured and many-layered. When people look at the Internet, they may see Big Brother's threat to the inner self, or echo the critics who damn television for turning the self into a commodity and selling it back to people. Or they may see a way to create many alternatives and indeed many different selves: the MUD and hypertext worlds. This interplay of fears and possibilities will continue to surface as people debate the future of privacy in the Information Age.

PRIVACY AND THE U.S. CONSTITUTION

The colonists who came to America from England naturally shared the regard for privacy and individual rights of the English political reformers. For example, the Rhode Island Code of 1647 stated that "a man's house is to himself, his family and goods as a castle." On the eve of the American Revolution John Adams told a jury that "An Englishman's dwelling House is his Castle. The law has erected a Fortification around it. [19]" Indeed, one cause of the friction that led to the American revolt was that officers of the Crown frequently broke into colonists' homes to seize papers, having only the authority of a vague "general warrant."

The Constitution that came into effect in 1789 was primarily a blueprint for organization of government, with Congress, the executive branch, and the judiciary branch each being given specified powers. While such a structure may have implied that rights not given to the federal government remained with the states or the people themselves, a keen awareness of abuses that had been suffered under British rule had led to demands for explicit guarantees of individual rights. The result was the adoption of ten amendments, popularly called the Bill of Rights, in 1791.

Several of the amendments have something to say about privacy. In particular, the Fourth Amendment states that

> *The right of the people to be secure in their persons, houses, papers, and effects, against unreasonable searches and seizures, shall not be violated, and no warrants shall issue, but upon probable cause, supported by oath or affirmation, and particularly describing the place to be searched, and the persons or things to be seized.*

This language restates the "your home is your castle" idea, declaring a fundamental right of privacy that officers of the state can only overcome by having sufficient reason ("probable cause") to believe that a crime has been committed, and that the place to be searched is likely to contain specified evidence relating to the crime.

Other amendments in the Bill of Rights also touch upon privacy: The Third Amendment prevents the government from using private homes to house soldiers ("quartering") during peacetime. The Fifth Amendment includes a provision that "[no person] shall be compelled in any criminal case to be a witness against himself." In other words, the information locked inside a person's brain is private and cannot be forced out and used against that person.

While many state constitutions had similar provisions, it was generally held that the federal constitution restrained only the federal government, not the states. As the 20th century progressed, however, the Supreme Court began to decide that the provisions of the Bill of Rights also apply to the states. (This is called the "incorporation doctrine.") The definitive step was taken in *Brown v. Board of Education* (1954), where the court held that the guarantee of due process and equal protection of the laws in the Fourteenth Amendment applied to the states, in this case prohibiting separate (but not really equal) racially segregated schools. The broader implication of this decision meant that states would have to guarantee at least the same amount of protection for a right (such as privacy rights) as that provided in the federal constitution. (A state can—and often does—have a stronger protection than the federal one, but it cannot have a weaker one.)

At the same time federal rights were being extended to state and local governments, the scope of the right of privacy began to be increased and made more explicit. As changes in sexual mores clashed with older laws concerning abortion, contraception, and other intimate practices, the Supreme Court was

15

called on to resolve these issues in a series of landmark cases. In *Griswold v. Connecticut* (1965) the Supreme Court held that the government could not intrude into the decision of a married couple to employ means of birth control: this was soon extended to unmarried couples. The area of sex and reproduction thus became part of a "zone of privacy"—matters that belong to the autonomy and liberty of the individual and should be beyond the reach of government. *Roe v. Wade* (1973) extended this zone of privacy to include the decision to have an abortion. (It should be noted that such privacy rights are not absolute, just very strong, with a "compelling" state interest required before they can be abridged. In *Roe* the state gets more scope to regulate abortion as the pregnancy progresses.) The most fundamental decision of all—whether to continue or end one's life—was also given to the individual in *Cruzan v. Director, Missouri Department of Health* (1990) where a person's clearly stated wishes not to receive life-prolonging treatment were to be weighed against the State's interest in protecting life. (As a result most states soon passed laws that recognized "living wills," in which individuals could formally state their wishes.)

INFORMATION PRIVACY

The traditional rights of privacy focused on creating a zone—a house or a person—that was protected from intrusion by the government except under specified circumstances. *Griswold, Roe, Cruzan,* and other decisions focused not on a physical zone but a sphere of activity—sex, reproduction, and health care decisions that would be presumed to be private. In both cases, the emphasis was on preventing intrusion. But as the quotation at the start of this chapter suggests, there is also a kind of privacy that focuses on the flow of *information* about a person, and the person's ability to decide who will get the information and how it will be used. It is the issues that arise from the impact of technology on information privacy that are the focus of this book.

PRIVACY AND TELECOMMUNICATIONS

Before the mid-19th century most communication was either directly spoken between two persons or in the form of writing (usually mail). The invention of telecommunications—the telegraph and telephone—allowed for instant communication across great distances, but that communication was subject to stealthy eavesdropping. (Indeed, both sides in the American Civil War had spies who were given the job of tapping telegraph lines.)

This new technology threatened to blow a hole in the Fourth Amendment. The Constitution said that government agents couldn't go into a house and seize letters without a warrant, but of course it said nothing about messages traveling outside the house in a telephone wire. In *Olmstead v. United States* (1928), the Supreme Court decided that as long as the police placed the tap on an outside wire rather than entering the house, the tap was not unconstitutional. But Justice Brandeis, dissenting from the decision, argued that in order to be true to the *intent* of the Constitution to protect people in the privacy of their homes, the language should be reinterpreted (or expanded) to include the new technology of the telephone.

It took more than a generation, but in 1967 the Court adopted Brandeis' reasoning in *Katz v. U.S.* It stated that a person had a reasonable "expectation of privacy" in making a call from his or her home telephone and that therefore the police would have to get a warrant to tap the line. Expectation of privacy became a key test that would be applied to other privacy questions. In many cases, however, the courts have decided that an individual does not always have a reasonable expectation of privacy, for example:

- Checks and bank records are not private because they flow between banks as part of ordinary commerce (*United States v. Miller*, 1976).

- Garbage at the curb or materials stored in an open field are not private (*California v. Greenwood*, 1988; *Oliver v. United States*, 1984).

- It is permissible for a police helicopter to peer through a hole in a roof to look for marijuana plants (*Florida v. Riley*, 1989).

These and other cases reveal a constant process of balancing the right of privacy against the goal of law enforcement and crime reduction. When the majority of the public is convinced there is a serious threat to public safety, they are likely to be willing to sacrifice privacy in order to get more effective law enforcement. Many critics point to the "War on Drugs" campaign as being the driving force behind a relentless diminishing of the right of privacy: of course, other justifications have also been given for favoring surveillance over privacy, such as the struggle against communism during the cold war, alarm about the activities of civil rights and antiwar protesters in the 1960s, international terrorism in the 1980s, and right-wing militia activity in the 1990s.

Another round in the privacy battle began in December 1998, when the Federal Deposit Insurance Corporation (FDIC) published a proposed regulation called "Know Your Customer." This regulation would build on the list of customer information already collected under the Bank Secrecy Act. The law would require that banks:

- Determine their customers' "source of funds"
- Determine their customers' "normal and expected" transactions

- Monitor transactions to determine if any are "inconsistent" with the profile of normal and expected transactions
- Report any "suspicious activity" to federal investigators

The ACLU, the California Bankers' Association, and many privacy organizations raised an outcry about what they see as a new dimension in intrusiveness. Since the Supreme Court has decided (in *Miller*, 1976, and other cases) that individuals do not have a Fourth Amendment interest in their bank records, the battle was fought mainly in the political rather than the legal arena. There, a public campaign by opponents flooded the FDIC with more than 250,000 letters and e-mail, and the proposed regulations were withdrawn in March 1999.

The emergence of new technologies also tends to encourage reinterpretation of traditional rights. Just as tapping the telephone line was considered at first not to be a "real" intrusion on privacy, some people have not considered words displayed on web pages to be "real" speech that is entitled to protection under the First Amendment. In response to this tendency that says constitutional guarantees do not apply to the new media of communication, civil libertarians have proposed making privacy protections more general. For example, constitutional scholar Lawrence Tribe has proposed a constitutional amendment that would read as follows:

> *This Constitution's protections for the freedoms of speech, press, petition, and assembly, and its protections against unreasonable searches and seizures and the deprivation of life, liberty, or property without due process of law, shall be construed as fully applicable without regard to the technological method or medium through which information content is generated, stored, altered, transmitted, or controlled.*[20]

PRIVACY AND THE DATA EXPLOSION

Telephone taps and surveillance technology have threatened to penetrate the zone of privacy around the individual, but the explosive growth of computer databases beginning in the late 1960s has increased the threat to privacy in a different way—by creating large amounts of information about the details of people's lives while providing little control over how this information may be used. Much of the database explosion came from government agencies that both needed and could afford huge mainframe computers for processing records for tax, Social Security, and a growing number of welfare programs. Large banks and insurance companies soon followed suit. Computerization offered governments the ability to manage an increasingly complex system of regulations and entitlements, while private business sought cost savings by replacing labor-intensive manual record-keeping systems with automated ones.

Public concern about an electronic Big Brother grew during the 1970s. But while the popular image was of a giant government computer stockpiling every scrap of data about every person, the real threat was more subtle and complex. In 1977, the U.S. Privacy Protection Study Commission warned that "The real danger is the gradual erosion of individual liberties through the automation, integration, and interconnection of many small, separate record-keeping systems, each of which alone may seem innocuous, even benevolent, and wholly justifiable."[21]

In other words, the threat was not Big Brother, but a swarm of "little brothers" who spend 24 hours a day gossiping with one another. The development of desktop computers and general-purpose computer networks in the 1970s and 1980s would make it easy to collect, distribute, use—and misuse—the information being gathered by government agencies and private businesses.

In 1972, in response to such concerns, the Advisory Committee on Automated Personal Data Systems to the Secretary of the Department of Health, Education, and Welfare suggested some basic principles for protecting privacy in the new Information Age:

1. There must be no personal data record-keeping systems whose very existence is secret.
2. There must be a way for an individual to find out what information about him/her is on record and how it is used.
3. There must be a way for an individual to correct or amend a record of identifiable information about him/her.
4. There must be a way for an individual to prevent information about him/her that was obtained for one purpose from being used or made available for other purposes without his/her consent.
5. Any organization creating, maintaining, using, or disseminating records of identifiable personal data must guarantee the reliability of the data for their intended use and must take precautions to prevent misuse of the data.

These are still the guiding principles for privacy advocates today, and they have been embodied in important legislation such as the Privacy Act of 1974, the Electronic Communications Privacy Act of 1986, and the Freedom of Information Act of 1964. But as will be seen throughout this chapter and in many works cited in the bibliography in Chapter 7, privacy advocates believe that the actual protection of the privacy of personal information falls far short of these goals in many respects.

All indications are that the public has become more, not less, concerned about privacy even as the boom in online services and the Internet has dazzled the public eye. A 1997 telephone survey conducted by *Money* magazine reports that 74 percent of the public are somewhat or very concerned about threats to their privacy, and 29 percent have experienced at least one serious invasion of their own personal privacy. About two-thirds of the respondents said they were more worried about their privacy than they were five years ago.

CONSUMER PRIVACY

The average person makes dozens of purchases each week. Many small purchases are anonymous, such as putting a quarter into a rack and taking out a newspaper or buying a quick burger at a fast-food place. But most purchases involving more than a few dollars are accomplished with a check or, more often, a credit card.

Until after World War II, credit cards were issued by a particular business such as a department store or an oil company, and could be used only for purchases from that vendor. In 1949, however, Diners Club came out with the first general-purpose credit card that could be conveniently used by travelers at a variety of restaurants, hotels, or other establishments. By the 1950s, the Carte Blanche and American Express credit cards had been introduced, and the 1960s brought Bankamericard (later Visa), and Master Charge (later MasterCard). With the 1970s came the "debit card" in the form of the automatic teller machine (ATM) card, and later, debit cards for use in stores.

Cash purchases require no information except a simple receipt. Checks are more complex, but essentially the only requirement is a way to verify the identity of the check writer and the sufficiency of the bank balance. Use of credit cards, however, represents an open-ended series of loans. People who make loans want to make sure they will be repaid, and that means keeping track of information such as the following:

1. *Identifying information:* name and spouse's name, Social Security number, address, and telephone number
2. *Financial status:* amount of income (present and past), employer (present and past), occupation, sources of income
3. *Credit history:* previous types, extent, and sources of credit granted
4. *Existing lines of credit:* payment habits, outstanding obligations and debts, extent of current lines of credit

5. *Public Record Information:* lawsuits, judgments, tax liens, bankruptcies, arrests [in some cases], and convictions
6. *Prior requesters:* names of subscribers who requested information on the individual in the past.[22]

Only powerful computers have the capacity to track these details for millions of borrowers in almost "real time," over a telephone network that enables merchants to accept the credit card and receive instant credit verification.

The largest nongovernmental database of personal information are those of the agencies that provide the credit information to credit card companies and merchants. TRW, Equifax, and Trans Union collectively maintain about 500 million records on 160 million people. The "master key" that retrieves an individual's record is usually the person's Social Security number. (Ironically, Social Security cards, until the 1970s, carried a warning that read "For Social Security Purposes—Not for Identification.")

IDENTITY THEFT

A woman opens her credit card statement and gasps in shock. Thousands of dollars worth of purchases are listed on the pages. They range from a color TV to an expensive camera to designer clothes. The problem is that she hadn't bought a single one of these items. Someone has invaded her privacy—indeed, has taken over her identity, bought goods in her name, and ruined her credit.

How could this happen? There are many ways: A criminal may have found her Social Security number somewhere, perhaps on a bill filched from her mail or her garbage. Or, by posing as a legitimate merchant, he obtained her credit report—or maybe he got a copy from a not-so-legitimate merchant who sold the report "on the side." Or perhaps the whole operation was accomplished on the Internet, with the information obtained from a "data broker" or "super bureau" that makes a good living by providing such information for a fee.

Once he had the credit report, he had all the information needed to apply for a credit card in her name—or several credit cards, for that matter. Substituting his address for hers, he ordered merchandise delivered to his home. (In earlier times, when credit card purchases were nearly all made over the counter, the need to forge a signature may have been an obstacle, but 800 numbers and the Internet make it easy to order anything with just the credit card number and the expiration date.)

21

Identity theft may not yet be as common as pickpocketing, but in 1997 the Secret Service reported 9,455 arrests for this offense, and many such crimes go unreported. (Indeed, some police departments are reluctant to take reports from the cardholder because they consider the actual "victim" to be the bank that issued the credit card.)

Cardholders who report credit card fraud as soon as they are aware of it are generally liable only for the first $50 worth of bogus purchases. But the same system of linked computers that makes it easy for criminals to tap into private information makes it hard for the victims to restore their good credit. The illicit purchases and credit balances spread throughout the system and end up in the credit bureau files, to be reported as bad credit.

Even without fraud, errors can easily creep into credit files—about a third of all files examined turn out to have mistakes. Sometimes credit information for two people with similar names can become intermixed. Errors can have serious consequences ranging from failure to obtain a home mortgage to being turned down by a prospective employer as a "deadbeat." A number of states have sued credit bureaus to make them comply with requirements that errors be promptly corrected. In addition, the Federal Trade Commission (FTC) sued one bureau, Equifax, and won an agreement to improve error correction procedures.

OTHER PRIVACY INTRUSIONS

Identity theft for financial gain is not the only intrusion to which databases make people vulnerable. The personal information of politicians and celebrities is fair game for opponents or for the tabloid media. When today's high-tech private investigators want to track someone down, they use a keyboard or a mouse, not shoe leather. The author of a book about finding personal information online boasts that

> *In a few hours, sitting at my computer, beginning with no more than your name and address, I can find out what you do for a living, the names and ages of your spouse and children, what kind of car you drive, the value of your house, and how much you pay in taxes on it. From what I learn about your job, your house, and the demographics of your neighborhood, I can make a good guess at your income. I can uncover that forgotten drug bust in college. In fact, if you are well-known or your name is sufficiently unusual, I can do all this without even knowing your address.*[23]

Even an ordinary person can fall victim to a stalker or abusive spouse who can use a Social Security number or other identifying information to get the target's address. There are, of course, legitimate reasons for police and private investigators to use databases to track down individuals, such as to determine a person's assets in a divorce or in some other legal action, or to get someone to pay child support. The main problem is that there is little to stop the illegitimate user from accessing the same data resources. The sources of data and the ways to obtain it are many, and the existing regulations and safeguards are far from comprehensive. And data in a networked computer is only as secure as the weakest link in the chain of users.

Modern telecommunications also create vulnerabilities. Cordless telephones are actually low-power radio transmitters, and calls on them can be picked up several hundred feet away. Cell phone calls can be picked up by scanners that are now illegal to sell but not illegal to own, as former House Speaker Newt Gingrich found out when his conference call was taped after being accidentally picked up by a nearby motorist. (Fortunately the newer digital, encrypted cell phone systems are much less vulnerable.)

MARKETING PERSONAL INFORMATION

When someone buys some groceries at a supermarket, the information needed to process the credit card transaction is not the only information that passes through the check stand. Anyone who belongs to a popular supermarket "discount club" creates a record of every item purchased, combining the information scanned from the items at the register with the person's identifying information in the store's computer. The supermarket can use this information to create coupons instantly to entice someone who likes Kellogg's corn flakes to try the house brand instead. The information can also be used to target the customer for direct-mail campaigns. This same process can occur at a visit to a department store, an auto dealer, or any time a consumer fills out a product registration or warranty card. (People who call 800 numbers can also have their phone number revealed by Caller ID and then looked up in a "reverse directory" to yield an address for a mailing list.)

Why is so much information collected about everyone's daily purchases? Because, as one observer has noted, "Laws on privacy may vary from country to country, but the laws of economics do not. The laws of economics in the information age say that information has value—it is a product that can be sold, just like socks, cars, and toothpaste."[24]

In addition to stores using information about consumer purchases for their own marketing, the information is often sold to other businesses or to agencies that package it and sell it to other direct-mail marketers. While the compiling and use of mailing lists are not new, modern database technology makes consumer information a much more valuable product because it can sort, select, and customize it in so many ways. For example, a mail-order catalog company can target just those women who might be interested in a new line of larger-size clothes.

In the late 1980s and early 1990s, the reselling of personal information came to public attention through a few high-profile cases. The Lexis-Nexis database company, for example, admitted that it paid credit bureaus for Social Security numbers and credit information on millions of Americans, which they packaged and sold to direct marketers. Lexis-Nexis was sued in a consumer class action suit and was required to remove the Social Security numbers, as well as agreeing to remove anyone's name, from their database on request.

In 1991, software developer Lotus Development Corporation and Equifax, a major credit bureau, announced plans to market a CD-ROM database called Households that contained names, addresses, and marketing information on 120 million consumers. But after 30,000 people wrote or called demanding that their names be removed, the companies abandoned their plans.

The marketing of personal information, however, usually goes on below the surface. For example, New York State investigators investigating the credit bureau TRW discovered that it had been taking the records it received from transactions through American Express and packaging and reselling the information to direct mailers. Such undisclosed reselling of information has become a major focus for regulatory action and legislation.

THE INTERNET: OPPORTUNITIES AND VULNERABILITIES

In many ways the Internet is a shopper's dream come true. By surfing the web, a consumer can obtain detailed information on just about any product or service, even enlisting the aid of a "robot shopper" to find the best prices. Items can be ordered with a credit card and a few keystrokes. (There is little risk in dealing with a known company that uses a "secure" web server that encrypts credit card information sent over the phone line, but credit card information can be stolen by bogus sites or when sent by e-mail.) As the 1990s draw to a close the Internet has become a mainstream billion-dollar market with more than ten million consumers buying things online.

But the Internet also adds another way to scoop up huge amounts of information from and about consumers. Many web sites store an identification file called a "cookie" on the user's hard disk. They can then combine that information with the web server's log of all the web pages the user views. The result is a detailed profile of what the user has bought and is likely to be interested in. The cookie file can save the user time (by making it unnecessary to resubmit credit card and address information for each order) and can also be used to "customize" the site with the user's preferences and to offer shopping suggestions. On the other hand, the information can also be used to generate spam (electronic junk mail) or it can be sold to other marketers (creating more spam).

When the FTC surveyed 1,400 web sites, it found that 92 percent collected data about visitors, while only 14 percent revealed how that data is used. The collection of data without notification is considered to be a violation of privacy by many people, and it is another focus of proposed legislation.

MARKETING TO CHILDREN

People tend to be especially concerned when they learn that their children are being asked for personal information on the web. A watchdog group called the Center for Media Education notes that children are big business—they spend about $80 billion a year themselves, and influence an additional $160 billion worth of spending by their parents. The Center surveyed a group of popular web sites that were especially targeted to children and found that 90 percent of them asked for some form of personally identifying information. Forty percent of the sites offered some sort of incentive such as a free gift to encourage kids to supply information. Twenty-five percent of the sites used the information to send e-mail to the kids later. And virtually none of the sites explained what they would do with the information or asked for parental permission. A larger survey by the FTC in late 1997 yielded similar results.

The potential for abuse extends beyond junk mail or marketing that parents may consider to be inappropriate. A TV reporter successfully ordered 5,500 names and addresses of children from a marketing company called Metromail—using the name of Richard Allen Davis, a convicted child murderer.

CONSUMER PRIVACY LEGISLATION

Public concern about vulnerability in the online world has spurred an unprecedented number of proposed laws to regulate collection of information from consumers, particularly information involving children.

The Fair Credit Reporting Act of 1971 requires credit bureaus to provide consumers copies of their credit records for a nominal fee (or for free, if the person has been turned down for credit, insurance, or employment on the basis of the report). It limits the use of credit reports to credit, insurance, employment, or another "legitimate business need." Consumers have the right to resolve disputes about particular information that they feel to be in error. The law does have numerous exceptions and limitations, however, and many states have passed stronger laws to fill the gap. Legislation has been proposed that would ban credit bureaus from selling personal identifiers such as mother's maiden names, birthdates, unlisted phone numbers, and Social Security numbers.

The collection and distribution of information by marketers has been largely unregulated. As the 1990s draw to a close, however, this is likely to change. The FTC has already taken several steps to put businesses on notice to reform their practices. The agency declared in July 1997 that the collection and sale of information from children without due disclosure and parental consent is an "unfair practice" under Section 5 of the FTC Act. In August 1998, the FTC settled a complaint about information collection and distribution against GeoCities, a popular web site that offers free e-mail and web pages to individuals and families. As part of the settlement, GeoCities agreed to post a clear privacy statement to explain its policies, and it also agreed to obtain parental consent before collecting any information from children under 12 years of age. These requirements are likely to be enshrined in law soon.

INDUSTRY INITIATIVES AND SELF-REGULATION

Reacting to the calls for regulation, online industry groups such as the Business Software Alliance and the Consumer Electronics Manufacturers Association have begun to embrace voluntary privacy standards. An organization called TRUSTe is certifying web sites that provide clear privacy statements that explain what information is gathered and what will be done with it, as well as what a consumer can do if he or she is not satisfied. Some free market advocates have argued that such disclosures are sufficient to provide privacy protection: consumers who don't like a site's privacy policy can shop elsewhere. Many privacy activists, however, believe that consumers should not be forced to make such choices, and that, at the least, a minimum of federal standards is necessary. Clinton administration officials have stated their willingness to "give the market a chance" to come up with voluntary standards, but by late 1998 the FTC was expressing its impatience with what it sees as the slow pace of reform.

MEDICAL PRIVACY

A man goes into the hospital for treatment of prostate cancer. A month later he receives mail from a drug company about their cancer treatment drug.

An employer searches pharmacy records for employees who have purchased more than $100 worth of drugs per month. The employer examines the records further to find people who were using Retrovir, a drug used to treat AIDS.

A woman's genetic testing reveals that she has a gene that indicates a high risk of her developing breast cancer. What happens if those test results are learned by her insurer? Her employer?

Since ancient times doctors have professed a code of ethics that goes back to the Hippocratic Oath: "Whatsoever things I see or hear concerning the life of men, in my attendance on the sick or even apart therefrom, which ought not be noised abroad, I will keep silence thereon, counting such things to be as sacred secrets."[25]

The doctor-patient relationship is central to this ethic, which assures people that they can seek medical treatment without having the details of their medical conditions revealed. Today, however, the doctor is only one of a large number of people and institutions involved in the delivery of health care. The tremendous growth in the cost of medical treatment has resulted in third parties—employer and insurance companies or the government—paying for most health care.

The flow of information is crucial to health care today. Doctors and pharmacists believe that access to comprehensive medical records is essential for providing better care and for protecting patients from taking dangerous combinations of prescription drugs. The managers of the government-run Medicare program need to track medical records to assure quality of care and to prevent fraud, which is estimated to run up to hundreds of millions of dollars each year. Insurance companies and health maintenance organizations (HMOs) claim they can use information systems to improve efficiency and hold down costs by eliminating wasteful and unnecessary treatments.

As a result of these concerns, so many people have joined the chain along which medical records pass that one writer has suggested revising the Hippocratic Oath to read as follows:

> *Whatever I see or hear in my attendance on the sick or even apart therefrom will be divulged to physicians, nurses, aides, surgeons, anesthesiologists, dietitians, physical therapists, admitting clerks, billing clerks, utilization review personnel, discharge planners, records coders, medical records filing staff, chaplains, volunteers, performance evaluators, insurers, medical transcriptionists, accrediting agencies, public health officials, other government officials, social workers, and employers. AND to whomever else requests them for whatever reason.*[26]

The clearinghouse for medical information is the Medical Information Bureau (MIB), which has a role similar to a credit agency. The government runs its own huge database for Medicare patients. As part of an HMO reform proposal, the Clinton administration proposed a national databank in which every person would have a "universal health care identification number." But the existence of a single central database accessible by a single key number would put all of a person's privacy eggs in a single vulnerable basket. Loudly expressed privacy concerns resulted in the Universal Health ID proposal being withdrawn, at least for now.

THE POTENTIAL FOR ABUSE

Despite the crucial importance of medical records for so many people, Donna E. Shalala, Secretary of Health and Human Services, has noted that "Our private health information [is] being shared, collected, analyzed, and stored with fewer federal standards than video store records."[27] A 1993 report by the federal Office of Technology Assessment referred to existing regulations as a "patchwork" of federal and state laws that was inadequate for protecting consumers.

Survey results tend to confirm the perception of a lack of control and sufficient safeguards for medical records. In a 1993 Louis Harris poll, 25 percent of respondents reported that they believed their medical records had been improperly disclosed, and 34 percent of health care professionals believed that records are given to unauthorized persons "somewhat often." The extent of undiscovered abuses may be much greater.

Disclosure of medical records to outside persons can harm people in many ways. Politicians or celebrities can be embarrassed by reporters or opponents digging into details of their medical history, such as treatment for mental illness. A job applicant can be turned down because the prospective employer obtains records that include a diagnosis for an expensive condition such as AIDS or cancer and doesn't want the new hire to increase the company's insurance premiums. Insurers can turn down applicants or cancel policies for the same reason. (A 1997 survey by University of Illinois researcher David Linowes found that 35 percent of employers used information, such as that derived from medical insurance claims or requests for leave, to help make hiring, firing, or promotion decisions.)

PROTECTING MEDICAL PRIVACY

Concerns about medical privacy and the abuse of medical records are combining with other issues raised by the practices of HMOs, such as concerns about denial of treatment and the second-guessing of doctors by clerks.

In 1998, the Clinton administration and members of Congress proposed regulations that would give people much more control over who gets to see their medical records. People would be assured better access to their own medical records and the ability to correct false information they find. Insurance companies would be forbidden from discriminating against people whose family medical history or genetic information suggests that they may develop a serious illness. Many states are adopting similar regulations. (In addition, antidiscrimination laws and the Americans with Disabilities Act, or ADA, can provide protection in some cases.)

As with other privacy issues, there is the need to strike a balance. If regulations are too restrictive, the system may become less efficient, more unwieldy, and still more expensive, which would make medical care even less affordable. But it is difficult to balance visible injuries against individuals with these more diffuse concerns.

PRIVACY IN THE WORKPLACE

A department store installs a peephole in a restroom because employees may be using their bathroom breaks to conceal stolen goods.

Alana Shoars, e-mail administrator at Epson America, discovers that a supervisor has been printing hard copies of all the e-mail that had been sent by her and other employees.

An employer uses detectives and informants to seek information to weed out employees who smoke, drink, or pursue adulterous sexual relationships.

After health, work is probably the next highest priority for most people. Many of the same driving forces—such as cost reduction and efficiency—are driving employers to monitor employees in ways that raise serious privacy concerns.

The assault on privacy often begins before a person even enters the workplace. Employers want stable, reliable employees and try to weed out "potential problem hires." But intrusive psychological tests can ask many questions about religious beliefs and sexual practices that have no connection with job duties. (Some of these tests are attempts to replace the use of polygraphs, or lie detectors, which have been banned for most kinds of employment.) Tests have been generally upheld in the courts, although antidiscrimination laws do regulate the collection and use of information relating to protected matters such as race, gender, disability status, and in some jurisdictions, sexual orientation.

EAVESDROPPING ON E-MAIL

Once on the job, workers who talk to the public on the phone (such as airline reservation agents) often have their calls recorded for "quality control" purposes. Sometimes, however, personal phone calls are also listened to by supervisors. Video surveillance of employees such as store clerks is also common. The many workers who use computers are often monitored by software that can keep track of how fast they type, how long they let the machine sit idle, or what locations they visit on the Internet. Most such monitoring is legal, but it may have a negative effect on the morale of workers who feel they are "living in a fishbowl." Unions have sometimes made workplace privacy a labor issue in contract negotiations.

The growing use of e-mail has led to some of the biggest privacy controversies. Alana Shoars sued Epson America for breach of her and her fellow workers' privacy. She argued that they had an "expectation of privacy," the key test used by courts. She said that since workers had to use private passwords to access their e-mail system, it was reasonable for them to think that their messages would be kept private. Epson, on the other hand, argued that the e-mail system was just another business tool like a phone or a copier. Since it was provided only for business purposes, workers had no reason to suppose that they could use it for private personal messages. In July 1992, the court agreed with Epson's position and threw out the lawsuit. This decision is in keeping with the general trend in workplace privacy issues: generally, workers do not have an expectation of privacy in the office, and employers can monitor activities (including e-mail) as long as the monitoring has a reasonable, business-related purpose.

Another privacy case arising from an e-mail system involved the U.S. Navy. In 1993, when President Clinton and Congress compromised on the issue of whether to allow gays to serve in the military, they decided that the watchwords would be "Don't Ask, Don't Tell, Don't Pursue." But in 1997, when navy officers suspected that Chief Petty Officer Timothy McVeigh (no relation to the Oklahoma City bomber) was the author of gay-related statements in an online "profile" on America Online, they obtained his identity from AOL. McVeigh sued and won a court order to block the navy from discharging him, arguing that the navy had violated the Electronic Communications Privacy Act.

A 1994 survey by the Society for Human Resource Management found that 36 percent of respondents search employee e-mail for business necessity or security. More than 70 percent believe that an employer should reserve the right to read anything in the company's electronic-communications system. Only about a third of employers, however, had an e-mail policy that spelled out acceptable e-mail practices for employees and described the monitoring procedures used by management. Since then, publicity and the urgings of experts have led more companies to establish policies for the use of e-mail as well as access to the World Wide Web.

LEGAL AND REGULATORY TRENDS

Ironically, many employers point to the legal system itself as the reason why they need to monitor employees and read their e-mail. Employers have been increasingly held liable for sexual harassment, discrimination, and workplace violence. (The number of sex, race, disability, and age-discrimination suits brought by workers has more than doubled from over 10,700 in 1992 to 23,000 in 1996.) A harassing e-mail sent by one employee to another can turn into a million-dollar liability problem for the employer.

One possible defense to such suits is to show that the employer has been "diligent" in discovering potential abuses and correcting them. But the same diligence that may prevent harassment claims can also be viewed as an invasion of privacy and become itself the subject of a lawsuit. Employers are unlikely to escape this dilemma and can only seek to craft policies that are most in keeping with recent court decisions. Employees may gain protection under proposed regulations that would require that monitoring be disclosed, that it be more strictly business related, and that information gained through monitoring not be disclosed to other parties. In general, however, it is safest for employees not to use business facilities for personal messages and to avoid including any information in e-mail that might cause trouble if disclosed, keeping in mind that supposedly "deleted" e-mail can be recovered by administrators in most systems.

PRIVACY AND GOVERNMENT AGENCIES

The government is in a paradoxical position with regard to privacy. On the one hand, legislatures and courts have provided a growing number of guarantees of privacy rights in some areas. On the other hand, the government is itself the single largest gatherer and user of information about individuals, and its own practices have long been a concern of privacy advocates. As the Privacy Protection Study Commission reported in 1977:

> *Accumulations of information about individuals tend to enhance authority by making it easier for authority to reach individuals directly. The voracious appetite of investigators for information causes [authorities] to collect and retain virtually any personal data uncovered unless the collection or retention is* clearly *illegal. This attention to avoiding what is improper, rather than accomplishing only what is necessary and proper, leads investigative agencies into abuses of citizens' rights.*[28]

THE "UNIVERSAL ID" DEBATE

As with commercial information gatherers, the threat to privacy does not come only from isolated abuses, but from the pervasiveness of the system as a whole and the lack of built-in safeguards. Many bureaucrats themselves see the system as being unmanageable. The problem of keeping up with the information needs of government agencies has a tempting solution in the creation of a giant, centralized database for all information about an individual that could be constantly updated and placed at the disposal of each agency for its own particular needs. In 1965, a limited version of this idea, the federal Data Service Center (also called National Data Bank) was proposed as a means to correlate all government data to allow for statistical research.

Such proposals have always resulted in strong opposition. During the 1960s and 1970s, the FBI conducted extensive counterintelligence programs (or COINTELPRO) that spied on Martin Luther King, Jr., and other civil rights and antiwar leaders. The Watergate scandal, of course, revealed that the Nixon White House was routinely using government agencies ranging from the CIA to the IRS to spy on or coerce political opponents. Scandals and accusations of misuse of information by government agencies have regularly arisen even in recent years, such as the discovery that the Clinton White House had been keeping FBI files for 400 Republicans who had worked there during the Bush administration. Such events have made many people keenly suspicious of any further centralization of government record keeping. Thus in 1998, the Clinton administration withdrew the "Universal health identification number" from its proposed HMO reforms due to strong public opposition. Similar universal IDs have also been proposed as a way of preventing illegal aliens from working in the United States.

The tendency to "federalize" crimes and social problems continues to lead to expansion of government information systems and thus of threats to privacy. Examples include the cross-matching of state and federal records to find persons who have failed to pay child support, the "instant background checks" for gun purchasers under the Brady Act, and the battle against welfare fraud. In each case proponents argue either that there is no privacy problem or that the goals of the legislation justify a minimal invasion of privacy. Privacy advocates, however, are concerned that the accumulation of seemingly minor intrusions on privacy may reach a point where the individual loses confidence in both privacy and the ability to hold the government accountable.

THE PRIVACY ACT OF 1974

The privacy concerns of the Watergate era culminated in the passage of the Privacy Act of 1974. The act embodied fundamental principles that were intended to make government agencies disclose their information-gathering and distribution activities and to give citizens the ability to learn what information had been collected about them and to correct any errors. But over the past two decades privacy advocates have pointed to what they consider poor implementation and lack of enforcement. Since the act did not appropriate any funds for privacy enforcement, most major government agencies did not appoint anyone to oversee implementation. Without an enforcement mechanism, agencies were essentially the judges of their own compliance. As ACLU Legislative Director John Shattuck remarked during congressional hearings in 1983, "the rule limiting disclosure of personal information without the subject's consent has been all but swallowed up by its exceptions, particularly the broad exception for undefined 'routine uses.'"[29]

Nevertheless, the Privacy Act of 1974 did provide citizens who suspect the government has inappropriate or inaccurate information about them with a useful if cumbersome tool. The citizen can try to determine which agency may have the information and file a request for it. Information involving law enforcement or intelligence activities, however, may be blocked from disclosure.

FREEDOM OF INFORMATION AS A PRIVACY ISSUE

One effective defense against government invasion of privacy is the ability to find out what the government is doing with all information it collects. The Freedom of Information Act of 1966 has allowed intrepid reporters and ordinary citizens to uncover important information about controversial government activities such as medical experiments and the handling of radioactive waste. The FOIA does allow the government to refuse to release information related to national security, intelligence activities, criminal cases, and other areas. As a result, documents retrieved by FOIA requests sometimes come back with many areas blacked out. Critics of the FOIA point to the frequent delays in obtaining information and the difficulty of appealing when requests are refused.

THE ENCRYPTION DEBATE: PRIVACY, LAW ENFORCEMENT, AND NATIONAL SECURITY

Technology itself offers a powerful way to protect privacy: encrypting information so it can't be read except by the intended recipient. An important impetus for the computer revolution was the race during World War II to decode German and Japanese messages that had been encoded using mechanical cipher machines. After the war, the growing conflict between Western nations and the Soviets led to the development of increasingly sophisticated forms of encryption.

Until the 1990s, the use of encryption was pretty much restricted to the government and to certain businesses with powerful computers and special communications systems. A much more "user friendly" encryption system was offered in 1991 by a programmer-activist named Phil Zimmermann. He released a program called Pretty Good Privacy, or PGP. This program uses a kind of coding called public key cryptography in which the decoding keys come in a pair that has a special relationship: text encoded using one of the keys can only be read using the other key.

A person can distribute one key in the pair, called the public key. Anyone using the public key can encode a message that can be read only by the person holding the corresponding private key. The private key itself need never be sent anywhere, so no one can steal it. Further, if one receives a message encoded with a person's private key, one can be sure it was sent by that person. The private key can thus serve as a "digital signature" that verifies the identity of the sender.

Public key cryptography and PGP together with increasingly powerful personal computers offer a way to protect electronic privacy. E-mail or data files that have been encrypted can't be read by nosy bosses, hackers, or industrial spies. But such messages can't be read by the FBI, the National Security Agency, or the local police, either. This meant that traditional search warrants might become useless. Computer security expert Dorothy Denning painted a grim picture of the consequences:

> *If we fail to pass legislation that will ensure a continued capability for court-ordered surveillance, systems fielded without an adequate provision for court-ordered intercepts would become sanctuaries for criminality wherein Organized Crime leaders, drug dealers, terrorists, and other criminals could act with impunity [no fear of punishment]. Eventually, we could find ourselves with an increase in major crimes against society, a greatly diminished capacity to fight them, and no timely solution.*[30]

Federal authorities tried to prevent Zimmermann from distributing his PGP program by classifying it as a "munition" [war material] that was restricted from export. Nevertheless copies of PGP soon appeared throughout the Internet and the government eventually gave up its investigation of Zimmermann when they could not prove that he had anything to do with the distribution.

The encryption debate, however, is far from over. While the government continued to ban the export of the more secure encryption programs, the FBI suggested in 1991 that the government require that all telephone and computer companies that did business with the government include a special device called the Clipper Chip in their systems. The Clipper Chip would provide powerful encryption, but with a catch: the government would retain a key that it could use to read any message encrypted by the device. Privacy advocates and industry groups alike strongly objected to the Clipper Chip proposal. They argued that there was no independent proof that the encryption system was secure and no way to make sure the government did not abuse its ability to read the code. Further, American manufacturers argued that being forced to include a possibly compromised device would make them less competitive with their foreign counterparts who could provide better encryption. The Clipper proposal went through a number of revisions, eventually being replaced with a proposal that would use no chip but would require that a "key escrow" agent hold a copy of each user's code key so the government could read data after obtaining a court order.

The encryption issue remains unresolved at the end of the 1990s, but as a practical matter it is unlikely that the use of encryption on the global Internet can be prevented by government action. On balance, privacy advocates believe that widespread use of encryption prevents more crime by protecting sensitive business data from industrial spies and hackers than it facilitates by being used by the occasional terrorist or gangster.

Encryption can be used to hide information, but new computer hardware might instead reveal too much information about the user. In early 1999, the giant computer chip maker Intel revealed that its forthcoming Pentium III microprocessors would have unique serial numbers built in. Advantages for both corporate and consumer PC users were touted. For example, managers trying to keep track of hundreds of computers could query them electronically and keep track of the location of each machine. The built-in IDs could also be used to protect online consumers by matching customers with their machines, making it harder for an identity thief to place orders.

For privacy advocates, however, the built-in IDs offered a dangerous opportunity for surveillance and tracking of individuals. In online commerce, the ID might act like a hard-wired "cookie" that merchants could use to build detailed customer profiles that they could sell to other firms. The consumer might have no way to prevent his or her computer from betraying its identity. Groups such as gays and lesbians that have frequently experienced harassment or persecution also objected strongly to the chips.

In response to the outcry, Intel agreed to provide a "software patch" to deactivate the serial number feature. Privacy advocates remained unsatisfied, and urged a boycott of Intel products until the serial number feature is completely deactivated or removed from the chips.

Anonymity—sending e-mail through a service that disguises the identity of the sender can also be used to assure privacy. But just as encryption can be used both to protect legitimate privacy and to further criminal enterprises, anonymity can both protect political dissidents and make terrorists unaccountable for their threats. But, as with encryption, it would be difficult to impose controls on anonymity throughout the Internet without reorganizing the system to make it centrally controlled. Privacy advocates and civil libertarians, however, both strongly believe that one of the biggest strengths of the Internet is its decentralized diversity.

PRIVACY AS AN INTERNATIONAL ISSUE

The encryption debate highlights the importance of the fact that the Internet and the so-called Information Superhighway is truly a global structure. While federal or state regulators can require that Americans take certain steps to protect privacy, they have little or no control over what computer users in other countries do. Attempts to block, censor, or suppress information fail because there is no central traffic control, just a web of connections with innumerable possible paths.

PRIVACY PROTECTION IN THE EUROPEAN UNION

While the concept of privacy plays an important role in the American constitution, American federal privacy law is much weaker than the laws in most European nations. Most European nations, including France, Germany, and Great Britain enacted comprehensive privacy regulations starting in the 1970s. In 1995, the European Union approved a Data Protection Directive that unified privacy practices throughout member countries. In addition to providing strong controls over the collection and use of personal data, the EU directive prohibits data transfer between its members and other countries that do not provide "adequate" privacy protection. As a result, in 1998 the United States and the EU found themselves in a complicated negotiation process where American officials tried to assure their European counterparts that the American system of federal and state regulations combined with voluntary industry standards was at least heading in a direction that should be acceptable to the Europeans. By the end of the year, that issue had been resolved only temporarily.

THE FUTURE OF INFORMATION PRIVACY

As the 20th century rushes to its conclusion, the Internet, online services, and information systems have taken center stage in our social and economic life. Privacy is one of the most important issues that comes into play when people look at the opportunities and risks offered by the new technology. The size and economic importance of the information industry as well as the depth of public concern have made privacy an enduring political issue. It is difficult to make any definite predictions about how privacy issues will be resolved in the coming decade, but it may be possible to identify trends that are likely to continue to be important:

- The proportion of commerce that will be carried out online will continue to grow, making risks of identity theft and invasion of privacy significant to more people.

- Public perception of privacy risks will drive increasing demands for regulation—particularly federal regulation.

- New legislation is likely to require disclosure of information-gathering practices and to require permission for resale of information (particularly for data involving children).

- Self-regulation efforts by businesses involved with collecting and distributing personal information are likely to become more uniform and widespread, but are unlikely to be effective enough to satisfy privacy advocates who demand government regulation.

- The federal government is unlikely to be able to stop the spread of strong encryption programs.

- Global pressures (particularly from Europe) will lead to international privacy standards.

- At the same time, the decentralized nature of the Internet will limit the effectiveness of regulations. Frustration with continuing privacy abuses may lead to regulations that don't take the realities of the Internet into account, and such regulations are likely to have unforeseen negative consequences.

- The protection of privacy rights is likely to be an important part of the health care reform agenda. Protection against the misuse and improper distribution of medical records is likely to increase.

- In the workplace, employer needs are likely to continue to win out over employee demands for privacy, but many separate battles are likely to be fought both in the courts and in labor negotiations.

- If people want privacy, they will have to become informed consumers, patients, information users, and citizens.

---

[1] Alan F. Westin, quoted in Fred H. Cate, Privacy in the Information Age. Washington, D.C.: Brookings Institution Press, 1997, p. 22.

[2] William Pitt, quoted in Philippa Strum. *Privacy: The Debate in the United States since 1945*. Fort Worth, Tex.: Harcourt, 1998, p. 116.

[3] Robert Ellis Smith, quoted in David Brin, *The Transparent Society*. Reading, Mass.: Addison-Wesley, 1998, p. 77.

[4] Alastair Fowler, *A History of English Literature*. Cambridge, Mass.: Harvard University Press, 1987, p. 184.

[5] Ralph Waldo Emerson, "Self-Reliance," *The Works of Ralph Waldo Emerson*. Available online. URL: http://americanway.com/emerson/works/

Essays:1st_Series_O2_Self-Reliance.htm. Posted 1998.

[6] Charles Darwin, quoted in Jack Meadows, *The Great Scientists*. New York: Oxford University Press, 1987, p. 167.

[7] Erik Davis, *Techgnosis: Myth, Magic + Mysticism in the Age of Information*. New York: Harmony Books, 1998, p. 67.

[8] George Orwell, *1984*, quoted in Harold Bloom, ed. *George Orwell*. New York: Chelsea House, 1986, p. 136.

[9] Cited in Simon Davies, *Big Brother*. London: Pan Books, 1996, p. 53.

[10] Arthur Kroker and David Cook, "Television and the Triumph of Culture," in Larry McCaffery, ed., *Storming the Reality Studio: A Casebook of Cyberpunk and Postmodern Fiction*. Durham, N.C.: Duke University Press, 1992, p. 233.

[11] Vince Juliano, "Computer Lib (& Dream Machines) by Ted Nelson A Review." Available online. URL: http://www.cla.lib.ct.us/cla/reviews/cmptrlib.html. Posted November 1996.

[12] Gary Gygax, et al., *Advanced Dungeons & Dragons Player's Handbook*. 2nd ed. Lake Geneva, Wis.: TSR, 1995, p. 10.

[13] Sherry Turkle, *Life on the Screen: Identity in the Age of the Internet*. New York: Simon & Schuster, 1995, p. 10.

[14] Julian Dibble, "A Rape in Cyberspace," *Village Voice*, December 12, 1993, p. 42.

[15] William Gibson, *Neuromancer*. New York: Ace Books, 1984, p. 51.

[16] Gibson, *Neuromancer*, excerpted in Larry McCaffery, ed. *Storming the Reality Studio: A Casebook of Cyberpunk and Postmodern Science Fiction*. Durham [N.C.]: Duke University Press, 1991.

[17] Brin, p. 87.

[18] Ibid., p. 110.

[19] Strum, *Privacy*, p. 116.

[20] Lawrence H. Tribe. "The Constitution in Cyberspace." Available online. URL: http://www=swiss.ai.mit.edu/6095/articles/tribe=constitution.txt. Posted November 14, 1994.

[21] Gelman, *Protecting Yourself Online*. San Francisco: HarperEdge, 1998. p. 35.

[22] From the federal Privacy Commission, quoted in American Civil Liberties Union, *Your Right to Privacy*. Carbondale, Ill.: Southern Illinois University Press, 1990, p. 119.

[23] Carole A. Lane, *Naked in Cyberspace: How to Find Personal Information Online*. Wilton, Conn.: Pemberton Press, 1997, p. 3.

[24] William Wresch, *Disconnected: Haves and Have-nots in the Information Age*. New Brunswick, N.J.: Rutgers University Press, 1996, p. 93.

[25] Quoted on the EPIC web site on medical privacy. Available online. URL: http://www.epic.org/privacy/medical/

[26] Dale Miller, quoted in Beth Givens, "Ten Privacy Principles for Health Care," URL: http://www.privacyrights.org/privprin.htm, Posted November 6, 1998.

27 Brin, p. 65.
28 Strum, *Privacy*, p. 148.
29 Ibid., p. 154.
30 Steven Levy, "Crypto Rebels," in Peter Ludlow, ed., *High Noon on the Electronic Frontier*. Cambridge, Mass.: MIT Press, 1996, p. 196.

CHAPTER 2

THE LAW OF PRIVACY

A SURVEY OF IMPORTANT PRIVACY LEGISLATION

Federal legislation, rather than state or local legislation, is more important for issues involving privacy in computer systems and computer communications, since electronic data often travels across state lines. State law, however, can both supplement and strengthen federal protections. State law takes over when interstate commerce and federal constitutional guarantees are not involved. State constitutions can also provide stronger protection than the federal law in some areas.

In the following survey, privacy legislation is categorized by general topic. Under each topic the federal legislation is summarized first, followed by a brief summary of the general trend in state legislation.

CONSUMER PRIVACY

Fair Credit Reporting Act

The Fair Credit Reporting Act (1970), as amended in 1992, (15 U.S.C. § 1681) begins with a justification for the need for regulating the preparation and distribution of credit reports:

> *(1) The banking system is dependent upon fair and accurate credit reporting. Inaccurate credit reports directly undermine the public confidence, which is essential to the continued functioning of the banking system.*
> *(2) An elaborate mechanism has been developed for investigating and evaluating the credit worthiness, credit standing, credit capacity, character, and general reputation of consumers.*

(3) Consumer reporting agencies have assumed a vital role in assembling and evaluating consumer credit and other information on consumers.

(4) There is a need to insure that consumer reporting agencies exercise their grave responsibilities with fairness, impartiality, and a respect for the consumer's right to privacy.

The law begins by describing legitimate, permissable uses for credit reports, such as responding to a court order, providing information directly to the individual named in the report, and a variety of "legitimate business needs" such as a person using a credit card or applying for credit, insurance, or employment. The law also prohibits "information brokers" from disclosing credit information without it falling under one of the legitimate purposes.

Credit bureaus and agencies are required to notify one another when a consumer disputes information in a report. The credit agency must have an effective procedure for reviewing and correcting information.

Fair Credit Billing Act of 1975

The Fair Credit Billing Act (15 U.S.C. § 1666) states that if a consumer tells a merchant about a problem or dispute concerning a bill, the merchant may not report the account as delinquent to a credit bureau or other agency. Installment credit or commercial credit are not covered by this law.

The Fair Debt Collection Practices Act of 1977

The Fair Debt Collection Practices Act (15 U.S.C. §§ 1692–1692o) addresses public concern about the often abusive and excessive practices of agencies that are hired to collect debts owed for consumer purchases, medical care, and other services. The law prohibits debt collectors contacting consumers at unreasonable hours (usually before 8:00 A.M. or after 9:00 P.M.) or places, or from coming to the debtor's place of employment if the collector knows that the employer disapproves. Debt collectors may not threaten violence or harm against "person, property, or reputation." They cannot publish a list of debtors (except to a credit agency).

Debt collectors cannot misrepresent themselves (such as by claiming to be an attorney), misrepresent the nature or the amount of the debt, misrepresent the nature of papers (claiming they are legal forms when they are not, or vice versa), or threaten that they will take actions that are in fact not legal to take. Various other similar practices are prohibited.

The debt collector must honor a request by the debtor to stop contacting him or her, though the collector can notify the debtor of consequences such as legal action. If the debtor claims the debt is not in fact owed, the collector must also stop pursuing the claim unless proof of the debt can be supplied.

Debt Collection Act of 1982

The Debt Collection Act of 1982 (public law 97-365, as amended) allows federal agencies to exchange information about recipients of government loans or grants, and to give such information to private collection agencies. It also gives the Internal Revenue Service the ability to obtain records showing the address of debtors, as well as requiring a Social Security number from every loan applicant.

Telephone Consumer Protection Act of 1991

The Telephone Consumer Protection Act of 1991 (47 U.S.C. § 227) requires that marketers maintain a list of consumers who do not wish to receive sales calls. Before making calls, the company must consult the list. If a person on the list is called anyway, he or she can receive damages. Recorded messages cannot be unsolicited (so marketers generally have a live person ask whether it is OK to play the recording). Sending of unsolicited faxes is also prohibited.

Telemarketing and Consumer Fraud and Abuse Prevention Act of 1994

The Telemarketing and Consumer Fraud and Abuse Prevention Act of 1994 (15 U.S.C. §§ 6101–6108) provides further protections against unwelcome or dishonest telephone sales pitches. It directs the Federal Trade Commission (FTC) to develop regulations that prohibit deceptive telephone advertising offers, calls that are repeated so that a reasonable person would feel harassed by them, and calls made at unreasonable hours. Callers must begin by clearly identifying the purpose of the call.

State Laws

Most state laws are similar to the federal statutes in their general principles and the commercial practices they regulate. Many state laws provide protection against merchants asking for (or writing down) addresses, phone numbers, or credit card numbers for the purpose of accepting checks. State laws generally require that consumers be given accurate copies of their files. Some state laws also regulate "credit doctor" services that offer to fix people's credit problems (many of these services charge high rates for obtaining information or making changes, things the individual has a legal right to do without charge.)

The following states* have laws relating to credit cards and credit investigations: Arizona, Arkansas, California, Colorado, Connecticut, Delaware, District of Columbia, Florida, Georgia, Iowa, Kansas, Kentucky, Louisiana, Maine, Maryland, Massachusetts, Minnesota, Montana, Nevada, New

---

* For this purpose, the District of Columbia is a "state."

Hampshire, New Jersey, New Mexico, New York, North Carolina, North Dakota, Ohio, Oklahoma, Pennsylvania, Rhode Island, Tennessee, Texas, Utah, Vermont, Virginia, Washington, and Wisconsin. Some example provisions include:

- **California:** adds to federal law the right to visually inspect actual files, and the right to sue for invasions of privacy.

- **Delaware:** like a number of other states, prohibits merchants recording credit card numbers on checks unless the credit card issuer is guaranteeing the check.

- **Georgia:** expands federal standards by requiring that each "consumer reporting agency" furnish upon individual request two complete reports per calendar year, free of charge.

- **Massachusetts:** bans use by credit agencies of arrest records over seven years old or bankruptcies over 14 years old.

- **Oklahoma:** requires that credit agencies preparing a credit report for a merchant first provide a copy of the report for the consumer to review.

- **Vermont:** requires that companies obtain the consent of a consumer before obtaining a credit report.

DRIVING RECORDS

Driver's Privacy Protection Act

The Driver's Privacy Protection Act of 1994 (18 U.S.C. § 2721) was passed in response to the murder of actress Rebecca Schaeffer by a stalker who apparently obtained her address through the California Department of Motor Vehicles. The law prohibits state DMVs from releasing personal information about license holders but makes many exceptions (such as for government agencies, insurance companies, and private investigators). The law is thus unlikely to prevent anyone who is willing to pay from obtaining information.

Existing protections seemed to be insufficient to head off abuses. In early 1999, three states—Florida, South Carolina, and Colorado—agreed to sell a combined total of 22.5 million driver's license photographs to Image Data LLD, a private antifraud company in New Hampshire. The company said it would use the photos to create a photo database that merchants could use to stop use of fraudulent ID for check cashing. But privacy advocates reacted quickly to the announcement, pointing out that none of the license holders had given permission for their photos to be used by a private company, and that the states had no right to market the pictures. State officials soon began to back away from the plan.

FINANCIAL PRIVACY

In *U.S. v. Miller* (1976), the Supreme Court ruled that an individual has no constitutional "legitimate expectation of privacy" in the records of financial transactions, such as deposits, withdrawals, checks, and funds transfers. However, in response, a number of laws have been passed that do provide real, though limited, privacy protection for financial records.

Bank Secrecy Act of 1970

The Bank Secrecy Act of 1970 (12 U.S.C. §§ 1951– and 31 U.S.C. §§ 1051–) is not, as the name might suggest, a law requiring banks to keep certain financial information confidential. Actually, it requires that banks keep track of a variety of kinds of transactions and report them to the federal government in an attempt to stop money laundering, drug-related transactions, or other illegal activities.

For example, transactions involving the movement of funds, currency, or credit in the amount of more than $10,000 out of the country must be reported, and individual travelers must report cash transactions of more than $10,000. ("Unusual" domestic currency transactions of more than $2,500 must be reported to the Internal Revenue Service.) Banks must also hold records of bank statements, checks over $100, and other transactions for at least five years. Banks must obtain Social Security numbers from customers for identification at the time an account is opened. In 1995, amended regulations (reflecting the Anti Money-Laundering Act of 1992) required additional tracking of wire transfers and other transactions.

Privacy advocates have objected to the widespread tracking of individual finances mandated by the Bank Secrecy Act. In *California Bankers' Association v. Schulz* (1974), the law was challenged on the constitutional grounds of freedom of association (First Amendment), unreasonable search and seizure (Fourth Amendment), and the right against self-incrimination (Fifth Amendment). The Supreme Court, however, upheld the law's constitutionality. The Electronic Funds Transfer Act of 1978 and the Right to Financial Privacy Act of 1978 (both discussed below) in part represented Congress' attempts to provide some privacy protection via regulation.

Electronic Funds Transfer Act of 1978

The Electronic Funds Transfer Act of 1978 (15 U.S.C. §§ 1693–1693r) regulates the use of the electronic banking systems that have largely replaced the traditional tellers and paper checks. Transactions included are those involving an "automated teller machine (ATM), point-of-sale terminal, automated clearinghouse, telephone bill-payment system, or home banking program."

All transaction systems by definition involve the transfer of information to parties other than the individual; however, an institution must inform the customer about circumstances in which financial information will be disclosed to a third party "in the ordinary course of business." Institutions are also prohibited from issuing unsolicited credit or ATM cards except as replacements or renewals for existing cards.

Right to Financial Privacy Act of 1978

Under the Right to Financial Privacy Act of 1978 (12 U.S.C. §§ 3401–) federal investigators must use proper legal process or "formal written requests" to obtain records of an individual kept by a financial institution such as a bank or credit card company, or financial records held by brokers, attorneys, or accountants. The affected individual must also be given notice in time to challenge the request for access. The Internal Revenue Service, in particular, is required to give 14 days' notice for any "administrative summons" to see financial records; during this time an individual can appeal to a federal judge to deny the summons.

The law also makes it illegal for an unauthorized individual to obtain information from a computer belonging to a financial institution, credit card company, or consumer reporting agency.

State Laws

Some states have enacted laws relating to banking privacy, with some stricter than federal laws. The following is a list of states with laws relating to bank records: Alabama, Alaska, California, Connecticut, Florida, Idaho (through court decisions), Illinois, Iowa, Louisiana, Maine, Maryland, Massachusetts, New Hampshire, North Carolina (through court decisions), Oklahoma, Oregon, Utah. Some example provisions include:

- **Alaska:** declares bank records to be confidential and not to be revealed except by court order or under applicable federal or state law, or to the holder of the negotiable instrument. Following the *Miller* decision in 1976, it added a provision that depositors must be notified of any request for records unless made under a search warrant.

- **Florida:** requires that banks with electronic funds transfer systems inform consumers about their privacy policies, including "protection against wrongful or accidental disclosure of confidential information"; prohibits use of Social Security numbers to identify individuals in electronic banking systems.

- **Maryland:** banks may not disclose financial records unless customer has authorized disclosure or records are subpoenaed. The subpoena must be given to the bank and the customer at least 21 days prior to disclosure.

- **New Hampshire:** requires that state and local investigators seeking financial or credit information about a bank customer describe the desired information "with particularity and consistent with the scope and requirements of the investigation."

GOVERNMENT RECORDS

Privacy Act of 1974

Growing concern about the misuse of the burgeoning government databases of information about individuals led to agreement on some basic principles for privacy protection. For example, the HEW (Health, Education, Welfare) Advisory Committee on Automated Personal Data Systems in a July 1972 report summarized these principles as follows:

1. *There must be no personal data record-keeping systems whose very existence is secret.*
2. *There must be a way for a person to find out what information about the person is in a record and how it is used.*
3. *There must be a way for a person to prevent information about the person that was obtained for one purpose from being used or made available for other purposes without the person's consent.*
4. *There must be a way for a person to correct or amend a record of identifiable information about the person.*
5. *Any organization creating, maintaining, using, or disseminating records of identifiable personal data must assure the reliability of the data for their intended use and must take precautions to prevent misuses of the data.*

The Privacy Act of 1974 (5 U.S.C. § 552a) attempts to implement these principles. In general it prohibits the release of federal information about an individual, but has a variety of exceptions including records used in the routine performance of the duties of an agency, use by the bureau of the census, statistical use when individuals cannot be identified from the records, historical records (the National Archives and Records Administration), and for law enforcement when properly requested. In 1983, the Privacy Act was amended to allow the government to give information about people who owe money to the government to credit agencies.

The "routine use" exception has been criticized as amounting to a major loophole in privacy protection. According to the ACLU, the law suffers from other defects that make it a weak guardian of privacy and one often ineffective in restraining the actions of government agencies.

In general, a federal agency must keep accurate track of any authorized disclosure of a record, and it must supply an individual upon request with any records pertaining to that individual, and provide the opportunity to correct erroneous information. However, records pertaining to law enforcement or intelligence activities may be withheld. The Freedom of Information Act, however, provides an alternative way to obtain some records.

Freedom of Information Act (FOIA)

The Freedom of Information Act (5 U.S.C. § 552) was enacted in 1966 and amended in 1974 and 1986. While the Privacy Act focuses on an individual's right to obtain records pertaining to him or herself, the FOIA attempts to make information about a wide range of government activities available to anyone willing to make the effort to request it. (In practice, there is considerable overlap between the laws, so a person seeking to find out what the government knows about him or her would ordinarily use both.)

Nearly all federal (but not state or local) agencies are subject to the provisions of the FOIA. However, there is no central clearinghouse where one can search for information; the person making the request has to determine which agency or agencies is likely to have the desired information, and issue a separate request for each agency. Agencies are required to respond within ten working days, indicating whether they will provide the information. In practice there is often a backlog of requests and thus considerable delay.

The government does not have to provide information if doing so would endanger national defense or foreign policy, reveal classified, or confidential information, or if releasing the information would harm the privacy of another individual. There is a process for appealing a decision not to release all or part of the information requested; appeals are often necessary.

Electronic Freedom of Information Act (EFOIA) of 1986

The EFOIA (5 U.S.C § 552, amended) attempts to update the Freedom of Information Act by responding to the vast growth in the use of computer databases and information systems by the federal government since the FOIA was enacted in 1966. The EFOIA requires that computerized records be made accessible in a way similar to paper records and that agencies reasonably accommodate requests to obtain records in computer-readable format.

Computer Matching and Privacy Protection Act of 1988

Besides the sheer growth in the size of databases, another concern of privacy advocates has been the ability to match or correlate records from several agencies in order to investigate a particular individual in depth. The Computer Matching and Privacy Protection Act of 1988 (5 U.S.C. § 552, amended) requires that agencies involved in computer record matching programs develop policies and procedures that must be approved by an Agency Data Integrity Board. If an adverse action is to be taken against an individual, the individual must be notified and given the opportunity to correct erroneous information. If government benefits are to be denied to an individual based on data found in a computer match, the agency must independently verify the data first.

State Laws

Most states have their own versions of the Freedom of Information Act. A similar concept is the "sunshine laws" that require many kinds of meetings to be held in public where people can find out how their government makes decisions.

The following is a list of states with laws relating to government use of databases involving personal information: Alaska, Arizona, California, Colorado, Connecticut, Florida, Georgia, Hawaii, Illinois, Indiana, Kentucky, Maine, Massachusetts, Minnesota, Mississippi, New Hampshire, New York, North Carolina, Ohio, Oklahoma, Utah, Virginia, Washington, Wisconsin. Some example provisions include:

- **Alaska:** has a set of protections in keeping with Fair Information Privacy principles. Each state agency must notify citizens from whom information is collected or sought: (1) what law allows the government to collect a given set of information, (2) what happens if the citizen refuses to provide the information, (3) what the government expects to do with the information (including to whom it may be disclosed), and (4) how the citizen can apply to correct information believed to be inaccurate.

- **California:** adds the right to sue a person for invasion of privacy if that person intentionally discloses information that he or she should have known came from a state or federal agency in violation of law.

- **Kentucky:** requires that any person shall have access to "any public record relating to him or her" in which he or she is specifically named.

- **Massachusetts:** requires that each state agency designate an individual responsible for its personal data systems and enact regulations involving outside access to information and the right of the individual to correct errors.

- **Minnesota:** Its Data Practices Act was the first comprehensive state privacy act. It includes telling individuals the purpose and intended use of information collected, the consequences of failing to provide it, and how to make corrections. Individuals must be given an opportunity to challenge information developed from "computer matching" before any action is taken.

- **Utah:** includes the federal Fair Information Practices standards in its state law. Categorizes personal information as public (accessible to anyone), private (involves personal information presumed confidential), confidential (medical and psychiatric), and protected (trade secrets or proprietary business information).

MEDICAL RECORDS

Occupational Health and Safety Act

The Occupational Health and Safety Act (29 U.S.C. § 657) allows workers to examine their occupational health records, but also requires that certain records be disclosed to the federal government when requested. Other laws such as the Rehabilitation Act (29 U.S.C. §§ 793–794) and the Vietnam Era Veterans Readjustment Act (38 U.S.C. § 2012) limit the disclosure of certain employee medical records.

The Privacy Act of 1974, which generally requires disclosure of federal records about an individual to that individual, includes medical records, but provides special procedures for releasing records to a physician instead of the individual in cases where the information may be harmful (such as to an individual's mental health.)

Federal agencies, such as the Department of Health and Human Services and the Public Health Service, as well as federally funded mental and substance abuse treatment centers, all have strict rules for disclosure of health information to third parties, with certain exceptions.

A considerable amount of new legislation is likely to emerge as part of the Health Maintenance Organization (HMO) reform. Protection of privacy and the right of individuals to see and review their records are likely to be part of such legislation.

State Laws

State laws tend to be strict about disclosure of individuals' medical records with certain exceptions. Patients generally have the right to examine their records, unless doing so might endanger their mental health. Many states provide special protections for confidentiality involving HIV/AIDs and the results of genetic testing.

The following is a list of states with laws relating to the handling of medical records: Arizona, California, Connecticut, Delaware, Florida, Hawaii, Illinois, Indiana, Iowa, Kansas, Maryland, Minnesota, Montana, Nevada, New Hampshire, New York, Rhode Island, Vermont, Washington, Wisconsin. Some example provisions include:

- **California:** full right of individual access to records except where a mental health professional refuses on grounds disclosure may harm the individual's health; in that case, the individual may designate another professional to examine the records. "No requester shall acquire medical information regarding a patient without first obtaining [written] authorization from that patient." (There are some exceptions including legal proceedings, law enforcement, medical research, and peer review.) AIDS test results are anonymous and must not be disclosed, even through subpoena. Employees are restricted in their use of employees' medical records.

- **Colorado:** defines medical records information as a "thing of value," and links it to the law against theft: "Any person who, without proper authorization, knowingly obtains a medical record or medical information with the intent to appropriate [it] to his own use or the use of another, who steals or discloses to an unauthorized person a medical record or medical information, or who, without authority, makes or causes to be made a copy of a medical record or medical information commits theft."

- **Florida:** health care providers must provide copies of medical records to the patient upon request, and may not disclose records to others without permission, except under subpoena.

- **Maryland:** allows doctors to report medical information to the state motor vehicle administration if it indicates the individual's driving may be impaired; requires that insurance claimants or applicants be given copies of their records (except those provided by a doctor, which are not available for five years, except with the doctor's consent).

- **Ohio:** makes doctor-patient relationship privileged, but requires disclosure of child abuse-related information to authorities. Provides that "No person shall be liable for any harm that results to any other person as a result of failing to disclose any confidential information about a mental health client, or failing to otherwise attempt to protect such other person from harm by any client."

- **Tennessee:** declares hospital records to be the property of the hospital, but requires access by the patient upon "good cause."

- **Washington:** requires that medical data collected by the state's health care financing system be used only for that purpose; requires that any state health ID be more secure (unique and accurate) than Social Security numbers.

SCHOOL RECORDS

Family Education Rights and Privacy Act of 1974

The Family Education Rights and Privacy Act of 1974 (20 U.S.C. § 1232g) applies to all school districts and colleges that receive federal funds (which most of them do receive). It guarantees students 18 years and older (and the parents of younger students) the right to see their school records. Each school system must have a procedure for challenging and correcting erroneous records.

The law also restricts the disclosure of school records to persons other than the parent or student, but there are many exceptions, including normal procedures that reflect a "legitimate educational interest." A 1994 amendment permits disclosure of records to the juvenile justice system; school officials are also by this amendment prohibited from revealing that records have been subpoenaed. School records can also be disclosed by the Department of Education to credit bureaus in cases of default on student loans, and statistical information can be compiled from student records for reporting crimes on campus.

Elementary and Secondary Education Act of 1978

Many conservatives have viewed the growing use of psychological testing and psychological exercises in public schools as educationally inappropriate and often as a form of propagandizing. This opposition led to an amendment in the Elementary and Secondary Education Act of 1978 that states, among other provisions, that "No student shall be required, as part of any [federally funded school] program, to submit to psychiatric . . . or psychological examination, testing, or treatment, in which the primary purpose is to reveal information concerning political affiliations; mental and psychological problems potentially embarrassing to the student or his family; sex behavior and attitudes; and illegal, anti-social, self-incriminating and demeaning behavior . . . without the consent of the student, or in the case of an unemancipated minor, without the prior written consent of the parent."

State Laws

Schools are largely regulated by states and school boards, not the federal government. While the federal constitution does apply to schools, and federal agencies can use their "power of the purse" to coerce states into following mandates, specific policies about the use and disclosure of student information vary considerably.

The following is a list of states with laws relating to school records: Arizona, California, Colorado, Connecticut, Delaware, Florida, Idaho, Illinois, Iowa, Kentucky, Louisiana, Maine, Maryland, Massachusetts, Michigan, Minnesota, Mississippi, Montana, Nebraska, Nevada, New Jersey, New York, North Carolina, North Dakota, Ohio, Oklahoma, Oregon, Rhode Island, South Dakota, Tennessee, Texas, Vermont, Virginia, Washington, Wisconsin, Wyoming. Some example provisions include:

- **California:** extends the state constitutional right of privacy to students in public institutions of higher education; gives parents an absolute right to examine their children's records in both private and public schools.

- **Maryland:** allows disclosure to the student or education officials of information concerning a student's academic achievement, biography, family, physical or mental ability, or religion.

- **Michigan:** prohibits disclosure by teachers, counselors, or other school officials of pupil information received in confidence, even in legal proceedings.

- **Ohio:** prohibits release of student files for any profit-making activity; allows release of mailing lists of high school students to military recruiters unless a parent or student objects.

- **Rhode Island:** makes it a misdemeanor to circulate without official permission any survey or questionnaire that is "so framed as to ask the pupils of any school intimate questions about themselves and/or their families, thus trespassing on the pupils' constitutional rights and invading the privacy of the home."

VIDEO RENTALS

Video Privacy Protection Act of 1988

Judge Robert Bork's nomination to the Supreme Court in 1987 became controversial in part because Bork did not believe that the language of the Constitution implied a right of privacy as declared in cases such as *Griswold v. Connecticut* and *Roe v. Wade*. Ironically, Bork's own privacy was invaded when a newspaper reporter obtained video store records that suggested Bork liked to watch pornography. Many members of Congress, while disagreeing over Bork's fitness for the Supreme Court, agreed that the titles of videos rented by an individual should be private information, as with the records of books borrowed at a public library. In response, they passed the Video Privacy Protection Act of 1988 (18 U.S.C. § 2710).

Under this law, a video store cannot disclose the titles or descriptions of the videos rented or purchased by a customer. If it does so, the customer can sue. The store may rent customer lists (without title information) if the customer has had the opportunity to remove his or her name from the list. Also, lists or compilations of titles or viewing preferences can be created for purposes of market surveys or other research provided that any information that could be used to link identifiable individuals to the records is removed.

Personal information can be disclosed "if the disclosure is incident to the ordinary course of business of the videotape service provider"—this is intended to allow for normal transaction processing. Personally identifiable information, however, must be destroyed not later than one year after the information is no longer necessary for the purpose for which it was collected.

WIRETAPPING, SURVEILLANCE, AND ENCRYPTION

Wiretap Act of 1968

The Wiretap Act of 1968 (Title 3 of the Omnibus Crime Control Bill) codified the Supreme Court's *Katz* decision by extending the protection of the Fourth Amendment against unjustified search and seizure to information traveling on a telephone line. It established the basic requirements for a search warrant for government interception of telephone communications. Recording calls by private individuals is not allowed unless all parties to the call give their consent.

Electronic Communications Privacy Act of 1986

In 1985, the congressional Office of Technology Assessment reported that "many innovations in electronic surveillance technology have outstripped constitutional and statutory protections, leaving areas in which there is currently no legal protection against . . . new surveillance devices." For example, the original wiretap law did not cover computer networks or data as opposed to voice communications. The ECPA (amending various sections of 18 U.S.C.) fills in this gap, covering radio-paging devices, electronic mail, cellular telephones, private communication carriers, and computer data transmissions (but not cordless phones).

Law enforcement agencies in turn became concerned that they would not be able to intercept computer transmissions using newer technology, particularly when encryption (coding) made the data unreadable. In 1994, the Clinton administration proposed the Communications Assistance for Law Enforcement Act (CALEA), which would require telephone companies to make sure their hardware would allow federal agents to conveniently tap into transmissions. Although FBI Director Louis Freeh insisted that the government would not abuse this access by increasing the number of taps, that number continues to rise rapidly and privacy advocates strongly oppose the CALEA and similar proposals.

State Law

State law varies with regard to private parties recording phone calls: 38 states allow any party to a conversation to record it without the consent of the other parties; 12 states require that all parties be notified and must give consent.

The following is a list of states* with laws relating to wiretapping or other forms of electronic surveillance: Alabama, Alaska, Arizona, Arkansas, California, Colorado, Connecticut, Delaware, District of Columbia, Florida, Georgia, Hawaii, Idaho, Illinois, Indiana, Iowa, Kansas, Kentucky, Louisiana, Maine, Maryland, Massachusetts, Michigan, Minnesota, Mississippi, Montana, Nebraska, Nevada, New Hampshire, New Jersey, New Mexico, New York, North Carolina, North Dakota, Ohio, Oklahoma, Oregon, Pennsylvania, Rhode Island, South Carolina, South Dakota, Tennessee, Texas, Utah, Virginia, Washington, West Virginia, Wisconsin, Wyoming. Some example provisions include:

- **Arizona:** It is a felony to intercept a wire or other oral communication without consent of one party or a court order based on probable cause.

- **California:** It is illegal to tap without consent of all parties, except in the case of telephone companies. A person may tap his or her own phone if a conversation relates to serious criminal activity and can be admitted at trial later. It is a felony for anyone except the parties involved in a telephone conversation to disclose it without permission. Cellular telephones and digital pagers are also covered. A device for "observing, photographing, recording, or amplifying" may not be installed in any place without consent.

- **Florida:** Taps permitted only by consent of both parties; illegal to advertise, mail, or possess tapping equipment.

- **Maryland:** Wiretaps [without consent of the parties in a conversation] are considered "contrary to public policy of this state and shall not be permitted except by court orders in unusual circumstances."

---

* For this purpose, the District of Columbia is a "state."

- **Oregon:** Tapping by law enforcers without consent of both parties requires a warrant, which must show probable cause that a crime "directly and immediately affecting the safety of human life or the national security has been committed or is about to be committed."

- **Washington:** Tapping generally requires consent of both parties, but one party can inform the other that the call is being recorded; police wiretapping requires consent of one party and a court order based on probable cause that a felony has been or is about to be committed.

WORKPLACE TESTING

Employee Polygraph Protection Act of 1988

The Employee Polygraph Protection Act of 1988 (29 U.S.C. § 2001) prohibits most polygraph tests by private employers (or imposes conditions that make the tests generally impracticable). Some exceptions are made for companies in the security (guard) business or in businesses involving drug manufacturing or sales.

State Laws

Most states prohibit or heavily restrict the use of polygraphs in employment, either when applying for a job or later. Most states permit some drug testing but with restrictions such as notification and the provision of treatment for employees who turn out to have a drug problem. There are generally restrictions on disclosure of test results outside the company. The following is a list of states* with laws relating to employment records: Alaska, California, Colorado, Connecticut, Delaware, District of Columbia, Florida, Hawaii, Illinois, Iowa, Maine, Massachusetts, Michigan, Minnesota, Nevada, New Hampshire, New Jersey, New York, North Carolina, North Dakota, Ohio, Oregon, Pennsylvania, Rhode Island, South Dakota, Tennessee, Utah, Vermont, Washington, Wisconsin.

The following is a list of states* with laws relating to polygraphs or other forms of testing: Alabama, Alaska, Arizona, Arkansas, California, Connecticut, Delaware, District of Columbia, Florida, Georgia, Hawaii, Idaho, Illinois, Iowa, Maine, Maryland, Massachusetts, Michigan, Minnesota, Mississippi, Montana, Nebraska, Nevada, New Jersey, New Mexico, New York, North Carolina, North Dakota, Oklahoma, Oregon, Pennsylvania, Rhode Island, South Carolina, Tennessee, Texas, Utah, Vermont, Virginia, Washington, West Virginia, Wisconsin.

Some example provisions of these laws include:

- **California:** Employees have the right to inspect all records and personnel files except for letters of reference and criminal investigation records.

- **Connecticut:** Employees have the right to inspect their records and either correct mistakes or file a rebuttal for disputed information; companies may give "truthful statements" that discredit an employee, but may not "blacklist" employees to prevent them from working in their industry. Urine tests for drugs can be administered only if there is "reasonable suspicion that the employee is under the influence of drugs or alcohol, which adversely affects or could affect such employee's job performance." Any positive result must be confirmed by two tests.

- **Louisiana:** A polygraph examiner must inform the person being tested that testing is voluntary and that refusal to take the test may not be grounds for termination. Examiners who fail to do so can lose their license.

- **Maryland:** Employers must include in application forms a notice that "an employer may not require or demand any applicant for employment or prospective employment to submit to or take a polygraph, lie detector, or similar test or examination as a condition for employment or continued employment."

- **Massachusetts:** Psychological "honesty tests" may not be administered in connection with employment.

- **Nevada:** Employers may not discriminate because an employee "uses a lawful product outside the premises of the employer." An employee may not be dismissed based on information provided by a "spotter" without a hearing or opportunity to confront the spotter.

- **North Carolina:** An employer may test for AIDS as part of an annual physical exam, and employees with the HIV/AIDS virus may be fired if there is a risk to others.

- **North Dakota:** All testing for HIV/AIDS must be confidential and by consent.

- **Rhode Island:** Urinalysis and blood testing for alcohol or drugs is permitted only when there are "reasonable grounds." Employers may not perform genetic tests.

- **Tennessee:** The law states that "No employer may take any personnel action based solely upon the results of a polygraph examination." Questions may not ask about sexual behavior or orientation unless (a) the question is relevant to the purpose of the exam, (b) the examinee gives written permission, and (c) the examinee has the right to explain any problematic results. Exams may not ask about religious, political, labor, or racial matters or anything that took place five or more years earlier, except for felonies and drug violations.

INTERNATIONAL PRIVACY LAWS

United Nations

The United Nations Universal Declaration of Human Rights (1948) is the philosophical basis for much of modern international law. It has the following privacy-related provisions:

> **Article 3:** *Everyone has the right to life, liberty, and security of person.*
> **Article 8:** *Everyone has the right to an effective remedy by the competent national tribunals for acts violating the fundamental rights granted him by the constitution or by law.*
> **Article 12:** *No one shall be subjected to arbitrary interference with his privacy, family, home or correspondence, nor to attacks upon his honor or reputation. Everyone has the right to the protection of the law against such interference or attacks.*

European Union

The European Union has emerged with one of the strongest and most comprehensive sets of privacy laws. The document has many "whereases" and details of implementation. However, the core of the legislation can be found in the following articles.

Article 6 describes the basic principles to be implemented in the EU's data policies:

> *Member States shall provide that personal data must be:*
> *(a) processed fairly and lawfully;*
> *(b) collected for specified, explicit and legitimate purposes and not further processed in a way incompatible with those purposes. Further processing of data for historical, statistical or scientific purposes shall not be considered as incompatible provided that Member States provide appropriate safeguards;*
> *(c) adequate, relevant and not excessive in relation to the purposes for which they are collected and/or for which they are further processed;*
> *(d) accurate and, where necessary, kept up to date; every reasonable step must be taken to ensure that data which are inaccurate or incomplete, having regard to the purposes for which they were collected or for which they are further processed, are erased or rectified;*
> *(e) kept in a form which permits identification of data subjects for no longer*

than is necessary for the purposes for which the data were collected or for which they are further processed. Member States shall lay down appropriate safeguards for personal data stored for longer periods for historical, statistical or scientific use.

Article 7 specifies the requirements for the gathering and processing of personal data:

Member States shall provide that personal data may be processed only if:
(a) the data subject has given his consent unambiguously; or
(b) processing is necessary for the performance of a contract to which the data subject is party or in order to take steps at the request of the data subject entering into a contract; or
(c) processing is necessary for compliance with a legal obligation to which the controller is subject; or
(d) processing is necessary in order to protect the vital interests of the data subject; or
(e) processing is necessary for the performance of a task carried out in the public interest or in the exercise of official authority vested in the controller or in a third party to whom the data are disclosed; or
(f) processing is necessary for the purposes of the legitimate interests pursued by the controller or by the third party or parties to whom the data are disclosed, except where such interests are overridden by the interests or fundamental rights and freedoms of the data subject which require protection under Article 1(1).

Article 10 specifies what must be disclosed to the individual about whom information is to be gathered:

Member States shall provide that the controller or his representative must provide a data subject from whom data relating to himself are collected with at least the following information, except where he already knows:
(a) the identity of the controller and of his representative, if any.
(b) the purposes of the processing for which the data are intended.
(c) any further information such as
—the recipients or categories of recipients of the data;
—whether replies to the questions are obligatory or voluntary, as well as the possible consequences of the failure to reply;
—the existence of the right of access to and the right to rectify the data concerning him insofar as they are necessary, having regard to the specific circumstances in which the data are collected, to guarantee fair processing in respect of the data subject.

The Law of Privacy

Article 25 deals with the interface between the EU and other countries. Its main concern is to ensure that data not be shared with countries that do not have similarly strict protections in place, since doing so could lead to improper disclosure or other abuses and ultimately defeat the purpose of the legislation:

1. *Member States shall provide that the transfer to a third country of personal data which are undergoing processing or are intended for processing after transfer may take place only if, without prejudice to compliance with the national provisions adopted pursuant to the other provisions of this Directive, the third country in question ensures an adequate level of protection.*
2. *The adequacy of the level of protection afforded by a third country shall be assessed in the light of all the circumstances surrounding a data transfer operation or set of data transfer operations; particular consideration shall be given to the nature of the data, the purpose and duration of the proposed processing operation or operations, the country of origin and country of final destination, the rules of law, both general and sectoral, in force in the third country in question and the professional rules and security measures which are complied with in those countries.*

Canada

The British Columbia, Canada Freedom of Information and Privacy Act has provisions that are similar to a combination of the U.S. Freedom of Information Act and the Privacy Act of 1974. Under "Purposes of this Act" it states that:

2. *(1) The purposes of this Act are to make public bodies more accountable to the public and to protect personal privacy by*
   (a) giving the public a right of access to records,
   (b) giving individuals a right of access to, and a right to request correction of, personal information about themselves,
   (c) specifying limited exceptions to the right of access,
   (d) preventing the unauthorized collection, use, or disclosure of personal information by public bodies, and
   (e) providing for an independent review of decisions made under this Act.

The Act applies to most records compiled by public agencies in the province, except for court records, records relating to legislative offices, some educational materials, and certain other exceptions. The "head of a public body must make every reasonable effort to assist applicants and to respond without delay to each applicant openly, accurately, and completely." It goes on to specify that the public body must extract a copy of a computerized record provided it is within normal technical expertise and not unduly burdensome.

After providing a mechanism for disclosure, the Act discusses circumstances under which information with which the government is not obliged to provide information (or indeed, is required to keep it confidential). It also discusses the need to give notice to third parties who may be harmed by a proposed disclosure (such as that of proprietary business information).

Protection of Privacy in other Countries

In general, the EU offers the strongest privacy protection, with countries in the British Commonwealth (such as Canada and Australia) also having high standards. These countries have stricter and more uniform regulation of private enterprise than the United States, but the greater centralization of government and weaker constitutional protection for free speech and the press may make it harder to disclose governmental abuses.

It is hard to compare the United States with other countries because it has both federal and state laws (and courts) that come into play under various circumstances. Regulation of the gathering and use of information by private enterprise is spotty, especially with regard to emerging Internet commerce. Because the United States tends to strike a balance toward freedom of speech and the press and away from government secrecy, governmental abuses can be more easily brought to light.

It is important to note that the right to privacy, like all rights, is dependent on a government not only providing constitutional guarantees, but being willing to abide by them. Dictatorships are unlikely to protect the privacy of their opponents, and parties involved in civil war are unlikely to have a regard for individual rights. China, the world's largest country, has little protection for privacy against the government, and the former U.S.S.R. has not yet replaced its post-Communist chaos with an effective system of legal guarantees.

COURT CASES

There are many cases in the Supreme Court and lower courts that hinge on some aspect of privacy. In keeping with the topic of this book, the selection of cases focuses on those that deal primarily with privacy violations involving the use (or abuse) of information, surveillance, or monitoring.

The Law of Privacy

OLMSTEAD V. U.S., 277 U.S. 438 (1928)

Background

During the Prohibition Era of the 1920s, federal agents waged a relentless war against bootleggers who sold illegal liquor. Agents suspected that Roy Olmstead was a major bootlegger, so they tapped the phone lines in the basement of a building where he had an office, and also tapped phone lines going into his home. The agents did not obtain court warrants before installing the taps. Using the taps, the agents gained evidence sufficient to convict him. After appeal, the case eventually reached the Supreme Court.

Legal Issues

Olmstead's defense claimed that the use of wiretaps violated Olmstead's constitutional rights under the Fourth Amendment, which states that "The right of the people to be secure in their persons, houses, papers, and effects against unreasonable searches and seizures shall not be violated, and no warrants shall issue but upon probable cause, supported by oath or affirmation and particularly describing the place to be searched and the persons or things to be seized." According to the defense, the wiretap was equivalent to a search and seizure of Olmstead's private office and home, and since it was done without a warrant, it was unconstitutional.

The defense also claimed that the prosecution's use of Olmstead's wire-tapped conversations violated the Fifth Amendment, which states (in part) that "No person . . . shall be compelled, in any criminal case, to be a witness against himself." According to the defense, using the wiretapped conversation forced him in effect to become an unwilling witness against himself.

Decision

The majority of the Court upheld Olmstead's conviction and rejected both constitutional challenges. With regard to the Fourth Amendment, the Court noted that "The Amendment itself shows that the search is to be of material things—the person, the house, his papers, or his effects. The description of the warrant necessary to make the proceeding lawful is that it must specify the place to be searched and the person or *things* to be seized." The Court noted that nothing physical had been seized. It also rejected the attempt to make an analogy between phone conversations and mail. While the mail is presumed confidential by the government, "The United States takes no such care of telegraph or telephone messages as of mailed sealed letters. The [Fourth] Amendment does not forbid what was done here. There was no searching. There was no seizure. The evidence was secured by the use of the sense of hearing, and that only."

The Court also insisted that "There was no entry of the houses or offices of the defendants. By the invention of the telephone fifty years ago and its application for the purpose of extending communications, one can talk with another at a far distant place. The language of the [Fourth] Amendment cannot be extended and expanded to include telephone wires reaching to the whole world from the defendant's house or office. The intervening wires are not part of his house or office any more than are the highways along which they are stretched."

The Court also rejected the Fifth Amendment challenge because Olmstead had not been forced or compelled to make the incriminating statements.

Impact

As a result of *Olmstead*, any protection against federal wiretapping would have to come through legislation (until the decision was reversed in *Katz v. U.S.* in 1967). State law, however, could restrict wiretapping by state or local law enforcement agencies.

Perhaps the most important impact of *Olmstead*, however, came from Justice Brandeis' dissenting opinion, which thrust the constitutional issue of privacy into the spotlight. While the Court majority had insisted on a literal interpretation of the Fourth and Fifth Amendments, Brandeis noted that "Since [*McCullough v. Maryland*, 17 U.S. 316, 1819], this Court has repeatedly sustained the exercise of power by Congress, under various clauses of that instrument, over objects of which the Fathers could not have dreamed." Brandeis cited examples of "modern" regulations that would have been considered oppressive or even absurd in earlier times, and insisted that like regulations, protections for rights such as privacy must also be updated when technology or other conditions change.

Brandeis noted that "When the Fourth and Fifth Amendments were adopted, 'the form that evil [of forced self-incrimination] had theretofore taken' had been necessarily simple. Force and violence were then the only means known to man by which a Government could directly effect self-incrimination. It could compel the individual to testify—a compulsion effected, if need be, by torture. It could secure possession of his papers and other articles incident to his private life—a seizure effected, if need be, by breaking and entry."

Brandeis insisted that courts must take changing conditions into account: "Subtler and more far-reaching means of invading privacy have become available to the Government. Discovery and invention have made it possible for the Government, by means far more effective than stretching upon the rack, to obtain disclosure in court of what is whispered in the closet."

The words of Justice Brandeis would prove to be prophetic as even newer technologies (such as video cameras, infrared scopes, and sophisticated "bugs") would become available to both government and private eavesdroppers, and the means of communication (and thus of potential self-incrimination) would come to include the teletype, the fax, and electronic mail.

GRISWOLD V. CONNECTICUT, 381 U.S. 479 (1965)

Background

During the 19th century, "anti-vice" crusaders succeeded in passing laws that made it illegal in most states to provide information about contraception (birth control) methods or to provide devices that could be used to prevent conception. By the 1960s, however, the invention of an effective birth control pill and freer attitudes about sex were leading to pressure to overturn restrictive laws.

Griswold, the Executive Director of the Planned Parenthood League of Connecticut, and the organization's medical director were convicted of violating Connecticut's anti-contraception law by providing birth control information and devices to clients. Griswold's attorneys appealed the conviction to the state court of appeals and then to the Connecticut Supreme Court, but both upheld the conviction. The case finally reached the U.S. Supreme Court.

Legal Issues

Griswold's appeal was based on the argument that the state anti-contraception law violated the Fourteenth Amendment to the Constitution. In part, this amendment states: "No State shall make or enforce any law which shall abridge the privileges or immunities of citizens of the United States; nor shall any State deprive any person of life, liberty, or property, without due process of law; nor deny to any person within its jurisdiction the equal protection of the laws."

This amendment had been passed originally just after the Civil War to ensure that the former Confederate states give their black citizens the same "privileges and immunities" afforded to whites. But the Supreme Court had gradually broadened its interpretation to find that the Fourteenth Amendment "incorporated" many of the rights in the first ten amendments (the Bill of Rights) and that the states as well as the federal government were required to respect these rights.

Griswold thus argued that the right of a married couple to make decisions about birth control was part of that couple's fundamental privacy: a right just as basic as freedom of speech or freedom of association, and thus incorporated in the Fourteenth Amendment. If the Court agreed, this meant that the state birth control law was unconstitutional and that the conviction would be overturned.

The state of Connecticut argued that the Bill of Rights made no mention of birth control nor indeed, of any "right to privacy." Therefore, no such right was incorporated in the Fourteenth Amendment, and the state was not prevented from outlawing birth control.

Decision

Justice William O. Douglas, writing for the majority, agreed with Griswold's argument. He disposed of the argument that privacy was not mentioned in the Constitution by noting that "The association of people is not mentioned in the Constitution nor in the Bill of Rights. The right to educate a child in a school of the parents' choice—whether public or private or parochial—is also not mentioned. Nor is the right to study any particular subject or any foreign language. Yet the First Amendment has been construed to include certain of those rights."

He then cited a number of cases in which the Court had established that such rights existed even though they are not specifically mentioned in the Constitution. For example, "In *NAACP v. Alabama*, 357 U.S. 449, 462 we protected the 'freedom to associate and privacy in one's associations,' noting that freedom of association was a peripheral First Amendment right. Disclosure of membership lists of a constitutionally valid association, we held, was invalid as entailing the likelihood of a substantial restraint upon the exercise by petitioner's members of their right to freedom of association."

Douglas went on to conclude that "The foregoing cases suggest that specific guarantees in the Bill of Rights have penumbras [shadows], formed by emanations from those guarantees that help give them life and substance. . . . Various guarantees create zones of privacy. The right of association contained in the penumbra of the First Amendment is one, as we have seen. The Third Amendment, in its prohibition against the quartering of soldiers "in any house" in time of peace without the consent of the owner, is another facet of that privacy. The Fourth Amendment explicitly affirms the "right of the people to be secure in their persons, houses, papers, and effects, against unreasonable searches and seizures." The Fifth Amendment, in its Self-Incrimination Clause, enables the citizen to create a zone of privacy which government may not force him to surrender to his detriment."

Douglas went on to note that the Constitution also says, in the Ninth Amendment, that "The enumeration in the Constitution, of certain rights, shall not be construed to deny or disparage others retained by the people." This made it impermissible to argue, as Connecticut had, that the lack of a specific "right of privacy" in the Bill of Rights meant that no such right existed.

Douglas thus replaced narrowly specific guarantees with "zones of privacy" that he believed were implied in the guarantees of the Bill of Rights. He insisted that something as intimate as the marriage relationship must stand at the center of the zone of privacy. The decision to use contraception (and thus the right to obtain information and devices) is thus protected by the Constitution.

Impact

The Griswold decision has had a major impact on how courts think about privacy. In effect, it elevates a "right of privacy" to as high a status as freedom of speech, freedom of association, the right against self-incrimination, and other items specifically mentioned in the Bill of Rights. The Court would go on to find a right to obtain an abortion (*Roe v. Wade*, 1973) and to make a decision about life-saving medical care (*Cruzan*, 1990). "Strict constructionists" such as Robert Bork would continue to oppose what they consider to be an illegitimate and subjective "creation" of rights by courts.

It is important to note, however, what *Griswold* did not do. While it created a broad right of privacy regarding personal decisions and intimate relationships, it refused to extend the right to make decisions or obtain information or devices to the marketplace or the public square. Indeed, as Douglas noted, "We do not sit as a super-legislature to determine the wisdom, need, and propriety of laws that touch economic problems, business affairs, or social conditions." In other words, the federal government or the states could still set safety standards for condoms or determine licensing requirements for birth control counselors.

After its brief moment in the sun, the Ninth Amendment has not often been used to argue for the existence of other rights that could limit government power. Instead, it has become part of a political debate over small versus big government.

KATZ V. UNITED STATES, 389 U.S. 347 (1967)

Background

As with Roy Olmstead, federal agents suspected that Charles Katz was engaging in illegal activity (in this case, conducting a multistate gambling operation by phone). The agents placed a "bug" on the outside of a phone booth that Katz was using. They then used the recordings as evidence to convict him for "illegal transmission of wagering information." The conviction was upheld on appeal, with the court citing the *Olmstead* case and noting that the police did not physically enter the area of the phone booth occupied by Katz.

Privacy in the Information Age

Legal Issues

As noted in the court's opinion, the petitioner seeking to overturn the conviction had raised two main issues:

A. Whether a public telephone booth is a constitutionally protected area so that evidence obtained by attaching an electronic listening recording device to the top of such a booth is obtained in violation of the right to privacy of the user of the booth.
B. Whether physical penetration of a constitutionally protected area is necessary before a search and seizure can be said to be violative of the Fourth Amendment to the United States Constitution.

Decision

The Court, however, refused to limit its consideration to the narrow question of just what part of the phone booth might be constitutionally protected. The general legal and social climate had changed considerably since *Olmstead*. During the 1950s and 1960s, the Supreme Court under Chief Justice Earl Warren had become much more willing to broadly interpret constitutional protections in the light of changing social conditions, whether with regard to civil rights (*Brown v. Board of Education*, 1954), privacy (*Griswold v. Connecticut*, 1965), protection against overbroad searches (*Mapp v. Ohio*, 1961), or against compelled self-incrimination (the famous *Miranda v. Arizona*, 1966, which led to the familiar warning heard endlessly on television cop shows). The courts were now heeding Brandeis' call for an explicit and robust constitutional right to personal privacy.

The Court declared that "the Fourth Amendment protects people, not places. What a person knowingly exposes to the public, even in his own home or office, is not a subject of Fourth Amendment protection. . . . But what he seeks to preserve as private, even in an area accessible to the public, may be constitutionally protected."

Looking to a previous Supreme Court decision (*Silverman v. United States*, 365 U.S. 505, 511), the Court noted: ". . . we have expressly held that the Fourth Amendment governs not only the seizure of tangible items, but extends as well to the recording of oral statements, overheard without any technical trespass under . . . local property law. Once this much is acknowledged, and once it is recognized that the Fourth Amendment protects people—and not simply 'areas'—against unreasonable searches and seizures, it becomes clear that the reach of that Amendment cannot turn upon the presence or absence of a physical intrusion into any given enclosure."

The justices had decided that it was not the existence of an enclosed place that created a right of privacy, but a person's engaging in an activity that he or she can reasonably expect to be private: "No less than an individual in a business office, in a friend's apartment, or in a taxicab, a person in a telephone booth may rely upon the protection of the Fourth Amendment. One who occupies [the booth], shuts the door behind him, and pays the toll that permits him to place a call is surely entitled to assume that the words he utters into the mouthpiece will not be broadcast to the world. To read the Constitution more narrowly is to ignore the vital role that the public telephone has come to play in private communication."

The Court therefore concluded that Katz's rights under the Fourth Amendment had been violated. Although the Court acknowledged that the government agents had probable cause to suspect a crime and conducted only enough surveillance to gather relevant evidence, it overturned the conviction because the agents had not obtained a warrant as required under the Fourth Amendment.

Impact

Since *Katz*, law enforcement officials generally have to obtain a warrant before beginning a wiretap or other surveillance of an individual's conversations. (In 1972 this requirement was extended by the courts to include even cases where the government believed there was a threat to "national security.")

There are some exceptions. In *United States v. David Lee Smith* (978 F. 2nd 171, U.S. App.), 1992, a court of appeals ruled that conversations on cordless telephones (which actually use radio waves to carry conversations) could be tapped by police without obtaining a search warrant. (Congress then passed a law to extend the warrant requirement to cover cordless phones, but not cellular ones.) Changes in technology thus have continued to challenge the boundaries placed around law enforcement activities by the courts. When the Justice Department concluded that the Wiretap Act of 1968 did not require a warrant for intercepting e-mail and other computer communications (because they were not aural or vocal in nature), Congress responded by passing the Electronic Communications Privacy Act of 1986.

There have been a number of cases (ranging from Watergate to the surveillance of left-wing groups and political enemies by the FBI) where the legal system seems to have been ineffective in preventing wiretapping abuses.

Some private wiretapping is permissible. Employers generally have the right to monitor employee conversations on company phones if the monitoring is for a legitimate business purpose, such as training or evaluation of employees' performance.

UNITED STATES V. MILLER, 425 U.S. 435 (1976)

Background

In 1970, Congress passed the Bank Secrecy Act, which required banks to report cash transactions over $10,000 and certain other transactions, and to keep copies of bank records such as deposit slips and checks for at least five years. The justification given for the legislation was that it would make it easier for law enforcement agencies to keep track of organized criminal activity such as the "laundering" of drug money.

In *California Bankers Association* (1970), the Supreme Court ruled that the transaction tracking provisions of the Bank Secrecy Act did not violate Fourth Amendment privacy rights. In *Miller* a related issue would be resolved: Were the Act's provisions making it easy for the government to obtain copies of a suspected person's bank records also constitutional?

On December 18, 1972, a deputy sheriff in Houston County, Georgia, responding to a tip, stopped a truck that turned out to contain distillery equipment and raw material for making liquor. About a month later, when a warehouse caught fire, firefighters and sheriff's deputies discovered a distillery and illegal liquor. Agents from the Treasury Department's Bureau of Alcohol, Tobacco, and Firearms investigated, and began to suspect a man named Mitch Miller as being leader of the bootlegging ring. They issued a subpoena to obtain Miller's records from two banks where he had accounts. The records showed that Miller had rented the truck, purchased a considerable amount of pipe (useful for distilling), and other materials. The leads and evidence provided by the records helped the government convict Miller of violation of liquor laws.

Legal Issues

Miller's attorneys argued that his bank records required a full-fledged subpoena similar to that used to get permission to search a person's home. (Such a subpoena would be issued by a judge and would specify what is being sought, and showing probable cause that a crime had been committed and that the suspected evidence was related to the crime.) The government argued that the Bank Secrecy Act authorized a much simpler subpoena issued by the U.S. Attorney. The basic issue was whether Miller's bank records were entitled to the full protection of the Fourth Amendment. If so, the Bank Secrecy Act would be unconstitutional and Miller's conviction could be reversed.

The Law of Privacy

The Fifth District Court of Appeals agreed with Miller and ruled that his rights had been violated by requiring a third party (the bank) to produce Miller's private papers without due process. The government appealed to the U.S. Supreme Court, arguing that Miller had no "Fourth Amendment interest" in his bank records, and that the Bank Secrecy Act did not violate the Constitution.

Justice Powell's majority opinion upheld the government. The Fourth Amendment refers to "the right of the people to be secure in their persons, houses, papers, and effects, against unreasonable searches and seizures . . ." But, Powell writes ". . . the documents subpoenaed here are not respondent's [Miller's] 'private papers.' . . . respondent can assert neither ownership nor possession. Instead, these are the business records of the banks." Harking back to the earlier decision in *California Bankers Association*, Powell notes that the bank is not "passively" holding records for the depositor, but rather, is a party in a business relationship with the depositor, and the bank records are property of the bank used to conduct its business with its customers.

Powell then turned to the possibility that the Bank Secrecy Act nevertheless allowed an impermissible invasion of Miller's privacy by making it too easy for the government to obtain if not papers, the private information contained in them. Powell notes that "Respondent urges that he has a Fourth Amendment interest in the records kept by the banks because they are merely copies of personal records that were made available to the banks for a limited purpose and in which he has a reasonable expectation of privacy." Thus the Fourth Amendment "expectation of privacy" test (from *Katz* and other cases) comes into play.

Powell rejects this challenge as well: "Even if we direct our attention to the original checks and deposit slips, rather than to the microfilm copies actually viewed and obtained by means of the subpoena, we perceive no legitimate 'expectation of privacy' in their contents. The checks are not confidential communications but negotiable instruments to be used in commercial transactions. All of the documents obtained, including financial statements and deposit slips, contain only information voluntarily conveyed to the banks and exposed to their employees in the ordinary course of business." Referring to earlier cases, Powell points out that there is no constitutional protection against information that was voluntarily revealed to a third party in the ordinary course of business being revealed to the government. Nor is their any protection against that third party being subpoenaed. Therefore, the Court ruled, Miller had no Fourth Amendment privacy right, and his conviction was upheld.

Impact

The *Miller* case is an example that shows that the robust privacy right seen emanating from the Constitution in *Griswold* and *Roe v. Wade* apparently does not pass from the bedroom to the checkbook. Further, the principle from *Katz* that changing technology from letters to telephone requires an expansion of privacy rights was not applied in *Miller*, despite the fact that banking might be considered as much of a necessity of modern life as the telephone.

Additionally, *Miller* can also be viewed as part of an ongoing seesaw battle between privacy rights and law enforcement interests. Congress passed the Bank Secrecy Act to help law enforcers fight organized crime. *Miller* upheld the constitutionality of the law. Yet while people have a strong interest in fighting crime, they also have shown a growing interest in protecting privacy. Congress, responding to these conflicting interests, passes some laws that limit privacy in favor of law enforcement and other laws that provide greater protection for privacy. The result of this conflict is that it is far from easy for the average individual to know what personal records or other information is protected, and from whom.

NEW JERSEY V. T.L.O., 469 U.S. 325 (1985)

Background

A teacher in a New Jersey public school noticed that T.L.O. (a 14-year-old girl) and another student were smoking in the school lavatory in violation of school rules. (Since the defendant was a minor, only her initials appear in court documents.) The teacher took her to the assistant vice principal. When confronted by the latter, T.L.O. insisted that she had not been smoking. He demanded to see her purse, which turned out to contain both a pack of cigarettes and a pack of the kind of cigarette papers commonly used by marijuana smokers. Continuing to search the purse, he found a pipe, marijuana, and a list of students and two letters that suggested that T.L.O. was dealing in marijuana.

Legal Issues

In juvenile court, T.L.O.'s attorney argued that the search had violated the Fourth Amendment. The court held that while the Fourth Amendment did apply to searches in schools, the search of T.L.O.'s purse met the standard of being "reasonable." The appeals court upheld the search, but the New Jersey Supreme Court reversed the decision, calling the search unreasonable. The case then went to the Supreme Court.

Decision

The Supreme Court noted that while parents are not bound by the Fourth Amendment, teachers are not just substitutes for parents, but also representatives of the State. As such, they are bound by the restrictions imposed by the Fourth Amendment.

The Court noted, however, that the need for "striking the balance between schoolchildren's legitimate expectations of privacy and the school's equally legitimate need to maintain an environment in which learning can take place requires some easing of the restrictions to which searches by public authorities are ordinarily subject." Thus school officials, unlike police, do not have to obtain a warrant before conducting a search, and do not have to meet the stricter standard of having "probable cause" to believe that there is criminal activity. Instead, they need only have "reasonable grounds for suspecting that the search will turn up evidence that the student has violated or is violating either the law or the rules of the school. And such a search will be permissible in its scope when the measures adopted are reasonably related to the objectives of the search, and not excessively intrusive in light of the student's age and sex and the nature of the infraction."

Impact

New Jersey v. T.L.O. established that on the one hand, students did have some expectation of privacy, but on the other hand, schools could conduct searches that were reasonably related to suspected violations of rules. Such practices as making students walk through a metal detector to prevent them from carrying weapons into the school have similarly been upheld as reasonably related to the school's need to provide a safe educational environment.

O'BRIEN V. PAPA GINO'S OF AMERICA, INC. 80 F. 2D 1067, 1072 (1ST CIR. 1986)

Background

A manager at a Papa Gino's restaurant in New Hampshire confronted an employee, saying that he had been seen using drugs outside of work. The employee took a polygraph test in which he was asked drug-related questions. The examiner said that he believed the employee was lying about his drug use, and the latter was fired. He sued the company.

Legal Issues

O'Brien argued that he had been forced to take the polygraph test or lose his job, and that the test included questions that were not related to his work. Papa Gino's argued that it had a legitimate interest in avoiding the risks caused by an employee who regularly uses drugs, even if the drugs are used only outside of work.

Decision

The jury found that the test and other investigative techniques used by Papa Gino's was "highly offensive to a reasonable person." It awarded $398,200 to O'Brien. The verdict was later upheld by the U.S. Court of Appeals for the First Circuit.

Impact

Public concern about the use of polygraphs and other devices that measure physical stress (such as voice analyzers) led to the passage in 1988 of the Employee Polygraph Protection Act. This law bans employers from using such devices in most cases.

O'CONNOR V. ORTEGA, 480 U.S. 709 (1987)

Background

Dennis O'Connor, director of Napa State Hospital in California, suspected that Dr. Magno Ortega, a psychiatrist and manager of a residency program for doctors, had improperly coerced residents into paying for a computer, and was also concerned that he was involved in sexual harassment. O'Connor instituted a number of searches of Dr. Ortega's office while the doctor was on administrative leave, seizing items that were later used against Ortega in proceedings before the California State Personnel Board.

Legal Issues

Dr. Ortega claimed that the search of his office violated the Fourth Amendment protections against improper search and seizure because he had a "reasonable expectation of privacy" in his office. O'Connor claimed that the search was a routine inventory checkup needed to secure state property and that it did not violate Ortega's privacy.

Decision

The district court upheld O'Connor, agreeing that there was no violation of privacy. The court of appeals, however, reversed that decision, holding that

Ortega did have a reasonable expectation of privacy and that the "routine inventory" defense was not applicable because such inventories had previously only been used for dismissed employees, not employees on leave.

O'Connor appealed the decision to the Supreme Court. In a 5–4 decision, the Court found that in keeping with "the realities of the workplace" a supervisor should not be expected to follow the same strict standards as a law enforcement officer. Work-related searches, the Court found, were "merely incident to the primary business of the agency." Requiring that a warrant be obtained for every search would "seriously disrupt the routine conduct of business." The Court held that the employer needed only to meet a standard of "reasonableness" before undertaking a search.

Impact

The *O'Connor* decision served notice to employees that their privacy rights were limited and that employers were not bound by the same rules as government officials or police officers. This did not mean, however, that employees had *no* privacy in the workplace. As the Court noted, "Not everything that passes through the confines of the business address can be considered part of the workplace context, however. An employee may bring closed luggage to the office prior to leaving on a trip, or a handbag or briefcase each workday. While whatever expectation of privacy the employee has in the existence and the outward appearance of the luggage is affected by its presence in the workplace, the employee's expectation of privacy in the contents of the luggage is not affected in the same way. The appropriate standard for a workplace search does not necessarily apply to a piece of closed personal luggage, a handbag, or a briefcase that happens to be within the employer's business address." Similarly, the Supreme Court majority agreed with the Appeals Court that Ortega had a "reasonable expectation of privacy" with regard to his locked desk and file cabinet, which he did not share with other employees.

Thus *O'Connor* did not fully resolve the question of what is private in the workplace, but it did provide some principles that could be applied to future cases.

ALANA SHOARS V. EPSON AMERICA, INC., NO. B 073234, LOS ANGELES SUPERIOR COURT (1990)

Background

Epson America e-mail administrator Alana Shoars discovered that her supervisor had been retrieving and printing out all the electronic mail sent by employees at the company's Torrance, California, office. When she told the general manager about her discovery and demanded that the practice be stopped, her supervisor fired her. Shoars then sued Epson for wrongful termination. (She also filed a class action suit for invasion of privacy, on behalf of herself and 77 other Epson employees whose e-mail had been intercepted.)

Legal Issues

Shoars' attorney argued that Epson had led her to believe that employee e-mail was considered private, and that the use of secret personal passwords for mail accounts reinforced that sense of privacy. He also argued that the interception of e-mail violated anti-wiretapping provisions in the state penal code.

Epson argued that the monitoring of e-mail was only for making sure the system was working properly. More fundamentally, they also argued that e-mail in a business was a facility provided solely for business purposes, and that Shoars and the other employees had no "expectation of privacy." Finally, they argued that the California anti-wiretapping laws did not apply to the new technology of electronic mail.

Decision

The trial court agreed that e-mail was not covered under California's wire-tapping laws, and that any protection for e-mail would have to be provided by new legislation. The court also threw out the class action suit, agreeing with Epson that there was "no sufficient legal or factual basis for extending the right to privacy to cover business-related communications." The appeals court agreed with the decision, but allowed Shoars to go ahead to trial on a separate suit for slander.

Impact

Although this was a state court decision rather than a federal one, the *Shoars* case follows the general pattern in favor of the employer for most workplace and e-mail monitoring cases. Activists who want to strengthen workplace privacy protection must generally direct their efforts not to the courts but to the legislature or to labor negotiations.

SOROKA V. DAYTON HUDSON CORP., 1 CAL. RPTR. 2D 77, 6 IER CASES (BNA) 1491 (APP. 1991)

Background

Sibi Soroka applied for a job as a security supervisor at Target Stores, which is owned by the Dayton Hudson Corporation. As part of his job interview, Soroka was given a "psychological inventory"—a written test that asked him about a variety of beliefs, feelings, and situations. As he worked his way through the test, he encountered questions such as the following:

> 3. *I looked up to my father as an ideal man.*
> 8. *I like Alice in Wonderland by Lewis Carroll.*
> 23. *When a person "pads" his income tax report so as to get out of some of his taxes, it is just as bad as stealing money from the government.*
> 73. *Maybe some minorities get rough treatment, but it is no business of mine.*
> 368. *I have no difficulty starting or holding my urine.*
> 466. *My sex life is satisfactory.*
> 492. *I am very strongly attracted by members of my own sex.*
> 506. *I believe in the second coming of Christ.*

Soroka became increasingly disturbed as he read. Some of the questions, such as 23, clearly tested for honesty. Question number 368, however, was clearly looking for health problems. Questions 466 and 492, inquiring into sexual matters, seemed to be none of the store's business, as did questions about social issues (73) or religion (506). Soroka finished the test because he needed a job, but he also made a copy of the test and showed it to an attorney. He decided to sue Target, not for personal damages, but to prevent them from giving anyone else such tests in the future.

Legal Issues

Soroka argued that the test was overly intrusive in seeking personal, intimate information, and thus violated the right to privacy in California's constitution (one of the strongest state privacy codes).

Target argued that shoplifting was a major problem, and that the store was trying to hire effective security personnel. On the other hand, the store was concerned about hiring persons to deal with the public in this sensitive job who were mentally or emotionally unstable or violent. If the store did not take measures to screen out such persons and one of its guards injured someone, the store could be sued for "negligent hiring." The store had adopted the psychological test (called Psychscreen) because it was part of the screening process used by many police departments. Finally, the store insisted that the applicant's privacy was protected because no one at the company ever saw an applicant's actual answer sheet, only a numerical score in each of several categories.

Soroka's lawyer replied that the security job was not all that high level or sensitive, and that there was no proof of the accuracy or reliability of the test. (He pointed out that police departments, unlike the store, conducted a much more extensive background investigation and that test was only a small part of their hiring procedure.)

Decision

Target filed to have the case dismissed, but the California Court of Appeals ruled that Soroka could take his lawsuit to trial. The court found that questions about such matters as sex or religion violated privacy, and that for such questions to be permissible, the store would have to show that it must be justified by a "compelling" interest and must serve a job-related purpose. Target had not met this high standard.

Target appealed to the California Supreme Court. That court agreed to take the case, and combined it with another case, *Hill v. NCAA*, which dealt with drug testing of student athletes. This combination of cases suggested that the court wanted to make a broader application of the right of privacy in the state constitution.

Meanwhile, the Americans with Disabilities Act (ADA) had been passed. Soroka felt that the health-related questions in the test would be illegal under the ADA. Target's attorneys also believed that a jury would be offended by some of the questions on the test. Target therefore agreed to settle the case for the considerable sum of $1,540,000.

Impact

Soroka caused many California employers to revise their employee screening procedures. Target, for example, replaced Psychscreen with detailed personal interviews and more extensive background checks. Meanwhile, the California Supreme Court ruled in the *Hill* case that the NCAA (the collegiate athletic association) was justified in requiring drug tests because it had a compelling interest in promoting the health and safety of athletes, and that the athletes had only a limited expectation of privacy.

In general, the court had determined that someone bringing a claim for invasion of privacy must show that there is a legally recognized privacy interest involved, that the person has a reasonable expectation of privacy in the particular circumstances, and that the invasion of privacy was sufficiently serious. For some kinds of invasion of privacy (such as intrusion on intimate or family relationships), the state must show it has a "compelling interest" justifying its action. In the case of employees and athletes, however, the privacy interest would be balanced against the organization's interests to see if the invasion of privacy is "reasonable."

The Law of Privacy

STEVE JACKSON GAMES, INC. V. UNITED STATES SECRET SERVICE, 816 F. SUPP. 432 (W.D.TEX. 1993)

Background

During the late 1980s, the term "computer hacker" entered popular vocabulary. While the term once referred to exceptionally skillful (if rather obsessed) young programmers, it had come to mean criminals who used their computer skills to break into computer systems for purposes of disruption or theft of valuable information such as credit cards or confidential documents.

In 1990, Secret Service agents organized a wide-ranging investigation of a hacker group called the Legion of Doom. They believed that the group had stolen a confidential document relating to BellSouth telephone company's emergency 911 phone system, which the company valued at almost $80,000. (In reality, the publication, far from being "confidential," was available to the public for only a few dollars.)

The agents learned that a copy of the BellSouth manual was being stored on a computer bulletin board called Phoenix. They downloaded a copy from that board, and then learned that the owner, Lloyd Blankenship, was also an operator of another bulletin board called Illuminati, which was operated by his employer, Steve Jackson Games, a company that published and sold role-playing and board games. Since Blankenship's board had much hacker-related conversation and material, Secret Service agent Tim Foley assumed that Illuminati was also a "hacker board."

On March 1, 1990, the agents raided Steve Jackson Games as part of a massive effort called Operation Sun Devil in which about 150 agents confiscated thousands of computer disks. They seized all of the computer equipment and files used by the company. After examining the contents of the computers, they discovered what they believed was a "how-to" manual for computer criminals. In reality, the document was the rule book for a role-playing game being developed by the company, called "GURPS Cyberpunk," in which players portrayed characters in a futuristic high-tech society.

Jackson asked the Secret Service to return his equipment after copying whatever files they needed, but the agency ignored his pleas. As a result of losing its equipment and having to reconstruct the files for its game, Steve Jackson Games was nearly forced into bankruptcy. Jackson sued the Secret Service for damages.

Legal Issues

The Secret Service argued that its agents had acted in good faith and had reasonable cause to suspect that the Illuminati bulletin board had a copy of the stolen BellSouth document.

Jackson's attorneys argued, however, that the Secret Service had violated the Privacy Protection Act of 1980, which states "Notwithstanding any other law, it shall be unlawful for a government officer or employee, in connection with the investigation . . . of a criminal offense to search for or seize any work product materials possessed by a person reasonably believed to have a purpose to disseminate to the public a newspaper, broadcast, or other similar form of public communication." They argued that the game book was a legitimate publication protected by the Privacy Act. They also accused the Secret Service of violating a law against the "interception" of private e-mail, which the agency had read and destroyed rather than allowing it to reach its intended recipients.

Decision

The court found that the Secret Service had violated Jackson's rights under the Privacy Act. "The Court does fault Agent Foley and the Secret Service on the failure to make any investigation of Steve Jackson Games, Inc., prior to March 1, 1990, and to contact Steve Jackson in an attempt to enlist his cooperation and obtain information from him as there was never any basis to suspect Steve Jackson or Steve Jackson Games, Inc., of any criminal activity, and there could be no questions regarding the seizure of computers, disks, and bulletin board and all information thereon, including all back-up materials would have an adverse effect (including completely stopping all activities) on the business of Steve Jackson Games, Inc., and the users of Illuminati bulletin board."

The judge further noted that "While the content of these publications are not similar to those of daily newspapers, news magazines, or other publications usually thought of by this court as disseminating information to the public, these products come within the literal language of the Privacy Protection Act." The court declined, however, to find that electronic mail had been "intercepted" in the sense meant by the relevant statute.

Jackson was awarded $50,000 in damages plus $1,000 "statutory" damages and attorney's fees. The mail interception issue was appealed by Jackson, but the appeals court found in favor of the Secret Service, stating that the seizing of "stored messages" in a computer fell under the part of the law that had already been dealt with in the preceding case.

Impact

The *Steve Jackson* case had a profound impact on both law enforcement and on the growing online community. Law enforcement was placed on notice that the First Amendment and privacy statutes had to be considered in dealing with computer communications and that although bulletin boards and e-mail don't "look like" traditional newspapers and letter mail, this does not mean they are not constitutionally protected.

For users of bulletin boards and the emerging Internet, the *Steve Jackson* case was a wake-up call about potentially devastating collisions between the seemingly abstract world of cyberspace and the realities of the legal and political system. Some users who were particularly affected included activists John Perry Barlow and Mitch Kapor, who founded the Electronic Frontier Foundation, a kind of high-tech ACLU, and attorney-activist Mike Godwin, who became immersed in cyberspace issues and would later play an important part in the struggle to prevent censorship on the Internet.

ARIZONA V. EVANS, 514 U.S. 1 (1995)

Background

Isaac Evans was stopped by Phoenix police because he was driving the wrong way down a one-way street. When asked for his license, Evans told police it had been suspended. The police checked records from their patrol car's computer and discovered an outstanding misdemeanor arrest warrant. Evans was arrested and his car was searched, yielding a bag of marijuana, and he was charged with possession. Later, however, the police discovered that the warrant had been quashed (dismissed) 17 days earlier, but that the computer record had not been updated to reflect the fact.

Legal Issues

Evans' attorney claimed that the bag of marijuana could not be used as evidence because the search had resulted from erroneous computer information. As a general rule, evidence that results from an improper search cannot be used at trial. This is called the "exclusionary rule."

Decision

The trial court agreed with Evans, but the appeals court reinstated the evidence because the mistake had not been made by the police but by a civilian employee. The Arizona Supreme Court then threw the evidence out again, because it concluded that the distinction between police and police employees was not significant, and that one intent of the rule against tainted evidence is to promote careful record keeping.

The case then went to the U.S. Supreme Court. That court said that regardless of whether the Fourth Amendment might be considered to have been violated, suppressing the evidence was not required when it resulted from a mistake not made by the police itself. The Court did not believe that enforcing the evidence exclusion rule would have any real effect on the accuracy of civilian employees.

Impact

Justice Ruth Bader Ginsburg dissented from the majority opinion, believing that "Widespread reliance on computers to store and convey information generates, along with manifold benefits, new possibilities of error, due to both computer malfunctions and operator mistakes. . . . Computerization greatly amplifies an error's effect, and correspondingly intensifies the need for prompt correction; for inaccurate data can infect not only one agency, but many agencies that share access to the database."

Public concern and pressure for legislation regulating the use of government records (including the ability to correct them promptly) suggests that the public is more in agreement with Ginsburg than with the court majority.

RAM AVRAHAMI V. U.S. NEWS & WORLD REPORT, CIRCUIT COURT OF ARLINGTON, VIRGINIA, NO. 95–1318 (1996)

Background

A Virginian named Ram Avrahami was receiving a lot of unwanted junk mail. When he subscribed to *U.S. News & World Report,* he deliberately misspelled his name so he could determine if the magazine would distribute his name without his permission. He then received a mailing from *Smithsonian* magazine using the misspelled name. He sued *U.S. News & World Report* for violation of a Virginia privacy statute (in the modest amount of $1,100).

Legal Issues

Avrahami's attorney argued that the magazine had violated the following language from the Virginia law: "Any person whose name, portrait, or picture is used without having first obtained the written consent of such person . . . for advertising purposes or for the purposes of trade, such persons may maintain a suit in equity against the person, firm or corporation so using such person's name, portrait, or picture to prevent and restrain the use thereof;

and may also sue and recover damage for any injuries sustained by reason of such use. And if the defendant shall have knowingly used such person's name, portrait or picture in such manner as is forbidden or declared to be unlawful by this chapter, the jury, in its discretion, may award exemplary damages."

Avrahami's complaint charged that the selling of his name to marketers without consent fit directly into this language, which refers to "name" as well as "portrait or picture."

The magazine disagreed, calling the suit frivolous and arguing that the language of the statute referred to such things as using a name or picture as advertising or in an endorsement, not the routine use of mailing lists by the direct mail industry.

Decision

When the case reached the circuit court the judge ruled against Avrahami, saying that selling a name in a mailing list is not the kind of use "for advertising purposes or for the purposes of trade" that the 1904 statute had in mind. Besides, it was the list itself, not a single name, that had enough value as a commodity for the courts to worry about.

Impact

Direct mailers ridiculed Avrahami's claims as frivolous. Connie F. Heatley, senior vice president of the Direct Mail Marketing Association also pointed out that "There are 98 million Americans who shop [through mail-order catalogs]. The fact is that people like Mr. Avrahami who don't want their names rented have a way to prevent that." (This can be done by sending one's name to the Direct Mail Preference Service. However, since Avrahami had misspelled his name in order to trace its distribution, the preference service would have been ineffective. Also, such services are not selective, blocking everything or nothing.)

Avrahami lost in the courts, but the argument over junk mail (and its online equivalent, "spam") is far from over. It is possible, though, that as more organizations go online, technology may allow a more selective and flexible way to block unwanted junk mail.

DANIEL BERNSTEIN V. U.S. DEPARTMENT OF STATE, 922 F. SUPP. 1426, 1428–1430, N.D. CAL. (1996)

Background

Daniel Bernstein was a mathematician who developed Snuffle, a new encryption algorithm—a method for encoding data by computer so it cannot be read without the code key. He wrote an academic paper describing the algorithm and prepared listings of the source code (the statements in computer language necessary to compile a program that implements the encoding scheme). He wished to present his paper at conferences, including those attended by foreign colleagues.

Encryption technology is regulated under the federal International Traffic in Arms Regulations (ITAR), which regulate the export of "munitions"—weapons or other military hardware. The federal Office of Trade Controls determined that Bernstein's paper was a defense item under ITAR and thus required a license for export. Because the decision seemed vague, Bernstein asked the agency to specify which part—the paper, the encoding system itself, the instruction for use, or the two source code listings—was restricted from export. The agency determined that all five components required a license.

Legal Issues

Bernstein was concerned that the mere act of lecturing about Snuffle or teaching people how to use it might be considered by the government to be illegal "exporting" of a munition. He therefore sued the Department of State, with his main claim being that the application of ITAR to his work violated the First Amendment of the Constitution because it regulated what he could write or speak about on the basis of its content—something the courts have generally forbidden the government to do.

The government lawyers moved that Bernstein's claim be dismissed. They claimed that Bernstein could not appeal the agency's decision in court because under federal law the designation of specific items as non-exportable under ITAR was not "justiciable" (subject to court consideration). Bernstein, however, said that he was not appealing the specific decision, but challenging the constitutionality of the ITAR statute itself.

Decision

Judge Marilyn Hall Patel agreed that the constitutional challenge should be heard. Because the federal agency had removed the paper itself from the restricted export list after Bernstein sued, Patel focused on the remaining issue of the computer source code. Bernstein's lawyer asserted that the source code is, like any other medium of writing, protected under the First Amendment, and that indeed, the fact that computer software can be copyrighted implies that it is a form of creative expression that is constitutionally protected.

The government's defense insisted that software was not a form of speech, because it didn't convey any human-understandable message but rather, just carried out actions in the computer. The government therefore argued that software was a form of *conduct* (like flag burning or nude dancing) that shouldn't be protected under the First Amendment—an issue which is itself quite controversial, of course.

The judge noted, however, that in form, source code at least *looks* like writing and that considering it to be "conduct" is an uncomfortable stretch. Once it is decided that source code is a language, the judge believed that "the particular language one chooses [does not] change the nature of language for First Amendment purposes. This court can find no meaningful difference between computer language, particularly high-level languages as defined above, and German or French. All participate in a complex system of understood meanings within specific communities. Even object code, which directly instructs the computer, operates as a 'language.' When the source code is converted into the object code 'language,' the object program still contains the text of the source program. The expression of ideas, commands, objectives and other contents of the source program are merely translated into machine-readable code." The judge also agreed that source code was analogous to other expressions of ideas protected by copyright law.

The judge decided that Bernstein had made "nonfrivolous" constitutional claims that the ITAR statute was overly broad and involved a "prior restraint" (preventing someone from speaking about something rather than simply holding them responsible for any violations of law later).

The government's motion to dismiss Bernstein's claims was denied. And on August 25, 1997, in a final ruling, Judge Patel declared the export restrictions to be unconstitutional and ordered the government not to enforce them. On May 6, 1999, Judge Betty Fletcher of the U.S. Circuit Court of Appeals in San Francisco upheld Patel's decision. In her ruling, she linked access to encryption technology directly to the protection of privacy and the protection of speech given by the First Amendment.

Impact

The *Bernstein* decision gave important protection to the right of free expression for computer scientists developing encryption algorithms or other programs that the government might want to suppress for national security reasons. Thus far, however, the export of actual products that contain only compiled programs, not source code, remains a major issue.

Seeing cryptography as an essential tool for privacy and liberty in the information age, privacy activists continue to challenge government restrictions on the distribution and use of powerful encryption programs. Meanwhile, the government attempted a final run around the issue by offering to provide an officially approved encryption device (the Clipper Chip) that included the capability for the government to read encrypted messages after obtaining a court order.

Timothy R. McVeigh v. William Cohen et al., Civil Action 98–116, United States District Court for the District of Columbia (1998)

Background

The Timothy McVeigh in this case is no relation to the convicted Oklahoma City bomber who shares the same name. He was a highly decorated navy chief petty officer, and the highest-ranking enlisted person aboard the nuclear submarine USS *Chicago*. On September 2, 1997, however, a civilian naval volunteer received an America Online e-mail in connection with a toy drive for the sub crew's children. She noticed that the message sender's online "handle" (a nickname used by users of many online systems) was "boysrch," presumably meaning "boy search." She looked the handle up in the AOL member directory and discovered that the owner of the account was named "Tim." Reading his "member profile," she noticed that he had listed favorite activities such as "collecting pics of other young studs" and "boy watching" and that he had listed his marital status as "gay."

At this point the volunteer only knew that someone who had some connection with the submarine was named Tim and had said that he was gay. She forwarded the mail to her husband, who was also a noncommissioned officer aboard the *Chicago*. The mail found its way to the boat's captain, Commander John Mickey, and a formal investigation began. The investigators suspected that "boysrch" was Timothy McVeigh, and they instructed a paralegal assistant to contact AOL to get information about the identity of that account. An AOL representative identified the customer as Timothy McVeigh.

McVeigh was then informed that the navy had obtained "some indication that he made a statement of homosexuality," which was a violation of the military's new "Don't Ask, Don't Tell, Don't Pursue" policy. This policy was the result of a political compromise that allowed gay people to serve in the military as long as they did not tell people about their sexual preference. In return, the military was not supposed to go out of its way to find and discharge gay personnel.

The navy conducted an administrative discharge hearing where the e-mail was the major item of evidence, and ordered that McVeigh be discharged from the navy on January 16, 1998. But the day before his discharge, McVeigh filed suit to win an injunction, or order from the court, blocking the discharge.

Legal Issues

In seeking the injunction, McVeigh argued that the order should be granted because discharge would cause him great harm by ending his naval career and losing his pension, and that he had a case that was likely to win in a later lawsuit. He said that the U.S. Navy had violated its own "Don't Ask, Don't Tell, Don't Pursue" policy because McVeigh had not "told" anyone about his sexual preference, that the navy should not have launched an investigation on the basis of a "handle" on an otherwise unidentified AOL account, and that in doing so, it had violated McVeigh's privacy.

Decision

Judge Stanley Sporkin agreed that McVeigh's anonymous e-mail was not the kind of revelation that should have triggered an investigation under "Don't Ask, Don't Tell, Don't Pursue." Further, he said, the navy had probably violated the Electronic Communications Privacy Act of 1986. As the judge explained, the ECPA says that the government can obtain information from an online service provider such as AOL "only if (a) it obtains a warrant issued under the Federal Rules of Criminal Procedure or state equivalent; or (b) it gives prior notice to the online subscriber and then issues a subpoena or receives a court order authorizing disclosure of the information in question." The U.S. Navy had not complied with either of these procedures.

Judge Sporkin therefore issued the injunction, blocking McVeigh's discharge. The navy, while not discharging McVeigh, relegated him to clerical duties and refused to allow him to return to his post on the *Chicago*. Judge Sporkin then told the navy that it had to restore McVeigh to his prior position (or an equivalent). The navy at first announced it would appeal the decision, but it then reached a settlement with McVeigh. In May 1998, McVeigh was promoted to master chief petty officer, gaining increased pension benefits as well as payment of his legal fees, and then was honorably discharged.

Impact

The *McVeigh* case did not address the issue of whether the "Don't Ask, Don't Tell, Don't Pursue" policy is itself constitutional, though it has probably discouraged aggressive pursuit of suspected gays by the military. As a privacy issue, however, *McVeigh* affirmed an important privacy right for users of all online systems under the Electronic Communications Privacy Act.

CHAPTER 3

CHRONOLOGY

This chapter presents a chronology of important events involving privacy issues, particularly issues related to information and telecommunications privacy.

1690
- John Locke writes *Two Treatises on Government*, in which he lays the basis that the government is accountable for protecting the rights of the individual.

1791
- The Bill of Rights to the U.S. Constitution is ratified, including the Fourth and Fifth Amendments, which protect citizens against unwarranted violation of privacy by the government.

1800s
- The Industrial Revolution and urbanization lead to new social rules defining places and activities that should be considered private.

1861
- The American Civil War begins, and new communications technology plays a vital role. The Union and Confederacy tap each other's telegraph lines.

1876
- Alexander Graham Bell introduces the telephone. The invention changes the nature of conversation and raises the question of whether phone conversations are presumed to be private.

1890
- The use of electromechanical punch card machines by the U.S. Census foreshadows the later development of computerized databases.

1928
- In *Olmstead v. U.S.*, the Supreme Court refuses to apply the Fourth Amendment to prohibit wiretapping without a warrant.

Chronology

1939
- World War II begins. Allies use primitive electronic computers to break codes from Axis cipher machines.

1948
- Claude Shannon of MIT writes a seminal paper on cryptographic theory, which ties into the growing interest in the field by government security agencies.

1952
- As the Cold War deepens, secret government cryptography efforts are assigned to the new National Security Agency (NSA).

1965
- In the *Griswold* case, the Supreme Court declares that the Constitution implies a right of privacy with regard to contraception.
- A proposed central government data bank arouses the concern of privacy advocates.

1966
- Congress passes the Freedom of Information Act, which provides a way for citizens to request many kinds of information about the operation of government.

1967
- Journalist David Kahn publishes *The Codebreakers*, arousing public interest in cryptography.
- The Supreme Court reverses the *Olmstead* decision, declaring that the government must get a warrant to wiretap a suspect (*Katz v. U.S.*).

1968
- Congress passes the Wiretap Act of 1968, codifying the previous year's Supreme Court decision in *Katz v. U.S.*

1969
- The ARPANET, funded by the Defense Department, comes online. At first restricted to government agencies and universities, it would eventually evolve into the Internet.

1970
- Congress passes the Fair Credit Reporting Act, giving consumers the right to request and correct information kept by credit bureaus.

1972
- The Advisory Committee on Automated Personal Data Systems to the Secretary of the Department of Health, Education, and Welfare states basic

principles for protecting privacy in the Information Age. These include disclosure of information-gathering activities, the right of individuals to correct information about them, and guarantees for accuracy and control of disclosure of information.

- The Watergate break-in and cover-up leads to greater public concern about the misuse of surveillance by the government.

1973

- In *Roe v. Wade*, the Supreme Court limits the ability of the government to regulate abortion, seeing an expanded area of privacy in intimate and family matters.

1974

- Congress passes the Privacy Act of 1974, implementing fundamental principles of privacy and access to government records.
- Congress passes the Family Education Rights and Privacy Act of 1974, which gives parents or adult students the right to access and correct their school records, as well as limiting disclosure to third parties.
- The Supreme Court upholds the Bank Secrecy Act, which requires that banks track many details of transactions in order to fight drugs and money laundering (*California Bankers' Association v. Schulz*).

1976

- Whitfield Diffie and Martin Hellman publish "New Directions in Cryptography," a paper that creates the basis for public-key cryptography.
- The Supreme Court declares that individuals have no "expectation of privacy" in their banking or other financial transactions (*U.S. v. Miller*).

1977

- The U.S. Privacy Protection Study Commission warns of the growing threat to privacy caused by large, increasingly interlinked computer databases.
- Congress passes the Fair Debt Collection Practices Act, which prohibits a variety of abusive activities by bill collectors.

1978

- Congress passes two laws to strengthen financial privacy: the Electronic Funds Transfer Act of 1978 and the Right to Financial Privacy Act of 1978.
- Ron Rivest, Adi Shamir, and Len Adelman at MIT fill in the gaps in the theory of public-key cryptography and create a cryptosystem that will be called RSA.

1985

- The Supreme Court rules that students are protected by the Fourth Amendment, but that schools can conduct "reasonable" searches without obtaining a warrant (*New Jersey v. T.L.O.*).

Chronology

1986

- Congress passes the Electronic Communications Privacy Act of 1986, which extends the protections of the Wiretap Act of 1968 to include computer data transmissions and e-mail.
- Congress passes the Electronic Freedom of Information Act (EFOIA), which applies freedom of information principles to requests for computerized government records.

1987

- The Supreme Court rules that employers can conduct "reasonable" searches in the workplace, but that employees do have an "expectation of privacy" in some areas (*O'Connor v. Ortega*).
- During the failed nomination of Robert Bork to the Supreme Court, the judge's video rental records are revealed by the press. This leads to the passage of the Video Privacy Protection Act of 1988.

1988

- Congress passes the Employee Polygraph Protection Act of 1988, which bans the use of lie detectors and similar devices by employers in most cases.
- Congress passes the Computer Matching and Privacy Protection Act of 1988, which provides appeals procedures and other protections for individuals threatened with loss of benefits based on computer matching of government databases (such as comparing tax records with welfare rolls).

1990

- A massive anti-hacker sweep by the Secret Service leads to the seizure of computers belonging to Steve Jackson, a game publisher. In 1993, a court rules the seizure violates protection for publishers under the Privacy Act of 1980, and awards Jackson modest damages.
- A California court rules that employers have the right to monitor workplace e-mail (*Alana Shoars v. Epson America, Inc.*).

1991

- In two cases the California Supreme Court balances the "reasonable" interests of the organization against the individual's right to privacy (*Soroka v. Dayton Hudson Corp., Hill v. NCAA*).
- Lotus and Equifax plan to offer a CD-ROM database of information on 120 million consumers, but withdraw the plan after public and privacy advocates object.
- Programmer-activist Philip Zimmermann releases Pretty Good Privacy, an easy-to-use encryption program. Government security agencies are not amused.

- The federal government proposes the Clipper Chip, a device that would provide data encryption but would also allow the government to read encrypted data. Privacy advocates and industry groups strongly oppose the proposal.
- Congress passes the Telephone Consumer Protection Act, which requires that telemarketers maintain a list of people who do not wish to be called.

1992

- The Justice Department promotes legislation that would force phone companies to add built-in wiretapping facilities to phone systems in order to facilitate government surveillance efforts. (The legislation failed, but was revived in 1994 as the Digital Telephony Act.)
- Congress passes the Fair Credit Reporting Act, strengthening protections for consumers in dealing with credit bureaus and users of credit information.

1993

- The first graphical web-browsing software is released. Use of the Internet by the general public starts to grow rapidly.
- A report by the federal Office of Technology Assessment criticizes the lack of safeguards for patients' medical information.

1994

- Congress passes the Telemarketing and Consumer Fraud and Abuse Prevention Act, which regulates deceptive or annoying practices by telemarketers.
- The Clinton administration proposes that telephone companies be required to build into their systems the capability for the FBI and other law enforcement agencies to tap phone lines automatically. Privacy advocates view the proposal as an invitation to widespread abuse.

1995

- The Supreme Court rules that computer mistakes made by a civilian employee do not taint evidence gathered by police relying on that record (*Arizona v. Evans*).
- The European Union's Data Protection Directive provides for strong privacy protection.
- *June:* The federal Privacy Working Group issues its *Principles for Providing and Using Personal Information.* The principles would influence many subsequent privacy regulations and policies.

1996

- "Electronic commerce" (e-commerce) grows, but identity theft becomes a bigger problem, with cases more than doubling since 1992.
- Ram Avrahami fails in his attempt to sue *U.S. News & World Report* for selling his name to marketers without his permission.

Chronology

1997

- *July:* The Federal Trade Commission warns marketers not to collect information from children online without disclosure and parental permission.
- *August 25:* A California district court rules that the source code (computer language) of Daniel Bernstein's cryptography program is protected by the First Amendment (*Daniel Bernstein v. U.S. Department of State*).
- *September:* An AOL user profile with gay-related sentiments triggers the investigation of U.S. Navy Chief Petty Officer Timothy McVeigh.

1998

- *January:* McVeigh wins a court order blocking the navy from discharging him. The order is based in part on the navy's probable violation of the Electronic Communications Privacy Act.
- *August:* The Federal Trade Commission settles a complaint against Geo-Cities, a major online service provider. The company agrees not to explain its privacy policies and agrees not to collect information from children without parental consent.
- *Fall:* American online businesses face being excluded from Europe because American privacy standards are much weaker than those of Europe. Negotiations continue in an attempt to resolve the issue.
- *December:* The Federal Deposit Insurance Corporation announces "Know Your Customer" regulations. The regulations, strongly opposed by bankers and privacy advocates, would require banks to create "profiles" of a customer's typical activity and to watch closely for "unusual" transactions. After the Libertarian Party and other opponents organized a campaign that flooded the FDIC with e-mail, the proposed regulations were withdrawn in March 1999.

1999

- *January:* The giant computer chip maker Intel arouses the concern of privacy activists when plans are revealed to include serial numbers in forthcoming Pentium III chips that could be used to track the location of computers.
- A federal jury brought in a verdict of more than $107 million against the operators of an anti-abortion web site that had listed the names and home addresses of abortion providers. The jury concluded the listings constituted threats that were not protected by freedom of speech.
- *February:* Faced by strong criticism from privacy groups, the states of Florida, South Carolina, and Colorado back down from their plans to sell drivers' license photos to a private company for use in preventing check fraud.
- *April:* Microsoft Corporation and the Electronic Frontier Foundation jointly propose new guidelines for the Privacy Preferences Project, which

would assure online consumers that businesses were adhering to industry privacy standards.

- The Federal Trade Commission issues regulations implementing legislation that in most cases requires parental consent for online gathering and distribution of information from children under 13.

- In response to privacy concerns, the federal Health Care Financing Administration scales back its plans to collect personal information from patients receiving home health care.

- The Federal Aviation Administration (FAA) proposes the use of computer-assisted screening procedures to select passengers for additional searches both randomly and on those who fit the profile of suspected terrorists. Privacy advocates argue that such searches are unreasonable and lack probable cause, thereby violating the Forth Amendment.

- *May:* The U.S. Ninth District Court of Appeals affirms an earlier district court ruling declaring that export restrictions on cryptographic "software and related devices and technology are in violation of the First Amendment on the grounds of prior restraint." The government files an appeal to the Supreme Court.

- *June 23:* In Congress, the House passes the Security and Freedom Through Encryption (SAFE) bill, which relaxes restrictions on expoting cryptographic software. It however, includes an amendment that would make it a crime to not decrypt information when ordered to do so by the government, a provision opposed by privacy advocates. Civil libertarians also object when, on the same day, the Senate passes a bill that requires schools and libraries that receive "E-rate" universal service funds to purchase and use filtering software wen providing service to monors. (The House had added a similar provision to the juvenile justice bill.)

- *July:* The Federal Trade Commission releases its report "Self-Regulation and Privacy Online." It reports that few commercial web sites are following basic informatin privacy practices, but recommends against further legislation to protect privacy. Privacy advocates decry this "laissez-faire" approach.

CHAPTER 4

BIOGRAPHICAL LISTING

This chapter offers brief biographical entries for a variety of persons who have played an important role in the development of privacy issues, from the technical side, through their fiction or nonfiction writing, or in litigation and activism. See Chapter 7, Annotated Bibliography, for more information on book titles cited.

David Banisar, policy analyst for the Electronic Privacy Information Center, formerly with the Computer Professionals for Social Responsibility. Banisar edits EPIC's publications *International Privacy Alert* and *EPIC Alert*, and is a contributing editor to *Privacy Times.* He is also editor of the annual *EPIC Cryptography and Privacy Sourcebook.*

John Perry Barlow, a retired Wyoming cattle rancher and Grateful Dead lyricist. Barlow found himself in the unlikely position of Internet activist and visionary of virtual communities. In response to the Operation Sundevil Secret Service raids and the seizing of Steve Jackson's computers, Barlow cofounded the Electronic Frontier Foundation, often described as an "ACLU for cyberspace."

Daniel Bernstein, mathematician and cryptographer. Bernstein wrote a cryptography-related paper and computer program and was told by the federal government that it was classified as a "munition" and could not be exported. Aided by John Gilmore and the Electronic Freedom Foundation, Bernstein sued and won a decision that declared that computer source code was a form of speech protected by the First Amendment.

Robert Bork, law professor and former solicitor general and acting attorney general of the United States during the Nixon administration. As acting attorney general he played a controversial role in the Watergate affair. He then became a judge in the U.S. Court of Appeals. Bork's nomination to the Supreme Court was embroiled in controversy, in part because he believed in a stricter, more literal construction of the Constitution and opposed the finding of a broad right of privacy (as had been done in *Roe v. Wade*). Ironically, Bork's own privacy was violated by the publication of his video rental records, which led to the passage of the Video Privacy Protection Act of 1988.

Louis Brandeis, chief justice of the U.S. Supreme Court, 1916–1939. Brandeis took a liberal position on antitrust issues and the right of the government to impose regulations such as minimum wage and maximum working hours. While supporting expanding government powers to control commerce, he took a libertarian position in favor of the individual in dealing with government power. In 1928, Brandeis wrote a dissent to the *Olmstead* decision in which he said that the Court must reinterpret the constitutional protection for privacy to take account of new technologies that threatened it.

David Brin, science-fiction author and writer on cyberspace and virtual communities. His book *The Transparent Society* (1998) promotes an unusual approach to the privacy issue. Brin argues that creating effective privacy protections is impossible due to the pervasiveness of new information and communications technology. Instead, activists should concentrate on putting individuals, the government, and corporations on a more equal footing by making sure that the watchers can be watched in turn.

Simon Gordon Davies, pioneer privacy activist, founder of Privacy International, A London-based worldwide privacy watchdog group. The group highlights privacy concerns and campaigns for stronger privacy protections. Davis is also Visiting Research Fellow at the London School of Economics and Political Science. Davies received a 1999 Electronic Frontier Foundatin Pioneer Award for his work.

Fred Cate, expert on privacy and information law, including international privacy. From 1994 to 1996 he chaired the Annenberg Washington Program's project on Global Information Privacy. He is author of the handbook *Privacy in the Information Age.*

Dorothy Denning, professor of computer science at Georgetown University. Denning is a widely recognized expert on data security and "information warfare." She has been involved in the Clipper Chip debate with cryptography activists.

Whitfield Diffie, cryptographer and developer of public key cryptography (with Martin Hellman and Ralph Merkle) in 1975. Diffie has become an activist for widespread use of cryptography to protect privacy, as well as a kind of elder statesman for the activists known as "cypherpunks." He is coauthor (with Susan Landau) of *Privacy on the Line: The Politics of Wiretapping and Encryption (1998).*

Amitai Etzioni, sociologist and founder of a movement called communitarianism that combines liberal social activism with conservative values of personal responsibility. In his recent book *The Limits of Privacy,* Etzioni criticizes what he sees as an overemphasis on individual privacy that can prevent society from dealing with problems such as terrorism, crime, and the spread of AIDS. He believes that government can use databases of personal information responsibly in carrying out social programs.

Louis H. Freeh, director of the FBI, appointed by President Clinton in 1993. Found himself in the center of major cases such as the Oklahoma City bombing and the 1996 Atlanta Olympics bombing. Freeh has expressed the FBI's concern that it be given sufficient means to conduct surveillance and carry out search warrants in the computer age. This has translated into such proposals as the Clipper Chip and the key escrow proposals, both vigorously opposed by privacy advocates.

William Gibson, science-fiction writer. His novel *Neuromancer* (1984) described a future in which people directly experienced a computer-generated world called cyberspace. Gibson and other science-fiction writers have explored the implications of such a world for privacy, anonymity, and even identity.

John Gilmore, cryptographer, activist, and cofounder of the Electronic Frontier Foundation. Gilmore is passionately involved in the development of free software and the promotion of cryptography to protect ordinary people's data from government surveillance. He organized a lawsuit (with the EFF) to overturn export regulations that were preventing Daniel Bernstein from publicizing his cryptography work. Among his attributed sayings is "the Net treats censorship as damage and routs around it."

Beth Givens, director of the Privacy Rights Clearinghouse in San Diego. Her background includes library and information science, telecommunications policy, and consumer activism (particularly with regard to utilities).

Mike Godwin, counsel to the Electronic Frontier Foundation. Godwin has been involved in numerous high-profile online issues including libel, intellectual property, privacy, and freedom of expression. He is best known for playing a major role in the successful court fight against the Computer Decency Act of 1996. He recounts his battles in *Cyber Rights: Defending Free Speech in the Digital Age.*

Emmanuel Goldstein, editor of *2600,* the "Hacker quarterly." His name is a pseudonym taken from the character in George Orwell's 1984. He has become a visible spokesperson for the virtues of hacking (in the original sense of creative exploration of computing) and an advocate for free access to information.

Al Gore, former representative and senator; vice president of the United States (1993–). Gore has taken a leading role as the administration spokesperson and advocate for developing the "information superhighway" and providing widespread access to the Internet. He has also promoted the administration's "bill of rights for the Information Age" proposals, including expanded consumer and patient privacy protections.

J. Edgar Hoover, director of the FBI from 1924 to 1972. He largely shaped the practices of the FBI, taking it from Prohibition to the radical tumult of the 1960s. Along the way, he organized high-profile efforts against gangsters and Communists, expanded the use of wiretapping, surveillance, and infiltration, which he often turned against political enemies, arousing civil liberties concerns.

Steve Jackson, designer and publisher of role-playing and board games. In 1990, his company's computers were seized by the Secret Service because of vague connections to a stolen phone company document. Jackson sued the government and eventually collected damages.

Mitch Kapor, entrepreneur and founder of Lotus Corporation, which was one of the early success stories in the personal computer revolution. He has a wide background in psychological and spiritual studies as well as computer science. In 1990, he joined with John Perry Barlow to found the Electronic Frontier Foundation to defend civil liberties in the Information Age.

John Locke, English philosopher and political scientist, 1643–1704; author of *Two Treatises on Government* (1690). Locke's writings were very influential in establishing constitutional government and the protection of individual rights. Locke believed that government held its power only so long as it fulfilled the people's need for security, and that individuals had inherent rights (such as the right to property). This creates fertile ground for the development of privacy rights.

Timothy McVeigh, chief petty officer in the U.S. Navy (not the same as the Oklahoma City bomber). His 17-year distinguished naval career was threatened in September 1997 when the navy obtained information from America Online that revealed that he was a user who had described gay-related interests in his user profile. McVeigh sued in 1998, arguing that the navy had violated the Electronic Communications Privacy Act. He won a court order blocking the navy from discharging him, and eventually retired with a promotion.

George Orwell (pseudonym of Eric Arthur Blair), British writer, 1903–1950. His novel *1984*, published in 1948, describes a world in which television and other technology is used by a totalitarian government for complete surveillance and control that extends to the use of language and thinking itself. Government thus acts as, what Orwell termed, a "Big Brother" who constantly watches over his younger siblings (the nation's citizens) making sure they don't "misbehave." Privacy advocates have noted that while a centralized Big Brother has not emerged (at least in the Western democracies), the abuse of technology to spy on and control the individual is a very real threat, although decentralized technology, such as the personal computer and the Internet, can also be used to resist totalitarian projects and to create alternative forms of community and governance.

Biographical Listing

John Postel, distinguished computer scientist and a major architect of the Internet. his interests ranged from the highly technical (data protocals and switching systems) to the realm of social communications (E-mail and multimedia conferencing services). Postel established the Internet Assigned Numbers Authority (IANA), which devised the system of address numbers on which the Internet relies for making connections. As a trustee of the Internet Society, Postel was involved with privacy concerns and received a posthumous 1999 Electronic Frontier Foundation Pioneer Award.

Howard Rheingold, editor of the *Whole Earth Review*, writer and pioneer in developing virtual communities. His book *The Virtual Community: Homesteading on the Electronic Frontier* (1993) recounts the development of many aspects of online life.

Marc Rotenberg, director of the Electronic Privacy Information Center and former head of the Washington office of the Computer Professionals for Social Responsibility. Rotenberg teaches information privacy law at Georgetown University Law Center and is a contributing editor to *Government Information Quarterly*, the *Computer Law and Security Report*, and the *Encyclopedia of Computer Science*. He is also secretary of Privacy International, an international privacy rights organization.

Susan Scott, technology analyst and publisher; former CEO of Upside Publishing. Scott is now executive director of TRUSTe, an organization that verifies and guarantees the privacy policies of online businesses.

Richard Stallman, founder of the Free Software Foundation, which promotes the cooperative creation and distribution of noncommercial software. This movement has been influential in providing alternative operating systems, promoting free access to technical information, and creating freely distributable software that is free from corporate or governmental control.

Clifford Stoll, an astronomer who became famous when he discovered evidence of computer tampering and began to pursue hackers. He has become a widely quoted critic of the supposed benefits of the Information Age, pointing out what he believes are profound social distortions caused by misuse of technology. His books include *The Cuckoo's Egg* (1995) and *Silicon Snake Oil* (1995).

Lawrence Tribe, noted constitutional expert and civil libertarian. In his address to the First Conference on Computers, Freedom, and Privacy (March 6, 1991) entitled "The Constitution in Cyberspace: Law and Liberty Beyond the Electronic Frontier," Tribe suggests that a new constitutional amendment might make it clear that the fundamental rights of free expression and privacy will be guaranteed regardless of the type of technology involved.

Alan Turing, mathematician and computer pioneer who developed fundamental theories of computation and helped build special computers for cracking German codes during World War II. After the war, he was a pioneer in exploring the possibility and implications of artificial intelligence. Ironically, the violation of his own privacy—the revelation of his homosexual activity—led to forced medical treatment and his apparent suicide.

Earl Warren, chief justice of the U.S. Supreme Court, 1953–1969. Warren played a major role in the expansion of civil rights and civil liberties, including the *Griswold* case, which established a right of personal privacy as implied in the language of the Constitution.

Philip Zimmermann, software engineer and cryptographer. Zimmermann developed the Pretty Good Privacy (PGP) program in 1991 and became embroiled in legal skirmishes with government agencies that tried to restrict its export. When the government dropped its legal efforts in 1996, Zimmermann founded a company to develop and market PGP.

CHAPTER 5

GLOSSARY

American Civil Liberties Union (ACLU) An organization founded in 1915 to protect the civil liberties asserted in the Bill of Rights. This mission has involved the ACLU in many privacy issues.

anonymity The online world allows opportunities to interact with people without identifying oneself. Anonymity is related to privacy in that it protects personal identity, and it can be a liberating experience. But anonymity creates the problem of lack of accountability for harmful actions.

Big Brother A pervasive, all-seeing government surveillance and control system; named after a character in George Orwell's *1984*.

Bill of Rights The first ten amendments to the U.S. Constitution. Of these, the Fourth, Fifth, and Ninth amendments have particular relevance to the protection of privacy.

bulletin board systems (BBS) Dial-up computers where users can leave messages or download or upload files. They became popular in the mid-1980s but have been largely superceded by the Internet.

Caller ID Telephone service that allows callers to know the phone number from which incoming calls originate. Raises privacy concerns when callers wish to remain anonymous.

ciphertext In cryptography, text that has been made unreadable by applying a code key and an encryption method.

Clipper Chip A proposed device that would provide encryption services but also allow the government to read encrypted messages.

COINTELPRO (Counterintelligence Program) Widespread FBI surveillance and infiltration of dissident groups (such as civil rights and antiwar activists) from the 1960s into the 1980s. When revealed, it fueled privacy concerns.

compelling state interest The strictest test applied by courts to see whether an invasion of privacy by the government is justified. It is applied, for example, to matters of contraception or abortion.

computer matching The comparison of two or more databases to find individuals who should be investigated: for example, matching a database of persons who are delinquent in paying child support with a database of tax refunds.

cookie A small file that some web sites write onto the user's hard disk. It can be used to recognize that user in subsequent sessions, customize the user interface, or to create a profile of that user that can be sold to marketers. It is the latter use that raises privacy concerns.

credit bureau A central clearinghouse for information about credit purchases and payments; the three major credit bureaus are TRW, Equifax, and Trans Union.

cryptography The science of code making (and code breaking).

cryptosystem A system for encoding text so that it can be read only by someone who has the key.

cyberspace The imaginary world experienced by online users. It can include many places such as schools, libraries, stores, game arenas, and private "chat" rooms that are analogous to their "real-life" counterparts.

cypherpunks Self-designation of a group of activists who promote the widespread use of cryptography to protect privacy, and who oppose government controls on the technology.

database An organized collection of information maintained on a computer system. It usually consists of a number of related files containing records that are further broken down into fields such as name, address, and Social Security number.

data broker A person or company that collects, packages, and sells computerized information (such as mailing lists). Data brokers have little specific regulation.

data mining The extraction of data (such as from consumer purchase records) that can be used or sold to marketers.

Data Protection Directive The European Union's comprehensive regulations (announced in 1995) governing the collection, disclosure, distribution, and access to computerized information.

DES A government-approved system for encoding text; comes in different strengths measured by the number of bits in the code key. First introduced in 1977, DES has come under attack as being too weak; the 56-bit DES has already been "cracked" by teams of programmers.

digital signature One of various methods of combining an individual's private encryption key with a message. Readers can use the individual's public key to verify that the message was created by that individual.

direct mailer An organization that gathers or obtains mailing lists and sends advertising to everyone on the list.

disclosure In privacy policies, the requirement that an organization reveal to affected persons what it intends to do with the information it collects. Also, the revealing of information collected from an individual to a third party.

"Don't Ask, Don't Tell, Don't Pursue" A controversial policy that allows gays to serve in the military if they don't reveal their sexual orientation. Authorities are not supposed to initiate investigations unless there is such a revelation. The policy has aroused privacy concerns, such as in the case of Chief Petty Officer Timothy McVeigh.

eavesdropping Listening to a conversation without the knowledge or consent of the participants. Wiretapping is eavesdropping on telecommunications; surveillance is the systematic surreptitious observation of someone or someplace.

electronic commerce The buying and selling of goods and services online, usually through web sites. It has been rapidly growing since the mid-1990s.

Electronic Communications Privacy Act of 1986 Federal legislation that extended the Privacy Act of 1974 to include most forms of telecommunications and data networks.

Electronic Freedom of Information Act of 1986 The Electronic Freedom of Information Act of 1986 extended the principles of the 1966 Freedom of Information Act to computerized records.

Electronic Frontier Foundation (EFF) A civil liberties organization founded by John Perry Barlow and Mitch Kapor in 1990 in response to government seizure of computers in the Operation Sun Devil hacker sweep. It quickly became involved in other issues, such as privacy and free speech.

Electronic Privacy Information Center (EPIC) A public interest research group founded in 1994, EPIC is concerned with issues of privacy and free speech in the online world, and includes a legal team as well as educational outreach.

e-mail (electronic mail) Messages sent to one or more individuals over a computer network.

encryption The process of applying a code key to text in order to create a message that cannot be read without the proper key.

Fair Credit Reporting Act of 1992 Federal legislation that sets basic requirements for the preparation and distribution of credit reports; regulates purposes for which reports can be disclosed and gives individuals the right to see and correct their reports.

Fair Information Principles Basic protections for privacy suggested by experts and advocates starting in the 1970s. They include disclosure of information-gathering activities and the right of an individual to view and correct records pertaining to him or her. The Privacy Act of 1974 attempted to implement these principles.

Federal Trade Commission (FTC) Government agency that sets many rules for how goods and services are bought or sold in the marketplace. It has proposed stronger privacy regulations, particularly where children are involved.

Fifth Amendment Part of the Bill of Rights. One clause prevents the government from forcing an accused individual to confess guilt; it has thus been interpreted as a protection of privacy.

Fourth Amendment Part of the Bill of Rights of the U.S. Constitution. It protects against law enforcement officers searching property or seizing evidence without a warrant.

Freedom of Information Act of 1966 Federal legislation that implements the principle that citizens have the right to know about government activities and see government records pertaining to them.

genetic information Information from tests that reveal genetic (hereditary) characteristics such as susceptibility to a particular disease.

hacker Originally, this term referred to an unusually skilled and often obsessed programmer; in recent years it has come to mean someone who illegally breaks into computer systems to destroy them or to steal information.

health maintenance organizations (HMOs) Health care providers that offer a package of health benefits through employers or directly to individuals. Their attempt to reduce high medical costs has led to a number of issues including privacy concerns.

Hippocratic Oath An ancient physician's oath that, among other things, promises that a doctor will not divulge information about a patient's medical condition to a third party.

home is your castle The idea enshrined in English law that any person's home should be protected against intrusion by the government except through proper legal process.

honesty test A psychological test designed to identify persons who have a tendency to lie, steal, or engage in other dishonest behavior. The tests have aroused concerns about both their validity and their abuse of privacy.

identity theft The use of stolen credit information (such as name, Social Security number, and bank account numbers) to assume another person's identity in order to make credit purchases or cash withdrawals.

incorporation doctrine Developed gradually during the mid-20th century, the principle that the Fourteenth Amendment guarantees of due process and equal treatment require the states as well as the federal government to enforce the guarantees in the Bill of Rights.

information privacy The aspect of privacy that focuses on the right of the individual to control how personal information is obtained or used.

International Traffic in Arms Regulations (ITAR) A regulation that has been used to restrict the export of encryption software; challenged in *U.S. Department of State v. Bernstein.*

Internet The rapidly growing worldwide interconnection of computers and networks that communicate using a standard protocol called TCP/IP.

Internet service provider (ISP) A company that offers connections to the Internet, usually for a monthly fee.

key A string of text (or piece of data) that when input into a coding system with the coded ciphertext, reveals the original message (plaintext).

key escrow The placing of a copy of a user's encryption key with a third party so it can be retrieved by law enforcement officials who have obtained a court order.

Ninth Amendment Part of the Bill of Rights. It states that "The enumeration in the Constitution, of certain rights, shall not be construed to deny or disparage others retained by the people." During the 1960s and 1970s, a majority of Supreme Court justices used the idea of unspecified rights to find that the Constitution implied a broader individual right of privacy regarding matters such as contraception, abortion, and reproduction.

online services Companies that set up computers with services such as message forums, chat rooms, and file libraries. Examples include America Online and CompuServe. These services were originally stand-alone, but during the 1990s they connected to the Internet and became value-added Internet service providers.

plaintext The result of decoding an encrypted message into readable text.

polygraph A device used to assess the truthfulness of statements by measuring symptoms of physical stress; commonly called a "lie detector."

Pretty Good Privacy (PGP) A popular software package that lets users encrypt their e-mail and other data files.

Principles for Providing and Using Personal Information Principles for information use originating from a committee of U.S. government agencies and published in 1995. Subjects covered include respect for individual privacy in collecting and disclosing information, informing affected persons about their rights and responsibilities, and offering the opportunity to correct incorrect information.

privacy The ability of an individual to prevent intrusion or to control the gathering or use of personal information.

Privacy Act of 1974 Basic federal law that regulates the distribution of information by federal agencies and the right of an individual to obtain (and possibly correct) records pertaining to him or her.

public-key certificate A digital record created by a certification agency using an individual's private key and other information, and containing the public key. An individual can verify the certificate's integrity and be assured that the public key belongs to the individual identified.

public-key cryptography A system where each user has two related code keys, one public and one private. The public key can be used by anyone to send a message, which can be read only by the user with the corresponding private key. The private key in turn can authenticate the user by creating a message that can be read by anyone with the public key.

reasonable expectation of privacy A test used by courts in deciding privacy cases. It describes circumstances (such as making a call in a phone booth) where a person should be allowed to assume that he or she is engaging in private conduct.

reasonable relationship A less rigorous test applied by courts to determine whether an invasion of privacy is justified. Applied, for example, to businesses monitoring employee performance, to determine if the monitoring has a reasonable relationship to business objectives.

reverse directory A telephone directory that can be used to look up the address corresponding to a phone number. It can be used by telemarketers to create mailing lists.

RSA An algorithm (method) for encoding text, using public-key cryptography (q.v.). Named for the last names of its developers at MIT (Rivest, Shamir, and Adelman).

Secure Server A web program that can be used by online consumers to place orders safely. Credit card information is encrypted so it cannot be read by hackers.

Super Bureau A company that offers (for a fee) the ability to obtain just about any sort of information about a person using government, credit, or other databases. A "bureau" sometimes obtains information under false pretenses.

surveillance technology General term for devices that allow a person's activities or conversations to be observed from a distance, such as through microphones, cameras, or infrared sensors.

telecommunications General term for electronic transmission of information, whether voice (phone), fax, or computer data.

telemarketer A salesperson who contacts consumers by telephone; often accused of deceptive or high-pressure tactics.

TRUSTe An organization that certifies the privacy practices of online businesses that follow its guidelines.

Universal ID Proposed single number that would uniquely identify an individual in all government databases. To some extent Social Security numbers have been used for this purpose. Its proposal arouses concerns because it in effect puts all a person's private information in one basket.

Glossary

virtual community The shared experience of computer users built up through prolonged interaction, such as through a bulletin board or a conferencing system.

web browser A program that lets users find and navigate through pages of information, graphics, etc., on the World Wide Web.

web cam A camera set up by a person to continually broadcast his or her activities to the Internet. The opposite of privacy; a form of electronic exhibitionism and perhaps a cultural artifact.

Wiretap Act of 1968 Federal law that extended Fourth Amendment privacy protections to telecommunications.

wiretapping The interception of telephone voice or data transmission by someone other than its intended recipient.

workfactor The number of operations required to break a cryptosystem: thus, a measure of the code's strength. This is only relative, however, as the power of available computers is rapidly increasing.

World Wide Web A system that links pages of text, graphics, sound, and other resources on the Internet to one another, giving each a unique address. A web browser can be used to display and navigate the pages.

PART II

GUIDE TO FURTHER RESEARCH

CHAPTER 6

HOW TO RESEARCH PRIVACY ISSUES

The tremendous growth in the amount of resources and services available through the Internet (and particularly, the World Wide Web) is providing powerful new tools for researchers. Mastery of a few basic online techniques enables today's researcher to accomplish in a few minutes what used to require hours in the library poring through card catalogs, bound indexes, and printed or microfilmed periodicals.

Not everything is to be found on the Internet, of course. While a few books are available in electronic versions, most must still be obtained as printed text. Many periodical articles, particularly those more than 10 years old, must still be obtained in "hard copy" form from libraries. Nevertheless, the Internet has now reached "critical mass" in the scope, variety, and quality of material available. Thus, it makes sense to make the Net the starting point for most research projects. This is particularly true regarding privacy issues. Since so many privacy concerns have arisen in connection with the Internet and other computerized information systems, many advocates of privacy rights have made the Internet their home base for organizing and education.

STARTING PLACES ON THE WEB

One basic principle of research is to take advantage of the fact that other people may have already found and organized much of the most useful information about a particular topic. For privacy issues, there are two web sites that can serve as excellent starting points for research.

The Electronic Privacy Information Center (EPIC) at http://www.epic.org is, according to its web site: "a public interest research center in Washington, D.C. It was established in 1994 to focus public attention on emerging civil liberties issues and to protect privacy, the First Amendment, and constitutional values." EPIC provides news of current developments (including court cases and pending legislation), as well as an extensive collection of guides and resources, including:

- *EPIC Alert*, an online newsletter, which can also be subscribed to by e-mail from the web page.

- A bookstore, where EPIC publications and other recommended books can be ordered.

- An online guide to "practical privacy tools" including aids for encryption and anonymity.

- An extensive collection of links to resources, including organizations, publications, and other web sites.

- A policy archives section, with pages of links for each topic.

The other privacy-related "megasite" is that of the Electronic Frontier Foundation (EFF) at http://www.eff.org. It is described as "a non-profit, non-partisan organization working in the public interest to protect fundamental civil liberties, including privacy and freedom of expression, in the arena of computers and the Internet." The EFF's home page provides links to the latest privacy-related news developments. Its information tends to be organized for easy use by activists. For example, a story about a privacy abuse or free speech case is often accompanied by links that can be used to respond to the situation, such as by participating in protests or contacting legislators.

Like EPIC, the EFF has extensive archives. (Indeed, the archives on the two sites are different enough that exploring both is a good way to get a very comprehensive survey of privacy-related resources on the Net.) The EFF archive categories most related to privacy are: "Legislation and Regulation," "Legal Cases," and "Privacy, Surveillance, and Cryptography."

Since both EPIC and the EFF are oriented toward activism, the researcher should take into account possible bias in the selection or presentation of materials. For example, in legal cases or legislative debates, the arguments opposed to the expansion of privacy rights may not be presented, although they may be available through some of the many links to other sites.

After delving into the resources offered by EPIC and EFF (either directly or through links), the researcher should note that many other privacy-related organizations and government agencies have web sites. (See Chapter 8 for details.)

Some initial exploration of major web sites plus browsing in books on general privacy law and policy (see Chapter 7 under "Privacy Law Reference" and "General Privacy Law and Policy") should provide the researcher with enough background to identify particular topics of interest that warrant further research. The bibliographical resources, databases, and other search tools described below can then be employed in a systematic way to find additional materials.

BIBLIOGRAPHIC RESOURCES

Bibliographic resources is a general term for catalogs, indexes, bibliographies, and other guides that identify books, periodical articles, and other printed resources that deal with a particular subject. They are essential tools for the researcher.

LIBRARY CATALOGS

Most public and academic libraries have replaced their card catalogs with online catalogs, and many institutions now offer remote access to their catalog, either through dialing a phone number with terminal software or connecting via the Internet.

Access to the largest library catalog, that of the Library of Congress, is available at http://lcweb.loc.gov/catalog/. This page explains the different kinds of catalogs and searching techniques available. A direct connection can be made using telnet to *locis.loc.gov*.

Yahoo! offers a categorized listing of libraries at http://dir.yahoo.com/Reference/Libraries/. Of course one's local public library (and for students, the high school or college library) is also a good source for help in using online catalogs.

With traditional catalogs, lack of knowledge of appropriate subject headings can make it difficult to make sure the researcher finds all relevant materials. Online catalogs, however, can be searched not only by author, title, and subject, but also by matching keywords in the title. Thus a title search for "privacy" will retrieve all books that have that word somewhere in their title. (Of course a book about privacy may not have the word "privacy" in the title, so it is still necessary to use subject headings to get the most comprehensive results.)

The basic subject heading for privacy is "privacy, right of." The LC Subject headings file breaks this heading down into the following subdivisions and cross-references:

Privacy, Right of
(TERM MAY BE SUBDIVIDED GEOGRAPHICALLY)*
Used for:
    Invasion of privacy
    Right of privacy
Narrower terms:
    Archives—Access control
    Confidential communications—Third parties
    Diaries in criminal evidence
    Hamsocn
    Personnel records—Access control
    Portraits—Law and legislation
    Public health—Statistical services—Access control
    Public records—Access control
    Records—Access control
Related terms:
    Computer crimes
    Confidential communications
Data protection—Law and legislation
    Secrecy—Law and legislation
Broader terms:
    Civil rights
    Libel and slander
    Personality (Law)
    Press Law
Call Number Ranges:
    JC596–JC596.2: Political theory

Once the record for a book or other item is found, it is a good idea to see what additional subject headings and name headings have been assigned. These in turn can be used for further searching.

BIBLIOGRAPHIES

Bibliographies in various forms provide a convenient way to find books, periodical articles, and other materials. Much of the material related to information privacy issues is quite recent, however, and the few book-length bibliographies still in print are pretty much out of date. However, many of the recent books described in Chapter 7 include extensive bibliographies (some annotated). EPIC, the EFF, and other web sites also include bibliographies.

---

* [That is, it can be specified by place, as in "Privacy, Right of—United States."]

BOOKSTORE CATALOGS

Many people have discovered that online bookstores such as Amazon.com at (http://www.amazon.com) and barnesandnoble.com (http://www.barnesandnoble.com) are convenient ways to shop for books. A lesser-known benefit of online bookstore catalogs is that they often include publisher's information, book reviews, and readers' comments about a given title. They can thus serve as a form of annotated bibliography.

On the other hand, a visit to one's local bookstore also has its benefits. While the selection of titles available is likely to be smaller than that of an online bookstore, the ability to physically browse through books before buying them can be very useful.

PERIODICAL DATABASES

Most public libraries subscribe to database services such as InfoTrac that index articles from hundreds of general-interest periodicals (and some moderately specialized ones). The database can be searched by author or by words in the title, subject headings, and sometimes words found anywhere in the article text. Depending on the database used, "hits" in the database can result in just a bibliographical description (author, title, pages, periodical name, issue date, etc.), a description plus an abstract (a paragraph summarizing the contents of the article), or the full text of the article itself.

Many libraries provide dial-in, Internet, or telnet access to their periodical databases as an option in their catalog menu. However, licensing restrictions usually mean that only researchers who have a library card for that particular library can access the database (by typing in their name and card number). Check with local public or school libraries to see what databases are available.

A somewhat more time-consuming alternative is to find the web sites for magazines likely to cover a topic of interest. (See Chapter 7 for some specialized periodicals in each subject category.) Some scholarly publications are putting all or most of their articles online. Popular publications tend to offer only a limited selection. Some publications of both types offer archives of several years' back issues that can be searched by author or keyword.

KEEPING UP WITH THE NEWS

It is important for the researcher to be aware of currently breaking news. In addition to watching TV news and subscribing to local or national newspapers and magazines, there are a number of ways to use the Internet to find additional news sources.

NEWSPAPERS AND NETNEWS

Like periodicals, most large newspapers now have web sites that offer headlines and a searchable database of recent articles. The URL is usually given somewhere in one's local newspaper. Yahoo! is also a good place to find newspaper links: see
http://dir.yahoo.com/News_and_Media/Newspapers/Web_Directories/.

Netnews is a decentralized system of thousands of "newsgroups," or forums organized by topic. Most web browsers have an option for subscribing to, reading, and posting messages in newsgroups. The Dejanews site (http://www.dejanews.com) also provides free access and an easy to use interface to newsgroups.

Some examples of privacy-related newsgroups include:

alt.privacy   General discussion of privacy topics
alt.security.pgp   The Pretty Good Privacy encryption program
alt.security and **comp.security**   Computer security
(has many subdivisions)
comp.security pgp.discuss   Discussion of PGP (Pretty
Good Privacy) software
alt.2600   Hackers and hacking
alt.privacy.anon-server   Setups for anonymous Internet use
comp.risks   Hidden risks and vulnerabilities of computer systems

MAIL LISTS

Mail lists offer another way to keep up with (and discuss) recent developments. Many organizations such as the Electronic Frontier Foundation maintain such lists, which you can subscribe to through the web site or by sending a specially formatted e-mail message using the instructions provided. The mailing list software automatically collates and distributes the e-mail messages.

Netnews and mail lists are generally most valuable when they have a moderator who keeps discussions focused and discourages "flaming" (the writing of heated or personally insulting statements).

SEARCHING THE WEB

A researcher can explore an ever-expanding web of information by starting with a few web sites and following the links they offer to other sites, which in turn have links to still other sites. But since this is something of a hit-and-miss proposition, some important sites may be missed if the researcher only "web surfs" in this fashion. There are two more focused techniques that can fill in the information gaps.

WEB INDEXES

A web index is a site that offers a structured, hierarchical outline of different subject areas. This enables the researcher to zero in on a particular aspect of a subject and find links to web sites for further exploration.

The best known (and largest) web index is Yahoo! (http://www.yahoo.com). The home page gives the top-level list of topics. Four of these are of particular use of researching privacy:

Computer and Internet: clicking on this topic leads to a variety of technical topics including encryption and data security, as well as the Internet, which has many facets including **Electronic Mail** and **Law**.

The **Government** category leads to **Law**, which offers, among other topics, **Cases** and **Privacy**.

Politics leads to **Political Issues**, which include **Censorship and the Net**, an issue that overlaps privacy concerns in many ways, as does **Health Care Policy**.

News and Media includes categories that provide links to newspapers, news services, and other ways to research current events.

In addition to following Yahoo!'s outlinelike structure, there is also a search box into which the researcher can type one or more keywords and receive a list of matching categories and sites.

Web indexes such as Yahoo! have two major advantages over undirected surfing. First, the structured hierarchy of topics makes it easy to find a particular topic or subtopic and then explore its links. Second, Yahoo! does not make an attempt to compile every possible link on the Internet (a task that is virtually impossible, given the size of the web). Rather, sites are evaluated for usefulness and quality by Yahoo!'s indexers. This means that the researcher has a better chance of finding more substantial and accurate information. (This advantage is also provided by sites like EFF and EPIC, of course.) The disadvantage of web indexes is the flip side of their selectivity: the researcher is dependent on the indexer's judgment for determining what sites are worth exploring.

Two other web indexes are LookSmart (http://www.looksmart.com) and The Mining Company's About.com (http://home.miningco.com).

SEARCH ENGINES

Search engines take a very different approach to finding materials on the web. Instead of organizing topically in a "top down" fashion, search engines work their way "from the bottom up." Basically, a search engine consists of two pieces of software. The first is a "Web crawler" that systematically and automatically surfs the net, following links and compiling them into an index with keywords (drawn either from the text of the sites themselves or from lists of words that have been flagged in a special way by the site's creators). The second program is the search engine's "front end": it provides a way to match user-specified keywords or phrases with the index and display a list of matching sites.

There are hundreds of search engines, but some of the most widely used include:

- Alta Vista (http://www.altavista.digital.com)
- Excite (http://www.excite.com)
- Hotbot (http://www.hotbot.com)
- Infoseek (http://www.infoseek.com)
- Lycos (http://www.lycos.com)
- Magellan (http://www.mckinley.com)
- NetFind (AOL) (http://www.aol.com)
- Northern Light (http://www.nlsearch.com)
- WebCrawler (http://www.WebCrawler.com)

Search engines are generally easy to use by employing the same sorts of keywords that work in library catalogs. There are a variety of web search tutorials available online [try "web search tutorial" in a search engine]. One good one is published by The Web Tools Company at http://thewebtools.com/tutorial/tutorial.htm.

Here are a few basic rules for using search engines:

- When looking for something specific, use the most specific term or phrase. For example, when looking for information about the PGP encryption program, use "PGP," not "encryption."

- When looking for a more general topic, use several descriptive words (nouns are more reliable than verbs). For example, "privacy medical records." (Most engines will automatically put pages that match all three terms first on the results list.)

- Use "wildcards" when a desired word may have more than one ending. For example, "crypto" matches cryptography, cryptographic, or the slang term "crypto" used by some people in the field.

- If applicable, try to use a commonly accepted phrase that is likely to be associated with that topic. For example, if researching the use of the legal principle of "expectation of privacy," use that phrase (use quotes, so it will be matched as a phrase).

- Most search engines support Boolean (*and*, *or*, *not*) operators that can be used to broaden or narrow a search.

- Use AND to narrow a search. For example, "internet AND privacy" will match only pages that have *both* terms.

- Use OR to broaden a search: "encryption OR cryptography" will match any page that has *either* term.

- Use NOT to exclude unwanted results: "cryptography NOT pgp" finds articles about cryptography that do not discuss PGP.

Since each search engine indexes somewhat differently and offers somewhat different ways of searching, it is a good idea to use several different search engines, especially for a general query. Several "metasearch" programs automate the process of submitting a query to multiple search engines. These include:

- Metacrawler (http://www.metacrawler.com)

- Inference FIND (http://www.inference.com/infind/)

- SavvySearch (http://www.savvysearch.com)

There are also search utilities that can be run from the researcher's own PC rather than through a web site. A good example is Mata Hari, a "shareware" (try before you buy) program available for download at http://thewebtools.com/.

FINDING ORGANIZATIONS AND PEOPLE

Lists of privacy-related organizations can be found on archive sites such as EPIC and EFF and index sites such as Yahoo! If such sites do not yield the name of a specific organization, the name can be given to a search engine. Generally the best approach is to put the name of the organization in quote marks such as "Americans for Computer Privacy."

Another approach is to take a guess at the organization's likely web address. For example, the American Civil Liberties Union is commonly known by the acronym ACLU, so it is not a surprise that the organization's web site is at http://www.aclu.org. (Note that noncommercial organization sites normally use the .org suffix, government agencies use .gov, educational institutions have .edu, and businesses use .com.) This technique can save time, but doesn't always work.

There are several ways to find a person on the Internet:

- Put the person's name (in quotes) in a search engine and possibly find that person's home page on the Internet.

- Contact the person's employer (such as a university for an academic, or a corporation for a technical professional). Most such organizations have web pages that include a searchable faculty or employee directory.

- Try one of the people-finder services such as Yahoo! People Search (http://people.yahoo.com) or BigFoot (http://www.bigfoot.com). This may yield contact information such as e-mail address, regular address, and/or phone number.

LEGAL RESEARCH

As information privacy issues continue to capture the attention of legislators and the public, a growing body of legislation and court cases is emerging. Because of the specialized terminology of the law, legal research can be more difficult to master than bibliographical or general research tools. Fortunately, the Internet has also come to the rescue in this area, offering a variety of ways to look up laws and court cases without having to pore through huge bound volumes in law libraries (which may not be accessible to the general public, anyway).

FINDING LAWS

When federal legislation passes, it becomes part of the United States Code, a massive legal compendium. Laws can be referred to either by their popular name or by a formal citation. For example, the Fair Credit Reporting Act is cited as 15 U.S.C. §1681, meaning title 15 of the U.S.C. code, section 1681.

The U.S. Code can be searched online in several locations, but the easiest site to use is probably the U.S. Code database at http://uscode.house.gov/. The U.S. Code may also be found at Cornell Law School (a major provider of free online legal reference material), at http://www4.law.cornell.edu/uscode/.

The fastest way to retrieve a law is by its title and section citation, but phrases and keywords can also be used.

Federal laws are generally implemented by a designated agency that writes detailed rules, which become part of the Code of Federal Regulations (C.F.R.). A regulatory citation looks like a U.S. Code citation, and takes the form *vol.* C.F.R. sec. *number* where *vol.* is the volume number and *number* is the section number.

Regulations can be found at the web site for the relevant government agency (such as the Federal Trade Commission or Federal Communications Commission).

Many states also have their codes of laws online. The Internet Law Library has a page of links to state laws at http://law.house.gov/17.htm.

KEEPING UP WITH LEGISLATIVE DEVELOPMENTS

Privacy protection is a fast-breaking field with many bills proposed in Congress and state legislatures each year. The Library of Congress catalog site (telnet: locis.loc.gov) includes files summarizing legislation by the number of the Congress (each two-year session of Congress has a consecutive number: for example, the 105th Congress was in session in 1997 and 1998). Legislation can be searched for by the name of its sponsor(s), the bill number, or by topical keywords.

For example, a search of the 105th Congress for the keyword "privacy" yielded 1,201 "hits." Narrowing it down to "online privacy" retrieves seven records, of which the first is:

1. H.R.3783: SPON=Rep Oxley, (Cosp=65); OFFICIAL TITLE: A bill to amend section 223 of the Communications Act of 1934 to require persons who are engaged in the business of selling or transferring, by means of the World Wide Web, material that is harmful to minors to restrict access to such material by minors, and for other purposes. FLOOR ACTION HAS OCCURRED.

Asking to display the item in full gets 10 pages of information, with the first page noting the title of the proposed law, the Child Online Protection Act. Besides the text of the law and its list of sponsors, a subcommand "chrn" yields a chronology listing what actions, if any, have been taken concerning the bill.

The Library of Congress THOMAS site (http://thomas.loc.gov/), provides a web-based interface that may be easier to use for many purposes. Summaries of legislation considered by each Congress can be searched by keyword or bill number. For example, if the researcher has read about the Child Online Protection Act but doesn't know the bill number, a keyword search for "child online protection act" gives the following:

1. H.R. 3783: A bill to amend section 223 of the Communications Act of 1934 to require persons who are engaged in the business of selling or transferring, by means of the World Wide Web, material that is harmful to minors to restrict access to such material by minors, and for other purposes. **Sponsor:** *Rep. Oxley-LATEST ACTION: 10/07/98 Measure passed House, amended.*

Clicking on the Bill number (3783) gives a screen with links to summary, text of legislation, current status, floor actions, and so on. Of course if one knows the number, one can go directly to this listing from the search screen by searching by number.

Privacy advocacy and industry-related sites also keep track of bills that affect them. For example, EPIC maintains a "Bill-Track" showing pending legislation (http://www.epic.org/privacy/bill_track.html).

FINDING COURT DECISIONS

Like laws, legal decisions are organized using a system of citations. The general form is: *Party 1* v. *Party 2, volume reporter,* [optional *start page] court (year).*

Here are some examples from Chapter 2:

Katz v. United States, 389 U.S. 347 (1967)

Here the parties are Katz and the United States government, the case is in volume 389 of the U.S. *Supreme Court Reports,* and the case was decided in 1967. (For the Supreme Court, the name of the court is omitted).

Daniel Bernstein v. U.S. Department of State, 922 F. Supp. 1426, 1428–1430, N.D. Cal. (1996)

Here the parties are Daniel Bernstein and the U.S. Department of State. The decision is in volume 922 of the *Federal Supplement* (which reports on cases in district courts). The court is the North California District Federal Court, and the case was decided in 1996.

To find a federal court decision, first ascertain the level of court involved: district (the lowest level, where trials are normally held), circuit (the main court of appeals), or the Supreme Court. The researcher can then go to a number of places on the Internet to find cases by citation and, often, the names of the parties. Some of the most useful sites are:

- The Legal Information Institute (http://supct.law.cornell.edu/supct/) has all Supreme Court decisions since 1990 plus 610 of "the most important historic" decisions.

- Washlaw Web (http://www.washlaw.edu/) has a variety of courts (including states) and legal topics listed, making it a good jumping-off place for many sorts of legal research.

- EPIC maintains a "Litigation docket" of pending court cases (http://www. epic.org/privacy/litigation/).

LEXIS AND WESTLAW

Lexis and Westlaw are commercial legal databases that have extensive information including an elaborate system of notes, legal subject headings, and ways to show relationships between cases. Unfortunately, these services are too expensive for use by most individual researchers unless they are available through a university or corporate library.

MORE HELP ON LEGAL RESEARCH

For more information on conducting legal research, see the "Legal Research FAQ" at http://www.eff.org/pub/Legal/law_research.faq. This also explains more advanced techniques such as "Shepardizing" (referring to *Shepard's Case Citations*), which is used to find how a decision has been cited in subsequent cases, and whether the decision was later overturned.

The Cyberlaw Encyclopedia (http://www.gahtan.com/techlaw/) provides law articles, cases, and other resources on a variety of legal issues affecting online computer use. Privacy is one of the available categories.

TOOLS FOR ORGANIZING RESEARCH

The vast amount of information on the Net can be both a blessing and a curse. It is easy to become swamped by the stream of new web sites and documents, bibliographical references, articles, and news postings. There are, however, some techniques and tools that can help the researcher keep materials organized and accessible:

- Use the web browser's "Favorites" or "Bookmarks" menu to create a folder for each major research topic (and optionally, subfolders). For example, folders used in researching this book included: organizations, laws, cases, current news, reference materials, and bibliographical sources.

- Use favorites or bookmark links rather than downloading a copy of the actual web page or site, which can take up a large amount of both time and disk space. Exception: if the site has material that will definitely be needed in the future, download it to guard against it disappearing from the web.

- If a whole site needs to be archived, obtain one of a variety of free or low-cost utility programs such as WebWhacker, that make it easier to download a whole site automatically, including all levels of links. But use the program judiciously: a site like http://www.eff.org has hundreds of megabytes worth of material.

- Where applicable, "subscribe" to a site so it will automatically notify you when new material is available.

- Use a simple database program (such as Microsoft Works) or perhaps better, a free-from note-taking program (such as the shareware program WhizFolders, available at http://skanade.simplenet.com/. This makes it easy to take notes (or paste in text from web sites) and organize them for later retrieval.

Finally, a word of caution about the Internet. It is important to critically evaluate all materials found on the Net. Many sites have been established by well-known, reputable organizations or individuals. Others may come from unknown individuals or groups. Their material may be equally valuable, but it should be checked against reliable sources. Gradually, each researcher will develop a feel for the quality of information sources as well as a trusty tool kit of techniques for dealing with them.

CHAPTER 7

ANNOTATED BIBLIOGRAPHY

Hundreds of books, thousands of articles, and thousands more Internet documents relating to privacy issues have appeared in recent years. Indeed, the rapidly increasing amount of material testifies to the growing importance of the privacy issue to businesspeople, information industry professionals, health care providers, lawyers, and legislators, as well as to the general public as citizens and consumers. This chapter lists a representative sampling of these sources, selected for:

- Clarity and usefulness to the general reader (thus most law journal and computer technical journal articles are omitted, except when they can serve as a useful overview for the lay reader).

- Recent publication (due to rapid development on both the technical and legal front, most works published before the early to mid-1990s are more or less obsolete, with the exception of those that emphasize general legal, philosophical, or moral issues).

- Variety (an attempt to include as many aspects and points of view as possible).

In order to organize this many-faceted topic, the bibliographies are presented by topic as follows:

- Privacy Law Reference
- General Privacy Law and Policy
- International Privacy Law
- Personal and Consumer Privacy
- Privacy for Children

- Medical Privacy
- Corporate and Workplace Privacy
- Privacy and Government Agencies
- Encryption, Surveillance, and Data Security

Within each of these categories, the works are grouped according to type:

- Books
- Periodicals
- Articles and Papers
- Internet Documents (specific articles, documents, etc., available primarily on the Internet)

Note that newspaper and magazine articles that were found to be available in Internet-accessible databases are listed under "Articles and Papers," not "Internet Documents." For such articles, the Internet address (URL) is given, generally that of the newspaper or news service. The actual document can be retrieved by typing a few keywords (such as author's last name and a few words from the title) into the site's search facility.

PRIVACY LAW REFERENCE

BOOKS

Cook, Earleen H. *Search and Seizure in School.* Monticello, Ill.: Vance Bibliographies, 1987.

Dworaczek, Marian. *Employee Privacy: A Bibliography.* Monticello, Ill.: Vance Bibliographies, 1989.

Freedom of Information Act Guide & Privacy Act Overview: September 1996 Edition. Washington, D.C.: Government Printing Office, 1996. Provides detailed guidance on the application of the Freedom of Information Act (FOIA) as well as privacy legislation.

"Privacy, Right of." *Britannica CD 98.* Summarizes the development of privacy in the U.S. Constitution and law.

Sanford, Bruce W. *Sanford's Synopsis of Libel and Privacy.* 4th ed. New York: Pharos Books, 1991. Provides a succinct summary of principles of libel and privacy law.

Smith, Robert Ellis. *Compilation of State and Federal Privacy Laws, 1997.* Providence, R.I.: Privacy Journal, 1997. Summarizes state and federal privacy-related legislation by topic. Topics include credit reporting and investigation, criminal justice data, polygraphing, and other tests used in employment.

Stewart, Alva. W. *Privacy in the Workplace: A Bibliographic Survey.* Monticello, Ill.: Vance Bibliographies, 1987.

Vance, Mary A. *Right of Privacy: A Bibliography.* Monticello, Ill.: Vance Bibliographies, 1988.

Watts, Tim J. *Confidentiality in the Use of Library Materials: A Bibliography.* Monticello, Ill.: Vance Bibliographies, 1989.

Watts, Tim J. *A Selected Bibliography on Workplace Privacy.* Monticello, Ill.: Vance Bibliographies, 1991.

White, Anthony G. *Confidentiality/Privacy: I. The Privacy Act of 1974: A Selected Bibliography.* Monticello, Ill.: Vance Bibliographies, c. 1982. A bibliography of works relating to the landmark Privacy Act of 1974.

———. *Confidentiality/Privacy Issues: A Bibliographic Update.* Monticello, Ill.: Vance Bibliographies, 1986.

WEB DOCUMENTS

American Law Sources Online. Available online. URL: http://www. lawsource.com/also/. A comprehensive collection of links to many free sources of information about American, Canadian, and Mexican law.

"Computers and Privacy." *Grolier's Multimedia Encyclopedia.* Available on CD or online at http://grolier.compuserve.com/grolier (membership required). Introduces the topic and provides bibliographies; also see article under "Privacy, Invasion of."

Electronic Frontier Foundation. "comp_crime_laws.list" Available online. URL: http://www.eff.org/pub/Legal/comp_crime_laws.list. Downloaded December 26, 1998. Provides state by state listing of criminal code numbers pertaining to computer crimes.

———. "Computer Crime Statutes" Available online. URL: http://www.eff.org/pub/Legal/comp_crime_us_state.laws. Posted May 1, 1995. Contains text of state laws relating to computer crime. Also available in PostScript format at URL: http://www.eff.org/pub/Legal/comp_us_ state_laws_table.ps. For the introduction to this page, go to URL: http://www.eff.org/pub/Legal/comp_crime_us_state_laws.readme.

———. "EFF Privacy, Security, Cryptography, and Surveillance Archive." Available online. URL: http://www.eff.org/pub/Privacy/. Updated on October 30, 1998. Provides a large collection of downloadable documents covering a variety of issues; also very useful for studying the historical development of privacy issues in the information age.

———. "Email Privacy Citations." Available online. URL: http://www.eff.org/pub/Legal/email_privacy.citations. Downloaded December 26, 1998. Contains citations from U.S. Constitutional and California Law that can be useful for developing privacy policies.

———. "The Legal List: Law-related Resources on the Internet and Elsewhere." Available online. URL: http://www.eff.org/pub/Legal/net_legal_resources. readme (for introduction) and http://www.eff.org/pub/Legal/net_legal_ resources.list (for body of file). Posted on March 17, 1994. Extensive list of legal-related organizations and other resources available online through WAIS, Gopher, mailing lists, newsgroups, and the World Wide Web.

———. "Legal Research FAQ." Available online. URL: http://www.eff.org/ pub/Legal/law_research.faq. Downloaded December 27, 1998. Explains how to research and cite legal cases.

Electronic Privacy Information Center. "EPIC Online Guide to Privacy Resources." Available online. URL: http://cpsr.org/cpsr/privacy/epic/ privacy_resources_faq.html. Updated February 10, 1996. Lists resources including organizations, publications, mailing lists and newsgroups, software tools, and other items of interest.

Jones Telecommunications and Multimedia Encyclopedia. "Update: Electronic Communications Privacy Act of 1986." Available online. URL: http://www.digitalcentury.com/encyclo/update/ecpa.html. Background. Downloaded January 4, 1998. Summarizes the provisions of the Electronic Communications Privacy Act of 1986. Also includes useful links to related online legal resources.

The 'Lectric Law Library. Available online. URL: http://lectlaw.com/. Downloaded January 4, 1998. A very extensive and well-organized (albeit somewhat irreverent) source for information, links, and text on a variety of legal topics.

The Privacy Page. Online at URL: http://www.privacy.org. Updated January 6, 1998. Web site with a collection of tools, resources, and current news on privacy issues from an advocacy viewpoint.

Privacy Rights Clearinghouse. "Amendments to the Fair Credit Reporting Act (USPIRG)." (Fact Sheet #6A). URL: http://www.privacyrights. org/fs/fsbacrdt.htm. Downloaded on December 28, 1998. Summarizes key 1996 provisions amending the federal Fair Credit Reporting Act, including strengthening procedures for correcting erroneous information but effectively weakening other provisions; also summarizes proposed provisions that were defeated in Congress.

Veeder, Stacy. "Email_priv.biblio." Available online: URL: http://www.eff. org/pub/Legal/email_priv.biblio. Downloaded December 26, 1998. Contains bibliography on e-mail privacy, consisting of papers from the 1990–1991 period.

World Wide Web Virtual Law Library. Sponsored by The Indiana University School of Law Library and the World Wide Web Virtual Library. Available online. URL:http://www.law.indiana.edu/law/v-lib/lawindex. html. Organizes documents by source (federal and state governments, etc.) or legal topic.

Yahoo! Online at URL: http://www.yahoo.com. Provides a comprehensive Internet subject directory and search engine. Relevant categories for computer privacy include:
Computers and Internet/Internet/Law/Privacy
Computers and Internet/Internet/World Wide Web/Security Computers and Internet/Security and Encryption

ZD Net. Online at URL: http://xlink.zdnet.com/.Computer-related news site by magazine publisher Ziff-Davis; has articles on encryption, Internet privacy, and related issues.

GENERAL PRIVACY LAW AND POLICY

BOOKS

Agre, Philip, and Marc Rotenberg, eds. *Technology and Privacy: The New Landscape.* Cambridge, Mass.: MIT Press, 1997. Collects expert essays that survey the development and current status of privacy issues and concerns from the standpoints of computer science, law, politics, and sociology.

Alderman, Ellen, and Caroline Kennedy. *The Right to Privacy.* New York: Knopf, 1995. Uses a wealth of cases and anecdotes to illustrate privacy issues including law enforcement abuses, privacy for intimate life, and privacy in the workplace.

Branscomb, Ann Wells. *Who Owns Information?: From Privacy to Public Access.* New York: Basic Books, 1995. Discusses how personal information gathered from daily transactions has become a "product" marketed on a vast scale, and offers suggestions for regaining control and accountability.

Brin, David. *The Transparent Society: Will Technology Force Us to Choose Between Privacy and Freedom?* Reading, Mass.: Addison-Wesley, 1998. Provocatively suggests that the battle for privacy is lost—but people can turn the tables and "watch the watchers" to prevent abuses.

Cantril, Albert H., and Susan David Cantril. *Live and Let Live: American Public Opinion About Privacy at Home and at Work.* New York: ACLU Foundation, 1994. Discusses polling data that give a good picture of changing public attitudes toward privacy issues.

Carroll, John Millar. *Confidential Information Sources: Public and Private.* 2nd ed. Boston: Butterworth-Heinemann, 1991. Surveys the growth in size and sophistication of government and corporate databases containing personal information, highlighting their increased threat to privacy.

Cate, Frederick H. *Privacy in the Information Age.* Washington, D.C.: Brookings Institution Press, 1997. Surveys privacy issues and regulations, American and international.

Decew, Judith Wagner. *In Pursuit of Privacy: Law, Ethics, and the Rise of Technology.* Ithaca: Cornell University Press, 1997. Provides a survey and analysis of legal and ethical approaches to the challenges instigated by development in information technology.

Easton, Joseph W. *Card-carrying Americans: Privacy, Security, and the National ID Card Debate.* Totowa, N.J.: Rowman & Littlefield, 1986. Examines the recurring proposals for a national ID card, including the various justifications and criticisms.

Ermann, David M., Mary B. Williams, and Michele S. Shauf. *Computers, Ethics, and Society.* 2nd ed. New York: Oxford University Press, 1997. Discusses ethical aspects of computer use, including privacy issues.

Etzioni, Amitai. *The Limits of Privacy.* New York: Basic Books, 1999. Argues that while privacy is important, other social values such as health and safety should not be sacrificed in favor of unlimited privacy.

Garrow, David G. *Liberty and Sexuality: The Right to Privacy and the Making of Roe v. Wade.* Berkeley, Calif.: University of California Press, 1998. Exhaustively analyzes the legal reasoning that led to the *Roe v. Wade* abortion rights decision. *Roe* represented an expansion of an assertion of privacy as a constitutional right in *Griswold v. Connecticut* and has an impact on expanding rights to information privacy.

Gottfried, Ted. *Privacy: Individual Right vs. Social Needs (Issue and Debate).* Brookfield, Conn.: Millbrook Press, 1994. Introduces the privacy debate to high school age readers by discussing court cases and issues involving law enforcement, abortion, birth control, medical privacy, and misuse of databases.

Hendricks, Evan, Trudy Hayden, and Jack D. Novik. *Your Right to Privacy: A Basic Guide to Legal Rights in an Information Society.* (An American Civil Liberties Union Handbook). Carbondale, Ill.: Southern Illinois University Press, 1990. Uses a question-and-answer format to provide guidelines on an individual's right to privacy with regard to government records, personal information, and the private sector.

Hixson, Richard F. *Privacy in a Public Society: Human Rights in Conflict.* New York: Oxford University Press, 1987. Explores the tension between the right of privacy and social needs through history and recent cases.

Annotated Bibliography

Inness, Julie C. *Privacy, Intimacy, and Isolation*. New York: Oxford University Press, 1992. Explores the roots of privacy in the need to protect the intimate, personal sphere of human life.

Keynes, Edward. *Liberty, Property, and Privacy: Toward a Jurisprudence of Substantive Due Process*. University Park, Penn.: Pennsylvania State University Press, 1996. Discusses privacy concepts in relation to assertion of individual rights in encounters with the power of the state.

Lin, Herbert S., ed., and Dorothy E. Denning, et al. *Rights and Responsibilities of Participants in Networked Communities*. Washington, D.C.: National Academy Press, 1994. Reports on the legal standards that apply to online information services and conferencing networks.

Ludlow, Peter, ed. *High Noon on the Electronic Frontier: Conceptual Issues in Cyberspace*. Cambridge, Mass.: MIT Press, 1996. Contains a variety of writings ranging from academic papers to provocative manifestos. Discusses issues such as privacy, encryption, copyright, and the development of virtual communities.

Lyon, David, and Elia Zuriek, eds. *Computers, Surveillance, and Privacy*. Minneapolis: University of Minnesota Press, 1996. Collection of essays exploring surveillance and privacy issues in the information age.

McLean, Deckle. *Privacy and Its Invasion*. Westport, Conn.: Praeger, 1995. Explores the origins of the idea of privacy and illuminates examples of threats to privacy in many aspects of life.

Regan, Priscilla M. *Legislating Privacy: Technology, Social Values, and Public Policy*. Chapel Hill: University of North Carolina Press, 1995. Describes the political process and the applications of public policy values to the complex problems that arise from changes in information technology.

Sadofsky, David. *The Question of Privacy in Public Policy: The Reagan-Bush Years*. Westport, Conn.: Praeger, 1993. Surveys developments in privacy law during the 1980s and early 1990s.

Schneier, Bruce, and David Banisar. *The Electronic Privacy Papers: Documents on the Battle for Privacy in the Age of Surveillance*. New York: John Wiley & Sons, 1997. Provides an extensive collection of source documents from the legal battles over privacy issues, including government and industry reports and papers. Includes secret documents pried loose under the Freedom of Information Act.

Seipp, David J. *The Right of Privacy in American History*. Cambridge, Mass.: Harvard University, Program on Information Resources Policy, 1978. Surveys historical development of American privacy law.

Smith, Robert Ellis. *War Stories: Accounts of People Victimized by Invasions of Privacy*. Providence, R.I.: Privacy Journal, 1993. Recounts particularly disturbing invasions of privacy of individuals during the 1980s and early 1990s.

Strum, Philippa. *Privacy: The Debate in the United States Since 1945.* Fort Worth, Tex.: Harcourt Brace College Publishers, 1998. Discusses the major aspects of the privacy issue including use of genetic information and Social Security numbers, access to public records, intrusions by law enforcement, the growing use of surveillance, and privacy in the workplace.

United States. Information Infrastructure Task Force. Information Policy Committee. Privacy Working Group. *Principles for Providing and Using Personal Information.* For sale by the U.S. Government Printing Office, Superintendent of Documents, June 1995. Reports from a broad-based group of government departments and expresses general principles of privacy, information integrity, and accuracy and completeness that should guide privacy policy and regulation; also takes into account recent European privacy regulations.

Wacks, Raymond, ed. *Privacy* (International Library of Essays in Law and Legal Theory. Areas, No. 19.1 and 19.2). New York: New York University Press, 1993. Consists of two volumes of essays, the first dealing with the development of the concept of privacy and the second dealing with the legal aspects of privacy.

Wawrose, Susan C. *Griswold v. Connecticut: Contraception and the Right of Privacy* (Historic Supreme Court Cases). Danbury, CT.: Franklin Watts, 1996. Explains the issues and decision in the *Griswold* case. While not directly related to information technology, *Griswold* helped establish an expanded right of personal privacy.

Weintraub, Jeff, and Kirshan Kumar, eds. *Public and Private in Thought and Practice: Perspectives on a Grand Dichotomy.* Chicago: University of Chicago Press, 1997. Provides a philosophical study of the distinctions between private and public that underly much of the current privacy debates.

Whitaker, Reginald. *The End of Privacy: How Total Surveillance is Becoming a Reality.* New York: New Press, 1999. Describes in great detail the systems of surveillance and monitoring that involve nearly every aspect of Americans' lives. Suggests that many people accept such intrusions as the price of consumer convenience.

PERIODICALS

Full Disclosure. Glen Roberts, ed. Box 734, Antioch, IL 60002. (708) 395-6200. URL:http://www.glr.com/glr.html. Monthly newsletter on privacy and surveillance issues.

Journal of Online Law. URL: http://warthog.cc.wm.edu/law/publications/

jol/. An electronic publication that features essays on various aspects of law relating to online communities.

Privacy Journal. Robert Ellis Smith, ed. P.O. Box 28577, Providence, RI 02908. (401) 274-7861. Journal on privacy law. Also publishes a useful annual compilation of federal and state privacy laws.

Privacy Times. Evan Hendricks, ed. P.O. Box 21501, Washington, DC 21501. (202) 829-3660. E-mail: pritimes@nicom.com. Biweekly newsletter on privacy law, of particular interest to legal and business professionals.

ARTICLES AND PAPERS

American Society for Information Science. "Information Privacy, Integrity and Data Security." *Bulletin of the American Society for Information Science,* vol. 22, June–July 1996, p. 2ff. Describes agenda for June 2–4, 1996, ASIS conference that met to discuss the social and technical issues involved with protecting privacy and data security.

Branscomb, Anne Wells. "Public and Private Domains of Information: Defining the Legal Boundaries." *Bulletin of the American Society for Information Science,* vol. 21, December–January 1994, p. 14ff. Discusses property rights as they apply to information, ranging from copyright to privacy law.

Budish, Armond D. "Who Knows What About You?" *Family Circle,* vol. 110, April 1, 1997, p. 34ff. Introduces consumer, medical, and workplace privacy issues.

Blyth, Myrna. "The Right to Privacy." *Ladies Home Journal,* vol. 112, November 1995, p. 194ff. Review of the book *The Right to Privacy* by Caroline Kennedy and Ellen Alderman; praises its nuanced, balanced approach.

Clausing, Jeri. "Administration Seeks Input on Privacy Policy." *New York Times.* np. Available online. URL: http://www.nytimes.com/. Posted on November 6, 1998. Comments on how the upcoming confrontation with strict European guidelines may be prompting the Clinton administration to move from emphasizing self-regulation to promoting legislation.

———. "Congress's Internet Agenda." *New York Times.* np. Available online. URL: http://www.nytimes.com/. Posted on September 1, 1998. Surveys pending congressional proposals in many areas of Internet use; includes issues such as encryption, privacy, and intellectual property.

———. "U.S. Plans New Internet Privacy Sweep." *New York Times.* np. Available online. URL: http://www.nytimes.com/. Posted on December 29, 1998. Reports that the Federal Trade Commission is preparing to do another survey to determine whether online businesses are complying with its guidelines for informing consumers about information gathering.

Privacy in the Information Age

"The Computers Have Eyes: How Private Is Private in the Digital Age?" *Playboy*, vol. 43, February 1996, p. 33ff. Interview with Andre Bacard, author of *The Computer Privacy Handbook*, who points out the extent of government and private snooping into the lives of ordinary Americans.

Etzioni, Amitai, and Nadine Strossen. "Should Americans Be Willing to Give Up Some of Their Privacy to Advance Policies that Are Generally Perceived to Be in Society's Best Interest?" *CQ Researcher*, vol. 7, March 21, 1997, p. 257. Debate between Etzioni, a communitarian philosopher, and Strossen, director of the ACLU that pits collective good against the individual right of privacy.

"The Eyes of Technology" [Editorial]. *San Francisco Chronicle*. March 14, 1999, p. 6. Summarizes recent events that show the pervasiveness of surveillance by government and data-gathering by businesses and raises questions about its ultimate extent.

Flood, Barbara. "The Emotionality of Privacy." *Bulletin of the American Society for Information Science*, vol. 23, February–March 1997, p. 7ff. Explores the importance of privacy to self-image and to the sense of control people have over their own lives.

Glancy, Dorothy J. "The Invention of the Right of Privacy." *Arizona Law Review* 21, 1979, np. Discusses the early development of legal concepts of privacy in America, particularly the opinions of Justice Brandeis.

Gormley, Ken. "One Hundred Years of Privacy." *Wisconsin Law Review*, 1992, np. Surveys a century's legal developments in the privacy field.

Healey, John. "Just Between Us: The Promises of New Technologies Also Pose a Threat to Personal Privacy." *Congressional Quarterly Weekly Report*, vol. 52, May 14, 1994, p. S41ff. Surveys emerging controversies arising out of new telecommunications technology and the information superhighway, pitting consumer privacy versus business productivity and law enforcement needs versus the use of encryption for communications privacy.

Herbert, Bob. "What Privacy Rights? Medical Records, Phone Calls, E-mail—Nothing Is Secure." *New York Times*, vol. 148, September 27, 1998, p. WK15. Contrasts the privacy people have with the reality that snoopers are everywhere.

Horn, Miriam. "Shifting Lines of Privacy." *U.S. News & World Report*, October 26, 1998. p. 57. Briefly summarizes the changing idea and experience of privacy in America since colonial times, in the light of recent media snooping and White House scandals.

Karaim, Reed. "The Invasion of Privacy." *Civilization*, October/November 1996, np. [also reprinted in Winters, Paul A., ed. *The Information Revolution: Opposing Viewpoints*. San Diego, Calif.: Greenhaven Press, 1998, pp. 151–158]. An overview of the history and development of the idea of

132

privacy with examples of how the right to privacy is becoming threatened in the Information Age.

Lassen, Nelson. "The History and Development of the Fourth Amendment to the United States Constitution." *The Johns Hopkins University Studies in Historical and Political Science*, Series LV, 1937. Surveys the early jurisprudence of the Fourth Amendment that played an important role in establishing privacy rights.

Lesser, Barry. "Information Protection Issues in the Information Economy." *Bulletin of the American Society for Information Science* 14, February/March 1988, pp. 21–22. Discusses the issues that arise with the growing use of information in business.

Milberg, S. J., S. J. Burke, H. J. Smith, and E. A. Kallman. "Values, Personal Information Privacy, and Regulatory Approaches." *Communications of the ACM* 38, December 12, 1995, pp. 65–74. Provides a detailed survey of information professionals in nine countries that compares privacy concerns and levels of regulation.

Mulligan, Deirdre, and Stephen J. Col. "Should the Federal Government Set Privacy Standards for the Internet?" *CQ Researcher*, November 6, 1998, p. 969. Debates whether a national privacy policy is desirable or feasible as a supplement to self-regulation.

Obser, Jeffrey. "Privacy Is the Problem, Not the Solution." *Salon*, June 26, 1997, np. [also reprinted in Winters, Paul A., ed. *The Information Revolution: Opposing Viewpoints*. San Diego, Calif.: Greenhaven Press, 1998, pp. 159–165]. Argues that the demand for privacy may be excessive and reflect "a fearful reaction to the collapse of trust in our culture" and that privacy laws may have a downside in protecting the criminal and corrupt from scrutiny.

Rothfelder, Jeffrey. "Twenty Facts About Privacy: Why the Price of Freedom Is Vigilance." *Playboy*, vol. 41, April 1994, p. 50ff. Outlines 20 examples of threats to privacy and suggests protective measures.

Sherill, Martha. "Private People, Public Lives." *Harper's Bazaar*, November 1995, p. 126ff. Review of the book *The Right to Privacy*, in which Caroline Kennedy and Ellen Alderman discuss a variety of troubling cases.

Spaeth, Harold J., and Edward Conrad Smith. "The Right to Privacy." Chapter in *Constitution of the United States*, Edition 1991, p. 133ff. Discusses the fundamental court cases that established a broad right of privacy in personal and family affairs.

Spinello, Richard A. "The End of Privacy: Companies That Collect Information for a Specific Purpose Can Resell or Reuse It for Other Purposes with Impunity." *America*, vol. 176, January 4, 1997, p. 9ff. Argues that existing laws are inadequate in protecting consumer, financial, and medical privacy; the article recommends legislation.

Talbot, Margaret. "Washington Diarist: Candid Camera." *The New Republic,* October 26, 1998, p. 42. Points out that while some people fight to keep their privacy, others put themselves in a fishbowl so that everyone on the Internet can see their lives. Does this kind of exhibitionism illuminate the nature of privacy?

"Top Security and Privacy Sites." *PC World,* vol. 16, September 1998, p. 187. A list of recommended web sites for privacy advocates, consumer and credit organizations, software tools, and other resources.

"We Know You're Reading This." *The Economist,* vol. 338, February 10, 1996, p. 27ff. Suggests that between the Big Brothers of government and a swarm of "little brothers" (paid snoops and hackers), privacy is in danger on many fronts.

Wilson, David L. "The Network Has Eyes: With Computers Tracking On-Line Activities, Users' Anxiety Over Privacy Grows." *The Chronicle of Higher Education,* vol. 41, July 21, 1995, p. A17ff. Describes the extent to which Internet sites can monitor a user's online activities—including which page of a document he or she may currently be reading.

INTERNET DOCUMENTS

Borella, Michael S. "Computer Privacy vs. First and Fourth Amendments Rights." Available online. URL: http://www.eff.org/pub/Legal/comp_ privacy_vs_rights.paper. Downloaded on December 26, 1998. Introduces the concept of cyberspace and then looks at cases where misuse of private databases and law enforcement databases such as the National Crime Information Center (NCIC) and even census records can lead to serious consequences for individuals.

"EFF 'Legal Issues—"Cyberspace Law for Non-Lawyers" Course' Archive." Available online. URL:http://www.eff.org/pub/Legal/CyberLaw_ Course/. Downloaded on December 26, 1998. [See files cyberlaw.13 through cyberlaw.25.] A series of lessons on the application of privacy principles and law to cyberspace, written for a lay audience.

Garfinkel, Simson L. "Introduction to Security: An Introduction to Computer Security for Lawyers." Available online. URL: http://www.eff. org/pub/Legal/comp_security_legal.article. Downloaded on December 26, 1998. Explains computer security issues for small businesses and law firms, including ways to safeguard data privacy.

Johnson, David R. "Dispute Resolution in Cyberspace." Available online. URL: http://www.eff.org/pub/Legal/online_dispute_resolution_johnson. article. Posted February 10, 1994. Argues that the special nature of cyberspace (such as its speed of interaction) means that new procedures need to be worked out for dealing with disputes, including determining jurisdiction and applicable law.

———. "Electronic Communications Privacy: Good Sysops Should Build Good Fences." Available online. URL: http://www.eff.org/pub/Legal/good_fences_johnson.article. Downloaded on December 26, 1998. Describes the provisions of the Electronic Communications Privacy Act of 1986 and how online system operators (Sysops) can comply with its provisions and protect users' privacy.

———. "Jurisdictional Quid Pro Quo and the Law of Cyberspace." Available online. URL: http://www.eff.org/pub/Legal/cyberjuris_quidproquo_johnson.article. Posted on July 12, 1994. Offers guidelines for determining jurisdiction over acts in cyberspace that frequently involve separate or uncertain jurisdiction. The article suggests a standard that would allow a jurisdiction to impose penalties in proportion to the offender's involvement with it, such as by using online means to block online offenses.

———. "Lawmaking and Law Enforcement in Cyberspace." Available online. URL: http://www.eff.org/pub/Legal/cyberlaw_johnson.article. Posted on April 27, 1994. Recommends self-regulation by cyberspace providers combined with a disclosure and agreement-based system for creating global rules that could apply to many participating systems.

———. "The New Case Law of Cyberspace." Available online. URL: http://www.eff.org/pub/Legal/new_cyber_caselaw_johnson.article. Posted May 17, 1994. Argues that the Net can evolve a "common law" of its own through the decisions and agreements of system operators and users.

———. "The Unscrupulous Diner's Dilemma and Anonymity in Cyberspace." Available online. URL: http://www.eff.org/pub/Legal/anonymity_online_johnson.article. Posted on March 4, 1994. Suggests that forming viable online communities requires limiting the use of anonymity because of the need for trustworthiness and accountability.

Levinson, Nan. "Electrifying Speech: New Communications Technologies and Traditional Civil Liberties." Human Rights Watch and the Electronic Frontier Foundation. Available online. URL: http://www.eff.org/pub/Legal/electrifying_speech.paper. Downloaded on December 26, 1998. The article urges that the core constitutional principle of applying rights to people, as opposed to places or technologies, be used to guarantee traditional rights in the new realm of cyberspace.

Loundy, David. "E-Law 2.0: Computer Information Systems Law and System Operator Revisited." Available online. URL: http://www.eff.org/pub/Legal/e-law.paper. Posted on September 30, 1994. Discusses liabilities and responsibilities for computer network system operators, including those arising under federal privacy legislation.

Privacy Rights Clearinghouse. "Privacy in Cyberspace: Rules of the Road for the Information Superhighway." (Fact Sheet #18). URL: http://www.privacy rights.org/fs/fs18-cyb.htm. Updated in December 1998. Introduces privacy issues in online communications (information services and the Internet); summarizes practices and applicable laws; describes features and gives advice.

Riddle, Michael H. "The Electronic Communications Privacy Act of 1986: A Layman's View." Available online. URL: http://www.eff.org/pub/Legal/ ecpa_laymans_view.article. Downloaded on December 26, 1998. Introduces and explains the provisions of the Electronic Communications Privacy Act of 1986 in nonlegal language.

Rose, Lance. "Cyberspace and the Legal Matrix: Laws or Confusion?" [Originally published in *Boardwatch*, June 1991]. Available online. URL: http.//www.eff.org/pub/Legal/cyberspace_legal_matrix.article. Downloaded on December 26, 1998. Describes the many conflicting systems of laws that might apply to online interactions and recommends an effort to establish well-designed national laws to minimize such conflicts.

Rotenberg, Marc. "The Law of Information Privacy: Supplement." Georgetown University Law School. Available online. URL: http://www.epic.org/ misc/gulc/materials/supplement.html. Updated on August 22, 1997. Provides an overview of legal aspects of information privacy.

Schlachter, Eric. "Cyberspace, the Free Market and the Free Marketplace of Ideas: Recognizing Legal Differences in Computer Bulletin Board Functions." Hastings College of Law and the Electronic Frontier Foundation. Available online. URL: http://www.eff.org/pub/Legal/cyberlaw_bbs_ free_market.article. Downloaded December 26, 1998. Suggests analogies for applying traditional legal principles to the actions of system operators and users of online bulletin boards.

Silverglate, Harvey. "Legal Overview: The Electronic Frontier and the Bill of Rights." Available online. URL: http://www.eff.org/pub/Legal/bill_ of_rights_online.paper. Downloaded on December 26, 1998. Describes the application of the protections in the First, Fourth, and Fifth Amendments of the U.S. Constitution to modern information technology.

Standler, Ronald B. "Privacy Law in the USA." Available online. URL: http://www.rbs2.com/privacy.htm. Updated on May 24, 1998. Summarizes the concepts and applicable laws for various aspects of privacy.

Tribe, Lawrence S. "The Constitution in Cyberspace: Law and Liberty Beyond the Electronic Frontier." Available online. URL: http://www. eff.org/pub/Legal/cyber_constitution.paper. Downloaded on December 26, 1998. Gives the keynote address at the First Conference on computers, Freedom and Privacy. Discusses the application of constitutional values and argues for maintaining their integrity in confronting changes in technological capabilities.

United States Department of Commerce. ["Safe Harbor" Proposal] Available online. URL: http://www.epic.org/privacy/intl/doc-safeharbor-1198.html. Posted on November 4, 1998. Government proposal that attempts to allow U.S. companies, which voluntarily agree to certain privacy principles, to gain a "safe harbor" that would allow them to operate in Europe despite new European Union regulations.

INTERNATIONAL PRIVACY LAW

BOOKS

Bennett, Colin. *Regulating Privacy: Data Protection and Public Policy in Europe and the United States.* Ithaca: Cornell University Press, 1992. Compares approaches to privacy and data protection in America and Europe.

Flaherty, David. *Protecting Privacy in Surveillance Societies: The Federal Republic of Germany, Sweden, France, Canada, and the United States.* Chapel Hill: University of North Carolina Press, 1989. Compares surveillance practices and privacy protection in a variety of North American and European societies.

Kahin, Brian, and Charles Nessen, eds. *Borders in Cyberspace: Information Policy and the Global Information Infrastructure* (Publication of the Harvard Information Infrastructure Project). Cambridge, Mass.: MIT Press, 1997. Discusses how differences in national laws make it difficult to cope with privacy issues in a network that ignores national boundaries. Includes discussion of commerce, security, and personal privacy.

Michael, James. *Privacy and Human Rights: An International and Comparative Study, with Special Reference to Developments in Information Technology.* Hampshire, United Kingdom: Dartmouth Publication Co., 1994. Surveys and analyzes the legal and ethical issues involved with the growth of data exchange, from a global perspective.

Moore, Barrington. *Privacy: Studies in Social and Cultural History.* Armonk, N.Y.: M. E. Sharpe, 1984. Surveys the concepts of privacy in many societies around the world.

Sieber, Ulrich. *The International Handbook on Computer Crime: Computer-Related Economic Crime and the Infringements of Privacy.* New York: John Wiley & Sons, 1987. Analyzes computer crime, including infringement of privacy, from a global perspective and with attention to the legal situation in each country.

Swire, Peter P., and Robert E. Litan. *None of Your Business: World Data Flows, Electronic Commerce, and the European Privacy Directive.* Washington, D.C.: Brookings Institution Press, 1998. Discusses the European Union Directive on Data Protection of 1998 and its implications, which could include preventing nonconforming American corporations from doing business in Europe.

PERIODICALS

International Privacy Bulletin. Dave Banisar, ed. Privacy International. 666 Pennsylvania Ave., SE #301, Washington, DC 20003. (202) 544-9240 URL: http://www.privacy.org/pi/. Includes reports on privacy-related developments in many countries.

Privacy Files. 1788 d'Argenson, Ste-Julie (Quebec), CANADA J3E 1E3. (800) 922-9151. E-mail: privacy.files@progesta.com. Canadian-based international newsletter on privacy issues. Offers "Privacy Files Abstracts" by free e-mail subscription: e-mail privacy.files@progesta.com; send message with "Add me to 'Privacy Files Abstracts' " and your name in the subject field.

Privacy Law and Policy Reporter. Level 11, Carlton Centre, 55–63 Elizabeth Street, Sydney, NSW 2000, Australia. Phone: +61-2-221-6199. Mainly covers privacy developments in Australia and New Zealand.

Privacy Laws and Business. Stewart Dresner, ed. 3 Central Avenue, Pinner, Middlesex HA5 5BT United Kingdom. Phone: +44-81-866-8641. Quarterly review of privacy law and issues from a European perspective.

ARTICLES AND PAPERS

Andrews, Edmund L. "European Law Aims to Protect Privacy of Data; Some Trade with the U.S. Could Be Disrupted." *New York Times*, vol. 148, October 26, 1998, p. A1. Explains that the United States has weak privacy standards compared to new European rules that require reciprocal provisions. This may exclude American companies from this important market.

de Bony, Elizabeth, and Margaret Johnston. "EU and U.S. Keep Data Flowing." *InfoWorld*, November 2, 1998, p. 57. Reports that the U.S. Department of Commerce and the European Union Commission have agreed that Europe will not block access from U.S. online sites while negotiations that attempt to reconcile weak U.S. privacy standards with much stricter EU policies continue.

Flaherty, David H. "The Emergence of Surveillance Societies in the Western World: Toward the Year 2000." *Government Information Quarterly* 5, no. 4, 1988, p. 377–387. Describes international trends toward more pervasive surveillance of individuals in developed countries.

Kaplan, Carl S. "Strict European Privacy Law Puts Pressure on U.S." *New York Times*. np. Available online. URL: http://www.nytimes.com/. Posted on October 9, 1998. Describes the new European Union Data Protection

Directive and its possible effects on access to Europe by U.S. online businesses that operate under much looser privacy standards.

Kuttner, Robert. "The U.S. Could Use a Dose of Europe's Privacy Medicine." *Business Week*, November 16, 1998, p. 22. Argues that the United States should adopt tougher privacy and junk e-mail/fax laws similar to those already in force in Europe.

Tutt, Nigel. "EC Revamps Data Privacy Rules." *Electronics*, vol. 67, July 11, 1994, p. 10. Describes new European rules covering telecommunications issues such as the use of ISDN, mobile phone services, and caller-ID.

Wilson, Des. "The Fact That Britain Is Finally Getting a Freedom of Information Act Is Almost Entirely Due to the Single-Mindedness of One Great Reformer." *New Statesman*, vol. 127, April 24, 1998, p. 19. Describes the efforts of reformer Maurice Frankel that are likely to result in Great Britain getting its first real freedom of information law.

INTERNET DOCUMENTS

Barnes, Douglas. "The Coming Jurisdictional Swamp of Global Internet-working." Available online. URL: http://www.eff.org/pub/Legal/anon_juris.article. Posted on November 16, 1994. Argues that as the Internet has expanded, so have conflicts and demands for legal solutions—but what does jurisdiction mean in a truly global interlinked communications network? The article also discusses the applicability of traditional doctrines of jurisdiction to the new medium.

European Commission. "European Commission Press Release: Council Definitively Adopts Directive on Protection of Personal Data." Available online. URL: http://www.privacy.org/pi/intl_orgs/ec/dp_EC_press_release.txt. Posted on July 25, 1995. Official statement introducing new European data privacy regulations.

———. "Final EU Data Protection Directive." Available online. URL: http://www.privacy.org/pi/intl_orgs/ec/final_EU_Data_Protection.html. Posted on February 2, 1995. Gives text of European Community data privacy regulations.

PERSONAL AND CONSUMER PRIVACY

BOOKS

Banks, Michael A. *Web Psychos, Stalkers, and Pranksters: How to Protect Yourself in Cyberspace*. Scottsdale, Ariz.: Coriolis Group, 1997. Discusses a variety of web-based scams as well as dangerous predators who haunt the "chat rooms" of online services. Uses colorful anecdotes and provides common sense tips.

Cavoukian, Ann, and Dan Tapscott. *Who Knows? Safeguarding Your Privacy in a Networked World*. New York: McGraw-Hill, 1996. Begins by explaining just how information is collected during each of life's daily transactions, and then offers suggestions for minimizing unnecessary and risky disclosure of information.

Charrett, Sheldon. *The Modern Identity Changer: How to Create a New Identity for Privacy and Personal Freedom*. Boulder, Colo.: Paladin Press, 1997. Discusses controversial techniques that can be used either to protect privacy or for criminal purposes; features a how-to for creating a new identity.

Fetherling, Dale, ed., and the Privacy Rights Clearinghouse. *The Privacy Rights Handbook: How to Take Control of Your Personal Information*. New York: Avon Books, 1997. Explains how consumers can take action to protect their privacy online and in dealing with corporations and government agencies.

Gelman, Robert B., with Stanton McCandlish. *Protecting Yourself Online: The Definitive Resource on Safety, Freedom, and Privacy in Cyberspace*. San Francisco: HarperEdge, 1998. Introduces online users to a variety of issues including free speech, privacy, and intellectual property based on advice prepared by the Electronic Frontier Foundation.

Goncalves, Marcus, and Arthur Donkers. *Internet Privacy Kit*. Indianapolis, Ind.: Que Education and Training, 1997. Provides encryption software and techniques for consumers to safely shop and communicate online.

Gurak, Laura J. *Persuasion and Privacy in Cyberspace: The Online Protests over Lotus Marketplace and the Clipper Chip*. New Haven: Yale University Press, 1997. Discusses the reaction to a Lotus Corporation database marketing proposal, which would have distributed personal consumer information nationwide, and a government proposal for the Clipper Chip that offered data protection but also a "back door" for government surveillance. Uses the two controversies as a way to explore the problematic debating techniques often used online.

Lane, Carole A. *Naked in Cyberspace: How to Find Personal Information Online*. Wilton, Conn.: Pemberton Press, 1997. Presents eye-opening "how-tos" for finding information about people from online sources—and for protecting oneself from other people's snooping.

Lesce, Tony. *The Privacy Poachers: How the Government and Big Corporations Gather, Use and Sell Information About You*. Port Townsend, Wash.: Loompanics, 1992. Focuses on the public and private "snoops" who use various techniques to obtain information that most people assume is personal and private.

Lynch, Daniel C., and Leslie Lundquist. *Digital Money: The New Era of Internet Commerce*. New York: John Wiley & Sons, 1995. Describes the technology and procedures that businesses can use to perform consumer transactions via the Internet, including privacy and security considerations.

Mandell, Lewis. *The Credit Card Industry: A History.* Boston: Twayne, 1990. Provides general background on the growth of the credit card industry and its impact on American life.

Mizell, Louis R., Jr. *Invasion of Privacy.* New York: Berkley Books, 1998. Provides detailed guidance for detecting and combating a variety of surveillance techniques at home and in the workplace, including cell phone eavesdropping and interception of e-mail.

Peterson, Chris. *I Love the Internet, but I Want My Privacy, Too!* Rocklin, Calif.: Prima Publishing, 1998. Begins with an overview of the benefits and threats brought about by the gathering of consumer and medical information. Gives the reader techniques for determining what personal information has been gathered online and how to prevent or limit its collection or distribution. Includes sections on common scams as well as protection for children.

Pfaffenberger, Bryan. *Protect Your Privacy on the Internet.* New York: Wiley Computer Publications, 1997. Guidelines and software for protecting privacy during online transactions, including control of the collection of "cookie" files by web site.

Rose, Lance. *Netlaw: Your Rights in the Online World.* Berkeley, Calif.: Osborne/McGraw-Hill, 1995. Guide to the laws affecting online computer lists, including privacy issues.

Scott, Gini Graham. *Mind Your Own Business: The Battle for Personal Privacy.* New York: Insight Books, 1995. Surveys the battles in recent years where privacy issues conflict with the goals of marketers, private investigators, police, and bureaucrats through narratives of a variety of actual cases.

Smith, Robert Ellis. *Our Vanishing Privacy: And What You Can Do to Protect Yours.* Port Townsend, Wash.: Loompanics, 1993. A collection of chapters that survey the major threats to personal and consumer privacy, including 20 "principles" to follow in order to maintain control over personal information.

Stewart, Marcia, Janice Portman, and Ralph E. Warner. *Every Landlord's Legal Guide: Leases and Rental Agreements, Deposits, Rent Rules, Liability, Discrimination, Property Managers, Privacy, Repairs and Maintenance, and Evictions.* Berkeley, Calif.: Nolo Press, 1997. Legal handbook for landlords; includes a section on the privacy rights of tenants.

PERIODICALS

Financial Privacy News. Dr. Styvesant J. Fishdt III, ed. 1293 Pavas 1200, Costa Rica; or SJO-966, P.O. Box 025216, Miami, FL 33182. E-mail: stephénw@sol.racsa.co. URL: http://apollo.co.uk/a/offshore/privacy.

Deals with asset protection and privacy through offshore banking and other techniques.

Low Profile. P.O. Box 84910, Phoenix, AZ 85701. Phone: 702-333-5942. Newsletter on asset protection and financial privacy.

Privacy and American Business. Bob Belair, ed. Two University Plaza, Suite 414, Hackensack, NJ 07601. Phone: (201) 996-1154. Covers privacy issues from the perspective of business and industry.

Privacy Newsletter. John Featherman, ed. P.O. Box 8206, Philadelphia, PA 19101-8206. E-mail: privacy@interramp.com. Consumer-friendly publication with anecdotes, background information, and tips on issues of consumer privacy.

ARTICLES

Allen, Michael. "Privacy Concerns Spark Criticism of Bank Rule." *Wall Street Journal,* December 10, 1998, p. B1. Discusses new proposals to have banks track more details of transactions to fight money laundering and objections from privacy advocates.

"Auditing Your Records: What You Don't Know Can Hurt You." *Consumer Reports,* vol. 61, November 1996, p. 60ff. Tells consumers how they can access their credit, insurance, medical, and other records and reports so they can find and fix potentially harmful errors.

Baig, Edward. "How to Practice Safe Surfing," *Business Week,* September 9, 1996, pp. 120–121.

Bank, David. "Some Worry About Privacy Aspects of the Information Superhighway." *Knight-Ridder/Tribune News Service,* February 16, 1994, p. 0216K0219. Discusses how new interactive TV systems might monitor everything a person watches or buys—with the information being passed to marketers, health insurers, or other organizations.

Bayne, Kim M. "Privacy Still Burning Web Issue: Marketers Scramble to Come Up with Self-Regulation Methods." *Advertising Age,* vol. 69, June 29, 1998, p. 37. Describes efforts by Metromail, Electronic Frontier Foundation, the Direct Marketing Association, and TRUSTe to develop privacy guidelines. These might include a way to reach targeted markets without revealing personal information to the marketer and a way for users to tell their web browser what standards to enforce. Also describes alternative guidelines such as those of the Online Marketing Alliance.

Beckett, Jamie, and Dan Fost. "FTC Sets Deadline on Internet Privacy Rules." *San Francisco Chronicle,* October 14, 1998, p. B1, B3. The Federal Trade Commission has notified the electronic commerce industry that it must set effective voluntary guidelines for Internet privacy or face the prospect of new legislation in 1999.

Beiser, Vince. "The Cyber Snoops: How Internet Gumshoes Breach Personal Privacy." *Maclean's*, vol. 110, June 23, 1997, p. 42. Describes the "data brokers" that can find out nearly everything about a person—for a price. Most of the information is actually publicly available and legal to obtain, but the practice raises privacy issues and the concern of the U.S. Federal Trade Commission.

Betts, Mitch. "Subscriber Privacy for Sale." *Computerworld*, vol. 28, October 10, 1994, p. 1ff. Investigates practices of America Online, Prodigy, and Compuserve; seeks to determine whether they give users enough notice about the gathering and selling of personal information, as well as making it clear that they can refuse to allow such distribution.

Blow, Richard. "Lock Your Windows." *Mother Jones*, vol. 23 no. 1, January–February 1998, p. 40(2). Discusses privacy issues arising from Microsoft's collecting consumer information from its expanding online services, such as the Sidewalk city guides and Expedia travel services.

Brinkley, Joel. "F. T. C. 'Losing Patience' with Business on Web Privacy." *New York Times*. np. Available online. URL: http://www.nytimes.com/. Posted on September 21, 1998. Reports that a recent survey of online sites by the Federal Trade Commission has found so many privacy problems that agency officials are no longer willing to wait long for the industry to come up with effective self-regulation.

———. "Judge Orders a Credit Bureau to Stop Selling Consumer Lists." *New York Times*, vol. 147, August 27, 1998, p. A1ff. Reports that in an action that may signal tighter restrictions, Judge James P. Timony of the Federal Trade Commission told the major credit reporting agency Trans Union Corporation that it could no longer sell consumer lists generated from its records.

Caruso, Denise. "Who Knows What About Whom on the Internet." *New York Times*. np. Available online. URL: http://www.nytimes.com/. Posted on April 13, 1998. Summarizes recent developments that highlight concerns about information-gathering by web sites.

Castelli, Jim. "How to Handle Personal Information." *American Demographics*, vol. 18, March 1996, p. 50ff. Describes the growing demand for privacy protection; suggests policies that can give consumers more control over their information and perhaps provide a competitive edge with privacy-conscious consumers.

Clausing, Jeri. "Coalition Announces Initiative for Online Privacy." *New York Times*. np. Available online. URL: http://www.nytimes.com/. Posted on October 7, 1998. Describes the Online Privacy Initiative, a major industry advertising campaign that seeks to educate users about how to protect their privacy.

———. "Proposed Standards Fail to Please Advocates of Online Privacy." *New York Times*. np. Available online. URL: http://www.nytimes.com/. Posted on June 2, 1998. Explores an industry software initiative called the Platform for Privacy Preferences (P3P), in which a site's disclosure would automatically be matched against the user's privacy settings. Al Gore expressed approval of the plan, but some privacy advocates consider it to be a cop-out and demand restriction or elimination of all gathering of personal information online.

———. "Trade Commission Says GeoCities Violated Privacy Rules." *New York Times*. np. Available online. URL: http://www.nytimes.com/. Posted on August 13, 1998. Reports that the Federal Trade Commission has concluded that the online service GeoCities gathered information from users despite its stated policy.

———. "U.S. Report on Net Commerce Set for Release; Key Recommendations Stress Self-Regulation." *New York Times*, vol. 148, November 30, 1998, p. C1. A federal interagency working group headed by Ira Magaziner will recommend some legislation, but take an overall approach of self-regulation by industry. Marc Rotenberg of the Electronic Privacy Information Center disagrees, saying strong laws are needed to protect consumers and to comply with new European Union regulations.

Clayton, Gary. "Eurocrats Try to Stop Data at the Border." *The Wall Street Journal*, November 2, 1998, p. A32. Describes the conflict between tough European privacy standards and weak U.S. regulations that may lead to American firms being blocked from access to the European online market.

"Consumer Privacy Legislative and Regulatory Initiatives." *Bulletin of the American Society for Information Science*, vol. 23, April–May 1997, p. 18ff. Summarizes Federal Trade Commission workshop and study of database practices, as well as proposals for regulating disclosure of information online.

"The Data Game: Sophisticated Marketing Wizards Can Track Just About Everything a Consumer Does." *Maclean's*, vol. 111, August 17, 1998, p. 14. Describes the "data mining industry" that gathers detailed information from credit cards, supermarket "clubs," and other sources and sells it to marketers who want to target certain kinds of customers.

Doherty, Brian. "Tangled Web Pages." *Reason*, vol. 29, November 1997, p. 21. Describes how federal government web sites often violate the government's own privacy rules, such as by collecting information without informing users or by putting "cookie" files on users' hard drives without permission.

Dowd, Ann Reilly. "Alert: New Threats to Your Privacy—And Some Help." *Money*, vol. 26, November 1997, p. 30. Briefly describes new threats to individuals' financial, medical, and workplace privacy and gives updates on proposed legislation.

Eisenberg, Rebecca. "The Net's Miracle Marketing." *San Francisco Examiner*, August 9, 1998, p. B–5, B–12. Reports that companies like Amazon.com are betting that consumers will love their ability to tailor product recommendations to their exact tastes and needs, but privacy advocates worry about the potential abuse of the detailed information that makes such custom services possible.

Fitch, Michael. "Here's How to Protect Your Wallet (and Your Privacy) from Online Pirates." *Money*, vol. 26, April 1997, p. 32. Gives consumer tips to protect privacy, such as using secure browsers and secure sites, avoiding unknown firms, not using online calculation features (that can store data secretly), and using software to replace one's address with "anonymous" and to wipe out "cookie" files that some sites store on the user's hard disk.

Flood, Barbara, and William Lutz. "Creeping Peoplebases: Database Developments and Privacy Loss." *Bulletin of the American Society for Information Science*, vol. 23, February–March 1997, p. 5ff. Describes how the ability to gather and combine information from many separate sources can create a "package" of information that can intrude deeply into the private life of an individual.

Flynn, Laurie J. "Company Stops Providing Access to Key Social Security Numbers." *New York Times*, June 13, 1996, p. B11. Reports that public outcry has led to the withdrawal of Social Security numbers from marketing databases.

———. "Group to Monitor Web Sites for Respect of Consumer Privacy." *New York Times*, July 16, 1996. Available online. URL: http://www.nytimes .com/. Reports that the Electronic Frontier Foundation and a group of Internet businesses have joined to create TRUSTe, an organization that will provide certification of privacy practices.

———. "Lexis-Nexis Flap Prompts Push for Privacy Rights." *New York Times*, October 13, 1996, np. Available online. URL: http://www.nytimes.com/. Reports that public outrage over the distribution of personal information by the Lexis-Nexis information service has led to demands for regulation by the Federal Trade Commission.

"Fraud in Credit Cards, Social Security on the Rise." (Associated Press) *San Francisco Chronicle*, May 27, 1998, p. A4. Reports that the growing fraudulent use of credit card and Social Security numbers is prompting proposed legislation that would restrict the distribution of such numbers and give victimized consumers an alternative to sometimes uncooperative banks.

Furchgott, Roy. "If Your Privacy's Invaded . . . Tough Luck." *Business Week*, no. 3565, February 16, 1998, p. 6. Claims that the privacy standards set by the Individual Reference Services Group are unclear and inadequate.

Gillmor, Dan. "Violating Privacy Is Bad Business." *Computerworld*, vol. 32, March 23, 1998, p. 38. Argues that it is shortsighted for companies to gather unnecessary information about their customers just to resell it. The result can be lost customers and perhaps onerous regulations.

Greene, Marvin J. "Who's Zoomin' Who on the Web? Internet Privacy Becomes a Major Issue for Concerned Cybernauts." *Black Enterprise*, vol. 28, no. 3, October 1997, p. 40(2). Points out that businesses want to use "cookie" files to track customer's choices and provide better service, but the practice raises privacy concerns. The article also reports on how a group of companies is proposing cookie standards that would assure privacy.

Grover, Varun, Liz Hall, and Scott Rosenberg. "The Web of Privacy: Business in the Information Age." *Business Horizons*, vol. 41, July–August 1998, p. 5ff. Surveys corporate, workplace, consumer, and medical privacy issues from the viewpoint of the business world, consumers, and government, and recommends encryption and other tools as reasonable solutions.

Gruenwald, Juliana. "Who's Minding Whose Business on the Internet?" *Congressional Quarterly Weekly Report*, vol. 56, July 25, 1998, p. 1986ff. Reports that the increase in online fraud and identity theft has led to a debate between advocates of government regulation and supporters of industry self-regulation.

"Guru Watch." *Inc.*, vol. 19, March 18, 1997, p. 18. Reports privacy consultant Ann Cavoukian's warning that businesses, particularly small businesses, should avoid collecting unnecessary information, both to avoid wasteful effort and to minimize exposure to possible lawsuits.

Hagel, J., and J. F. Rayport. "The Coming Battle for Customer Information." *Harvard Business Review*, January–February 1997, pp. 53–65. Reports on the high stakes of companies that seek to take advantage of the flood of personal information available to be collected online while resisting demands for regulation.

Hamburg, Jill. "Selling Your Privacy." *Working Woman*, vol. 22, October 1997, p. 84. Describes the selling of personal information by database service bureaus. Discusses proposed legislation that would outlaw the sale of Social Security numbers, unlisted phone numbers, or health-related information.

Hansell, Saul. "Big Web Sites to Track Steps of Their Users." *New York Times*, August 16, 1998. np. Available online.URL: http://www.nytimes.com/. Describes ambitious but controversial plan of a group of web companies to collect data about users; although personal identification information would not be gathered, privacy advocates worry about misuse.

Hansell, Saul. "Web Firms to Share Data About Users' Movements." *San Francisco Examiner and Chronicle*, August 16, 1998, p. A–11. Describes CMG Information Services' organizing a system called Engage in which

30 Internet sites will pool data about users' online selections. While they claim they will make it impossible to identify individual users, critics worry about lack of accountability.

Harris, Marlys. "Should I Pay $49 to Find Out What's in My Financial Records?" *Money*, vol. 25, February 1996, p. 31ff. Describes Privacy Guard, a service that will obtain an individual's credit, driving, medical, and other records—while these records can be requested directly from the relevant agencies, the convenience may be worth the cost.

Hawkins, Dana. "Politics of Privacy: Gore, Congress Talk but Will They Act?" *U.S. News & World Report*, vol. 125, August 10, 1998, p. 30. Contrasts the talk about protecting privacy with the defeat by health care interests of a bill that would limit the use of Social Security numbers.

Holding, Reynolds. "He Filled Out an Application—and Ruined His Credit." *San Francisco Sunday Examiner and Chronicle*, May 24, 1998, p. 3. Describes how a simple application to a health club led a California man into a morass of bogus credit charges and ruined credit, as well as a lawsuit to determine whether the club was responsible for not preventing the fraud.

"Internet Industry Lags in Privacy Protection: Report May Prompt Response from FTC." (Reuters) *San Francisco Chronicle*, June 4, 1998, p. D1. Summarizes an FTC survey that shows that most Internet sites don't disclose their gathering of user information, thus prompting privacy advocates to demand federal privacy regulations because they believe self-regulation is failing.

"Is Your Computer Spying on You?" *Consumer Reports*, vol. 62, May 1997, p. 7. Reports on DoubleClick, an advertising agency that records information about online browsing, including web searches on AltaVista, storing the information in a "cookie" file on the user's hard disk.

Johnson, Jeff. "Pushing and Pulling the First Amendment: E-mail, Web Content Shouldn't Be Subject to Same Regulations." *San Francisco Examiner*, August 9, 1998, p. B–5, B–12. Suggests that regulators should be careful to distinguish between web pages, which a user chooses to view, and "spam" e-mail that arrives unsolicited. The former should have stronger First Amendment protection.

Kalish, David E. "Demand Grows for Electronic Privacy Laws." *San Francisco Chronicle*, April 11, 1998, p. D2. Uses several anecdotes to illustrate online fraud and abuse; describes proposed legislation to give consumers greater control over their information.

Kaplan, Carl S. "Cable TV Privacy Law May Protect Web Surfers." *New York Times*, September 11, 1998. np. Available online. URL: http://www.nytimes.com/. Reports that a 14-year-old cable TV privacy law may also protect web users who access the Internet through cable modems.

Kelly, Tina. "You Can Search, but Can You Hide? Using the Net, Old Friends, Old Flames and Old Debts May Find You." *New York Times*, vol. 148, November 26, 1998, p. G1. Discusses the mixed blessings that come from the ability to find almost anyone through information in online databases.

Knecht, G. Bruce. "Reporter's Notebook: Is Big Brother Watching Your Dinner and Other Worries of Privacy Watchers." *Wall Street Journal*, November 9, 1995, p. B1.

Labaton, Steve. "U.S. Agency Cracks Down on Internet Investigators." *New York Times*, April 23, 1999, np. Available online. URL: http://www.nytimes.com. Reports on the Federal Trade Commission's crackdown on private investigators who advertise on the Internet and by doing so can obtain confidential information on individuals' bank and telephone records. Such investigators often call banks and falsely claim to be the individual being investigated or a relative.

Leiter, Lisa. "Data Flowing Freely onto Info Highway." *Insight on the News*, vol. 12, August 19, 1996, p. 20ff. Describes the proposed Electronic Freedom of Information Act of 1996.

Machlis, Sharon. "Web Sites Rush to Self-Regulate." *Computerworld*, vol. 32, May 11, 1998, p. 2. Reports that in response to demands for regulation, IBM and 50 other companies are trying to set up their own standards for protecting privacy. Advocates of regulation argue that it's too little, too late.

Machrone, Bill. "Trust Me?" *PC Magazine*, vol. 17, June 9, 1998, p. 85. Describes the TRUSTe privacy policy disclosure program, using the example of the Lands' End catalog company.

Magid, Lawrence J. "Justifiable Paranoia: Growing Databases of Unregulated Information Should Have You Spooked." *Bay Area Computer Currents*, May 18, 1998, pp. 41–42, 46. Gives a variety of web site links for researching consumer privacy issues.

Mannix, Margaret, and Susan Gregory Thomas. "Exposed Online: On the Web Your Personal Life Is Merely Marketable Data." *U.S. News & World Report*, vol. 122, June 23, 1997, p. 59ff. Reports that widespread concern about privacy abuses has led the Federal Trade Commission to demand quick action by the information industry to craft new privacy standards; describes the Open Privacy Standard proposed by more than 100 Internet companies that limits the types of information that can be distributed and requires online consent.

Markey, Edward J. "A Privacy Safety Net." *MIT's Technology Review*, vol. 100, August–September 1997, p. 29. Argues for both legislative and software-based approaches for protecting the privacy of web users.

Markoff, John. "Microsoft Will Alter Its Software In Response to Privacy Concerns." *New York Times*, March 7, 1999. Available online: URL: http://www.nytimes.com/. Describes registration procedures for Windows 98 and other Microsoft products that associate a unique ID number with information such as the user's name and address. This number allows the tracing of documents created in the programs back to the user. Privacy advocates warned that it could be used against whistle-blowers. In response, Microsoft agreed to change its registration procedures and to delete existing information in its user database.

Matlick, Justin. "There Is Not a Privacy Crisis on the Internet as Users Control Their Information: Self-Regulation Works." *Knight-Ridder/Tribune News Service*, August 11, 1998, p. 811K1056. Argues that new regulation is not needed to protect online privacy because consumers already have the power to refuse "cookies" and intrusive forms—and the market will respond.

Mendoza, Martha. "Little Black Box Monitors a Vehicle's Every Move." *San Francisco Chronicle*, December 31, 1998, p. B3. An inventor has come up with a "black box" that records many details of a driver's behavior, including speed and use of the accelerator. Parents can use the device to keep tabs on teenage drivers, but critics worry about its possible effects on trust within families and businesses.

Metcalfe, Robert M. "TRUSTe Uses Consents and Disclosures to Protect Privacy on the Internet." *InfoWorld*, vol. 19, November 10, 1997, p. 159. Describes a program where participating online businesses agree to disclose how they intend to collect and use the information they gather from consumers. In turn, participating businesses can display a "trust mark" or symbol on their web sites.

O'Connor, Rory J. "Congress Appears Ready to Enact Measures to Protect Personal Information." *Knight-Ridder/Tribune News Service*, February 6, 1997, p. 206K3314. Reports on pending privacy-related legislation in the 105th Congress.

O'Hara, Robert, Jr. "Research Firms Weave a Tangled Web to Net Private Information." *San Francisco Chronicle*, June 15, 1998, p. A8. Gives examples of online research services or data brokers who will obtain information about anyone for a fee by employing both legal sources and questionable methods such as "pretext calling."

Postrel, Virginia. "The Politics of Privacy." *Forbes*, vol. 161, June 1, 1998, p. S130. Argues that information arising out of interactions is shared by both parties—such as a consumer and a business—and that regulations that make it only the property of its originator should not replace the variety of arrangements offered in the marketplace.

"Privacy Matters: Who Knows What about You—And Why? There Is an Electronic File Somewhere Containing All Sort of Information about You and Your Family. . . ." *Current Events*, vol. 96, September 30, 1996, p. 1ff. Introduces information-gathering techniques, abuses, and privacy issues.

Richtel, Matt. "Despite Privacy Concerns, Free PC's Attract Many Consumers and Schools. (Companies Give Away Computers in Return for Demographic Information and the Right to Advertise on the Systems)" *New York Times*, February 25, 1999, p. G7. Reports that falling computer prices now allow companies to offer free PCs to consumers or schools in exchange for them viewing advertising while online. Privacy advocates worry that users of such systems may be required to provide extensive personal information for use by marketers.

Rifkin, Glen. "Information Technology: Privacy Matters." *Harvard Business Review*, vol. 72, July–August 1994, p. 8ff. Reports on a study, which concludes that protecting privacy has a low priority in most corporations and that existing privacy policies are often obsolete.

Robertson, Geoffrey. "A Triumph for Sir Humphrey." *New Statesman*, vol. 127, March 6, 1998, p. 24ff. Describes the British lawmaker's campaign to pass Britain's first real Freedom of Information Act; criticizes some shortcomings such as the exceptions given for files on individuals from security agencies.

Robischon, Noah. "My Week as an Internet Gumshoe." *Time*, vol. 149, June 2, 1997, p. 65. Confirms Senator Dianne Feinstein's contention that lots of personal information is available on the Internet by obtaining Feinstein's own family birth dates, legal records, unlisted phone number, and other information from a succession of free sources and information brokers.

Rosenfield, James R. "How to Avoid Data-Gate." *Sales & Marketing Management*, vol. 147, February 1995, p. 28ff. Suggests elements of a policy that will allow corporations to take advantage of the booming data market without raising privacy concerns.

Rothfelder, Jeffrey. "Dangerous Things Strangers Know About You." *McCall's*, vol. 121, January 1994, p. 88ff. Describes the ways people can find out about an individual's credit or medical history, suggests that people ask doctors and banks not to provide information to third parties without their approval.

———. "You Are for Sale." *PC World*, vol. 16, September 1998, p. 96. Gives examples of how marketers gather and cross-reference personal data to target consumers in ways that can amount to a startling invasion of privacy.

Rule, James, and Lawrence Hunter. "Privacy Wrongs: Corporations Have More Right to Your Data Than You Do." *Washington Monthly*, vol. 28, November 1996, p. 17ff. Uses anecdotes to show how personal information can be exposed to criminals, sold, or otherwise misused as part of a burgeoning data industry.

Rust, Michael, and Susan Crabtree. "Access, Privacy, and Power." *Insight on the News*, vol. 12, August 19, 1996, p. 8ff. Explores the trade-off between the power and convenience of computer technology and the ability it gives people to invade other peoples' privacy.

Screeton, Lisa Scott. "There's No Business Like Your Business: Protecting Consumer Privacy Online." *Business America*, vol. 119, August 1998, p. 29ff. Reports that only a small number of American web sites have formal privacy policies, but the European Union's privacy initiative may force many others to start taking privacy seriously.

Shapiro, Andrew L. "Privacy for Sale: Peddling Data on the Internet." *The Nation*, vol. 264, June 23, 1997, p. 11ff. Surveys the growing industry of online data marketing, and potential responses including government regulation, self-regulation, empowering consumers to contract for use of their data, and the use of encryption.

Smith, Kelly D. "How to Keep Your Finances as Private as Possible." *Money*, vol. 24, June 1995, p. 27. Gives basic steps for reducing the amount of information business and snoops can learn about an individual's credit and purchases and for making sure such information is at least accurate.

Smith, Rebecca. "Privacy Worries at the Grocer." *San Francisco Chronicle*. April 20, 1999, p. C1, C3. Discusses proposed bills in the California legislature that would limit the use of information gathered from holders of supermarket "club cards."

"Spy Hole: Private Investigators." *The Economist*, vol. 331, April 23, 1994, p. 61ff. Describes deceptive tactics used by private investigators in the United Kingdom; recommends stronger legislation to protect privacy.

Swartz, Jon. "Clinton Outlines Internet Growth Strategy." *San Francisco Chronicle*, December 1, 1998, p. C1–C2. Announces a multiagency administration privacy initiative by the Commerce Department, Federal Communications Commission, Small Business Administration, and possibly the World Bank to develop new high-speed Internet connections and incentives for self-regulation to strengthen privacy protections.

———. "Gore Proposes Bill of Rights for Online Privacy." *San Francisco Chronicle*, May 15, 1998, p. B2–B3. Describes Vice President Al Gore's call for "An Electronic Bill of Rights" that would give consumers control over how information about them is collected, as well as the ability to review and correct it.

Teinowitz, Ira. "DMA Campaigns for Privacy Rules." *Advertising Age*, vol. 68, May 19, 1997, p. 81. Describes the attempt of the Direct Marketing Association to create privacy standards to forestall expected Federal Trade Commission regulation.

———. "FTC Chief Asks Congress to Ensure Privacy on Web: Pitofsky Calls Voluntary Effort 'Disappointing'; Wants Parental OKs Required." *Advertising Age*, vol. 69, June 8, 1998, p. 53. Reports that Federal Trade Commission Chairman Bob Pitofsky has concluded that self-regulation by Internet sites has failed and that he wants immediate regulations to protect children from information-gatherers; he is willing to allow only a little more time for the industry to address adult privacy issues.

———. "FTC Expands Probe of Privacy Issues: Plan for Hearings Raises Concern over Effect on Database Marketing." *Advertising Age*, vol. 68, March 10, 1997, p. 43. Discusses possible forthcoming Federal Trade Commission actions from the point of view of marketers of database information; FTC regulations will likely require some form of consent from consumers before their information can be redistributed.

———. "Internet Privacy Concerns Addressed." *Advertising Age*, vol. 68, June 16, 1997, p. 6ff. Describes June 1997 hearings of the Federal Trade Commission (FTC) that may lead to new legislation to protect consumer and e-mail privacy.

———. "Online Privacy Rules Proposed to Ease Threat to E-Commerce: Self-Regulation Could Help Allay Consumer Fears." *Advertising Age*, vol. 69, April 27, 1998, p. 3ff. Describes the formation of the Privacy Alliance, an industry group that seeks self-regulation of privacy practices to forestall possible federal regulations and to comply with European requirements.

———. "Privacy Regulation Grows as Legislation Passes." *Advertising Age*, October 26, 1998, p. S16. Argues that the coming Congress will resume the push for Internet privacy legislation; some noncommercial sites may be unable to afford to comply with new laws, while some commercial sites are already budgeting for compliance.

Thompson, Mozelle W. "Where Are Privacy Guarantees?" (Open Forum). *San Francisco Chronicle*, November 10, 1998, p. A23. Argues that the electronic marketplace would be even bigger if consumers received better assurances of privacy, and that lack of privacy protection may keep American e-commerce firms out of the European market.

"Trial Opens in 'Baby Butcher' Web Site Controversy: Abortion Doctor List Seen as an Incitement." (Associated Press) *San Francisco Chronicle*, January 7, 1999, p. A6. Reports on a case where the creators of a web site that posted names and home addresses of abortion doctors are being sued by Planned Parenthood and others for inciting violence; the defense argues that the list is protected by the rights of free speech.

Verhovek, Sam Howe. "Creators of Anti-Abortion Web Site Told to Pay Millions." *New York Times*. February 3, 1999, np. Available online: URL: http://www.nytimes.com/. Reports on a verdict of more than $107 million against the operators of an anti-abortion web site that posted the names and addresses of doctors who provided abortions. The jury concluded that the site had gone beyond free speech to making threats that created an imminent danger of violence.

"Virtual privacy." *The Economist*, vol. 338, February 10, 1996, p. 16ff. Describes new privacy regulations for the European Union that would require companies to describe what they do with personal information, and ask for permission before obtaining it.

"Voluntary Ban on Personal Data." *Computerworld*, vol. 31, December 22, 1997, p. 8. The Federal Trade Commission announces that it favors self-regulation by information providers to keep sensitive information such as Social Security numbers out of general circulation.

Wagner, David. "High-Tech Snoops Get Real Personal." *Insight on the News*, vol. 12, August 19, 1996, p. 18. Argues that database and other technologies are racing ahead of the ability of the legal system to control their use, and that regulations against strong encryption leave users with easy-to-break codes.

Waldrop, Judith, and Mary J. Culnan. "The Business of Privacy." *American Demographics*, vol. 16, October 1994, p. 46ff. Describes the practices of responsible direct-mail advertisers who screen clients and provide recipients with a way to opt out of receiving "junk mail."

Warwick, Shelly. "Privacy and Policy." *Bulletin of the American Society for Information Science*, vol. 23, February–March 1997, p. 14ff. Argues that the failure to specify privacy rights makes the nation's information policy incomplete.

Wayner, Peter. "Reporting Practices Put WebTV on Defensive." *New York Times*, October 18, 1998. np. Available online. URL: http://www.nytimes .com/. Describes privacy concerns that have been raised about the gathering of information about users of Microsoft's WebTV product; the company says it is making sure identifiable personal information is not collected, but critics worry about the misuse of aggregated information.

Williamson, Debra Aho. "Privacy and Ad Revenue Issues Impede Growth." *Advertising Age*, vol. 68, June 16, 1997, p. 46. Argues that public concern about privacy may be reducing the effectiveness (and revenue) of Internet advertising; meanwhile, the marketing of personal information gathered online has been more profitable than expected.

Weber, Thomas E. "Net Interest: Browsers Beware—The Web Is Watching; but Your Privacy May Be Jeopardized Less Than You Think." *Wall Street Journal*, June 27, 1996, p. B8. Suggests that much of the concern about "cookie" files and other tracking of web users may be overblown.

Weise, Elizabeth. "Small Company Plays Large Role in Net Privacy." *New York Times*, June 14, 1997, np. Available online. URL: http://www. nytimes.com/. Describes Firefly, a maker of software that attempts to make it easy to collect user information while enforcing a privacy policy.

"You Are Being Tailed." *The Economist*, vol. 347, June 27, 1998, p. 62. Points out that everyone seems to agree that information abuse on the net is a serious problem. The article then asks the question: what is the solution—government regulation, industry self-regulation, or giving users more control over their own information?

Zamora, Jim Herron. "ID Bandits Reaping Millions." *San Francisco Examiner*, September 6, 1998, p. A1, A7. Describes how a growing number of "identify theft" rings use Social Security numbers and other information to steal consumers' identities and run up bills on their credit cards, potentially ruining their credit.

INTERNET DOCUMENTS

Johnson, David R. "Barbed Wire Fences in Cyberspace: The Threat Posed by Calls for Ownership of Transactional Information." Available online. URL: http://www.eff.org/pub/Legal/cyber_barbwire_johnson.article. Posted on April 4, 1994. Argues that giving individuals the property rights of their data may be an ineffective way to protect privacy because people would just trade away such rights for convenience or other incentives. Suggests strong, fully disclosed privacy policies as an alternative.

Methvin, David W. "Safety on the Net." *Windows Magazine*. Available online. URL: http://winmag.com/library/1996/0896/08c1_001.htm. Posted August 1996. Interactive version of cover story that deals with many aspects of safety and privacy for Internet users, including recommendations for proxies, firewalls, and other web security tools.

Pressman, Aaron. "Net Surfer Privacy Improves." Reuters/ZD Net, Available online. URL: http://www.zdnet.com/. Posted December 21, 1998. Reports that public concerns about Internet privacy have resulted in many sites displaying their privacy policies online. But many users are still leery of interacting with commercial Internet sites, and privacy advocates say the corporate policies are often vague and not backed by specific guarantees.

Privacy Rights Clearinghouse. "Anti-Spam Resources" (Fact Sheet #20).URL: http://www.privacyrights.org/fs/fs20-spam.htm. Downloaded on December 29, 1998. Gives a list of web sites that offer help and software tools for helping reduce the number of unwanted e-mail solicitations (spam).

———. "Are You Being Stalked? Tips for Your Protection" (Fact Sheet #14). URL: http://www.privacyrights.org/fs/fs14-stk.htm. Updated in August 1997. Recommends ways to deal with a stalker and ways to reduce the chance that a potential stalker might be able to access personal information. Also includes security recommendations from the Los Angeles Police Department.

———. "Caller ID" (Fact Sheet #19). URL: http://www.privacyrights.org/fs/fs19-cid.htm. Updated in August 1997. Describes the potential privacy effects of Caller ID and explains the blocking features that can be selected to preserve privacy.

———. "Coping with Identity Theft: What to Do When an Imposter Strikes" (Fact Sheet #17). URL: http://www.privacyrights.org/fs/fs17-it.htm.

Updated in December 1998. Explains what makes people vulnerable to identity theft and gives detailed instructions on how to minimize the risk and what to do if it happens.

———. "Cordless/Cellular Phones" (Fact Sheet #2). URL: http://www. privacyrights.org/fs/fs2-wire.htm. Updated August 1997. Explains how people can eavesdrop on wireless communications (cordless and cellular phones), the laws governing such eavesdropping and phone fraud, and technical measures for reducing it.

———. "How Private Is My Credit Report?" (Fact Sheet #6). URL: http://www.privacyrights.org/fs/fs6-crdt.htm. Updated November 1998. Explains the kind of information typically found in credit reports, who has access to them, and how to correct mistakes. Also covers check verification systems.

———. "How to Put an End to Harassing Phone Calls" (Fact Sheet #3). URL: http://www.privacyrights.org/fs/fs3-hrs2.htm. Updated in August 1997. Explains what can be done to stop or reduce harassing phone calls, including requests to the phone company, use of caller ID and screening, and other measures.

———. "Merchant Laws" (Fact Sheet #15). URL: http://www.privacyrights. org/fs/fs15-mt.htm. Updated in August 1997. Specifies what kinds of information merchants can legally require, optionally ask for, and are prohibited from asking for when an individual seeks to cash a check or make a credit card purchase. These descriptions are based primarily on California law.

———. "Privacy Survival Guide" (Fact Sheet #1). URL: http://www. privacyrights.org/fs/fs1-surv.htm. Updated November 1998. Provides a checklist of basic steps individuals can take to obtain copies of their credit, medical, and other information, as well as advice for minimizing privacy risks in a variety of types of daily communication and transactions.

———. "Reducing Junk Mail" (Fact Sheet #4). URL: http://www. privacyrights.org/fs/fs4-junk.htm. Updated October 1998. Explains the variety of ways in which the names and addresses of individuals are obtained by marketers from routine transactions; offers suggestions for removing one's name from specific lists and for reducing the amount of junk mail in general.

———. "Responsible Information-Handling Practices" (Fact Sheet #12). URL: http://www.privacyrights.org/fs/fs12-ih2.htm. Updated August 1997. Gives recommended practices for an organization's gathering, handling, securing, and distributing of information, stressing privacy and data security.

———. "Telemarketing Calls" (Fact Sheet #5). URL: http://www. privacyrights.org/fs/fs5-tmkt.htm. Updated August 1997. Explains how telemarketers get people's phone numbers and how to get them to stop calling; also summarizes the provisions of applicable laws.

———. "Your Social Security Number: How Secure Is It?" (Fact Sheet #10). URL: http://www.privacyrights.org/fs/fs10-ssn.htm. Updated in December 1998. Explains the value of Social Security numbers to snoops and identity thieves. The article also discusses circumstances under which the number can be demanded or requested and suggests ways to minimize use of one's number.

Swire, Peter. "Cyberbanking and Privacy: The Contracts Model." [Talk given at the Computers, Freedom and Privacy Conference, San Francisco, March 1997]. Available online. URL: http://www.osu.edu/units/law/swire1/cyber.htm. Argues that a purely market-driven approach to privacy is inadequate and that a government regulatory approach is inflexible and overcentralized; the article favors an approach that allows for the creation of enforceable contracts between consumers and businesses.

PRIVACY FOR CHILDREN

BOOKS

Carlson, Matt. *Childproof Internet: A Parent's Guide to Safe and Secure Online Access.* New York: MIS Press, 1996. Introduces parents to the Internet and its challenges, and offers practical suggestions for protecting children from inappropriate materials and predators.

Frazier, Deneen, with Dr. Barbara Kurshan, and Dr. Sara Armstrong. *Internet for Kids.* 2nd ed. San Francisco: Sybex, 1996. An introduction to the use of the Internet for young people. Useful for parents, but written for kids. It is filled with dozens of interesting projects.

Schroeder, Keith. *Life and Death on the Internet.* Menasha, Wisc.: Supple Publishing, 1998. Gives detailed guidance on how to protect children's privacy on the Internet; also deals with indecent material.

United States House Committee on the Judiciary Subcommittee on Crime. *Children's Privacy Protection and Parental Empowerment Act of 1996: Hearing Before the Subcommittee on Crime of the Committee on the Judiciary, House of Representatives, One Hundred Fourth Congress, Second Session. . . .* Washington, D.C.: U.S. G.P.O., 1997. Hearings on an important legislative initiative for federal protection of children's privacy.

Annotated Bibliography

ARTICLES AND PAPERS

Beckett, Jamie. "Web Sites Use Treats to Pry Data from Youngsters." *San Francisco Chronicle*, September 22, 1998, p. C1, C6. Congress holds hearings on regulating web sites that use cute graphics and "freebies" to entice kids to reveal personal information that can be used for marketing.

Brunais, Andrea. "We Need to Go the Extra Mile to Protect Children from Pedophiles, Even If It Means a Loss of Some Civil Liberties." *Knight-Ridder/Tribune News Service*, September 13, 1996, p. 913K3380. Argues that the right of privacy of some kinds of sex offenders is less important than the need to protect children. Supports creation of computer databases to track such offenders.

Caywood, Carolyn. "YA Confidential." *School Library Journal*, vol. 42, August 1996, p. 41. Advocates protecting the privacy of young adult library users by avoiding intrusive monitoring or use of Internet filter software.

Clausing, Jeri. "FTC Report on Online Privacy Draws Quick Criticism." *New York Times*, June 4, 1998. np. Available online. URL: http://www.nytimes.com/. Quotes privacy advocates who criticize the Federal Trade Commission for not acting immediately to protect children's privacy, instead deferring the matter to Congress.

———. "Senate Panel Debates Children's Online Privacy." *New York Times*, September 24, 1998. np. Available online. URL: http://www.nytimes.com/. Reports on the debate over proposed regulations for Internet sites that are directed at children; the industry pushes for a less cumbersome compromise that would allow sites to send children e-mail without consent if no information was being gathered.

Elliot, Stuart. "Marketers Told to Protect Children's Privacy Online." *New York Times*, September 14, 1998. np. Available online. URL: http://www.nytimes.com/. Warns that industry must move immediately to protect children's privacy online or face tough regulations.

———. "Watch What the Internet Asks Children, Sponsors Are Warned, or See the Government Step In." *New York Times*, vol. 147, September 14, 1998, p. C11. Reports that regulators are warning Internet sites for children that they'd better tighten up their policies about asking for personal information, or face increased regulation.

"Is Somebody Watching You?" *Current Events*, vol. 95, February 26, 1996, p. 3. Asks readers to consider the implications of schools using video cameras to catch kids engaging in violent or disruptive behavior. Some students like the reduction in violence, but others complain of a loss of privacy and an oppressive atmosphere.

157

Jabs, Carolyn. "Why Children Need Privacy." *Working Mother*, vol. 20, October 1997, p. 99ff. Describes the psychological importance of providing children with appropriate privacy.

Mendels, Pamela. "New Serious Side to Child's Play on Web: Privacy Protection Law Is Likely to Make Access More Difficult." *New York Times*, November 26, 1998. np. Available online. URL: http://www.nytimes.com/. Describes the Children's Privacy Protection Act of 1998 and how it is changing the way child-oriented Internet sites are interacting with children online.

———. "Sites Aimed at Children Collect More Than Just Hits." *New York Times*, June 29, 1998. np. Available online. URL: http://www.nytimes.com/. Describes how web sites ask children for information in games or promotions; although the information it does gather does not include personal identification, it is collected without parental consent and could result in marketing targeted at selected groups of young people and their families.

O'Connor, Rory J. "Groups Proposing Legislation to Ban Practice of Selling Information About Children." *Knight-Ridder/Tribune News Service*, May 21, 1996, p. 521K5249. Describes the push to pass strict laws regulating the selling of information about children, fueled by revelations of how easy it is for potential child molesters to obtain kids' names and addresses.

———. "Passions over Protecting Children, Maintaining Freedom Could Lead to Bad Internet Policy, Some Observers Warn." *Knight-Ridder/Tribune News Service*, March 25, 1998, p. 325K4536. Reports that privacy advocates warn that public hysteria over a few cases of Internet-based child molestation may give the FBI dangerous new wiretapping powers and lead to restrictions on the use of privacy-protecting encryption.

Quittner, Joshua. "Tell the Kids to Fib: A U.S Agency Says Laws Are Needed to Protect Children's Privacy Online. But You Can Do Better. (It Is Often Necessary to Encourage Children to Make Up Personal Information When Using the Internet in Order to Protect the Family's Privacy." *Time*, vol. 151, June 15, 1998, p. 86. Suggests that responsible marketers will come up with appropriate disclosure and privacy policies; meanwhile, parents should tell their kids that when web sites demand personal information, they can provide bogus answers.

Roberts, Richard L., Larry Rogers, and Sara M. Fier. "Duty-to-Warn: Implications for School Administrators." *The Clearing House*, vol. 71, September–October 1997, p. 53ff. Describes court cases that explore the legal conflict between school counselors and administrators' duty to warn potential victims of threatening behavior or deadly diseases like AIDS and their obligation to protect the confidentiality of their student clients;

points out that while court decisions have often been unclear or contradictory, administrators can take steps to create better policies.

Service, Robert F. "Bill Threatens Child Survey Research." *Science*, vol. 268, May 19, 1995, p. 967ff. Reports on researchers' opposition to a bill that would require parental consent for a variety of surveys done with children; opponents claim that the rules would make surveys much more expensive and might skew results of surveys on sensitive topics such as sex and drugs because parents of at-risk children may be less likely to give permission.

Sipe, Jeffrey R. "Confidentiality Laws Shield Bureaucrats, Not Children." *Insight on the News*, vol. 12, February 26, 1996, p. 38. Argues that laws supposedly designed to protect the privacy of children in the child welfare system are often being used to keep the public from discovering widespread neglect and abuses within the system itself.

Swartz, Jon. "FTC Seeks Online Privacy Law for Children." *San Francisco Chronicle*, June 5, 1998, p. B1–B2. Describes an FTC investigation that revealed that most web sites that collect personal information don't inform users about their practices; reports on proposed legislation that would require parental consent before information could be collected from children.

Teinowitz, Ira. "Kids Online Privacy Bill Moves Ahead Sponsors Agree to Limit Web Sites Being Regulated." *Advertising Age*, vol. 69, October 5, 1998, p. 69. Describes a compromise likely to lead to swift passage of a bill requiring commercial web sites to obtain permission before marketing information for children under 13; would also prohibit requiring information in order to enter a contest or get a prize.

Timberg, Craig. "Sex Offender Web Site Draws Fire in Virginia." (Reprint from *Washington Post*). *San Francisco Chronicle*, January 2, 1998, p. A4. Reports the controversy over Virginia's putting names and addresses of violent sex offenders on the World Wide Web; advocates say that it will help parents protect their children in ways the police cannot, but opponents believe it amounts to an additional punishment and may lead to vigilantism and loss of employment for ex-offenders who may be trying to reform.

Warren, Andrea. "Should Parents Spy on Their Kids?" *Ladies Home Journal*, vol. 112, November 1995, p. 114ff. Notes that as home drug test kits and other monitoring devices enter the market, it is tempting to spy on one's kids—but while parental supervision is important, not allowing children sufficient privacy can be damaging to their development.

"When the Web Gets Too Nosy." *Business Week*, no. 3582, June 15, 1998, p. 53. Discusses proposed legislation by the Federal Trade Commission that would give parents greater control over the gathering of information from their children online.

INTERNET DOCUMENTS

Center for Democracy and Technology. "Children's Privacy Headlines." Available online: URL: http://www.cdt.org/privacy/children/. Downloaded on January 5, 1999. Provides news items and articles regarding privacy of children.

Electronic Frontier Foundation. "Children's Privacy Protection and Parental Empowerment Act of 1996." Available online. URL: http://www.eff.org/pub/Security/Children/franks_child_priv_1997.bill. Posted January 24, 1997. Text of revised draft of proposed federal law for protection of children.

Galkin, William S. "Collecting and Using Information About Children Online." *Computer Law Observer*, no. 23, February 1997. np. Available online. URL: http://ei.cs.vt.edu/~cs3604/lib/Privacy/Children. Privacy. html. Describes legalities, practices, and approaches to the regulation of gathering of information from children by web sites and online services.

Privacy Rights Clearinghouse. "Children in Cyberspace" (Fact Sheet #21). Available online. URL: http://www.privacyrights.org/fs/children.htm. Updated December 28, 1998. Describes privacy issues involved in online marketing to children; gives many web links to organizations, surveys, and other resources.

MEDICAL PRIVACY

BOOKS

Dickson, Donald T. *Confidentiality and Privacy in Social Work: A Guide to the Law for Practitioners and Students*. New York: Free Press, 1998. Describes privacy issues and the procedures social workers should use to comply with relevant laws and protect both the agency and its clients.

Donaldson, Molla S., Kathleen N. Lohr, and Molly Donaldson, eds. *Health Data in the Information Age: Use, Disclosure, and Privacy*. Washington, D.C.: National Academy Press, 1994. Explains that large regional health databases can help researchers, hospital planners, and insurance companies provide more efficient service. The book also raises issues about the quality and accuracy of data and the potential for misuse.

Hubbard, Ruth, and Elijah Wald. *Exploding the Gene Myth*. Boston: Beacon Press, 1993. Gives a popular introduction to the uses—and limitations—of genetics and genetic testing.

Institute of Medicine (United States). *The Computer-Based Patient Record*. Washington, D.C.: National Academy Press, 1991. Describes the use of computerized medical records and the issues involved in their distribution.

Kevles, Daniel J., and Leroy Hood. *The Code of Codes: Scientific and Social Issues in the Human Genome Project*. Cambridge, Mass.: Harvard University Press, 1992. Explores the implications of the emerging ability to map the human genetic code, including social conflicts such as privacy issues.

National Research Council, Commission on Physical Sciences, Mathematics, and its Applications, Computer Science and Telecommunications Board, Committee on Maintaining Privacy and Security in Health Care Applications of the National Information Infrastructure. *For the Record: Protecting Electronic Health Information*. Washington, D.C.: National Academy Press, 1997. Describes the threat of invasion of patient privacy and abuse of medical records; makes recommendations for strengthening privacy protection.

Nelkin, Dorothy, and Laurence Tancredi. *Dangerous Diagnostics: The Social Power of Biological Information*. New York: Basic Books, 1989. Discusses the disturbing implications of the use (or abuse) of medical tests.

Rothstein Mark A., ed. *Genetic Secrets: Protecting Privacy and Confidentiality in the Genetic Era*. New Haven: Yale University Press, 1997. A variety of experts survey the legal and ethical issues raised by the growing ability to obtain detailed genetic information that can predict future health. Explores issues such as the implications for the doctor-patient relationship, availability and cost of insurance, and the conducting of medical research.

Saunders, Janet McGee. *Patient Confidentiality*. 3rd ed. Salt Lake City, Utah: Medicode, 1996. Presents guidelines for health professionals concerning what patient information can be released and to whom; organized by topic.

Suzuki, David T., and Peter Knudtson. *Genetics: The Clash Between the New Genetics and Human Values*. Cambridge, Mass.: Harvard University Press, 1989. Explores the impact of the new genetic knowledge on human values, including those of privacy and personal responsibility.

United States House of Representatives. Information, Justice, Transportation, and Agriculture Subcommittees of the House Committee on Government Operations, 103rd Congress, 1st Session, 1993. *Fair Health Information Practices Act of 1994*. Washington, D.C.: U.S. G.P.O., 1994. Covers congressional hearings on the Fair Health Information Practices Act of 1994.

United States House of Representatives. Information, Justice, Transportation, and Agriculture Subcommittees of the House Committee on Government Operations, 103rd Congress, 1st Session, 1993. *Health Reform, Health Records, Computers and Confidentiality*. Washington, D.C.: U.S. G.P.O., 1993. Covers congressional hearing on health information practices as part of health reform efforts.

United States House of Representatives. Information, Justice, Transportation, and Agriculture Subcommittees of the House Committee on Government Operations, 103rd Congress, 2nd Session, 1994. *Health*

Security Act. Washington, D.C.: U.S. G.P.O., 1994. Covers congressional hearing on the Health Security Act of 1994.

United States Office of Technology Assessment. *Protecting Privacy in Computerized Medical Information.* Washington, D.C.: U.S. G.P.O., 1993. Provides overview of issues and practices involving distribution of medical information records.

ARTICLES AND PAPERS

"Access to Medical Records Differs Across State Lines." *HealthFacts*, vol. 22, May 1997, p. 2. Notes that only 28 of 50 states allow patients access to their medical records and that rules differ from state to state; also discusses efforts to pass federal legislation for uniform access.

Allen, Bill, and Ray Moseley. "Predictive Genetic Testing: Ethical, Legal, and Social Implications." *USA Today* (Magazine), vol. 123, November 1994, p. 66ff. Discusses the implications of the increasing availability of tests that can reveal the probability that an individual may contract a serious disease in the future; discussion includes the increased need for confidentiality.

Andreae, Michael. "Confidentiality in Medical Telecommunication." *The Lancet*, vol. 347, February 24, 1996, p. 487ff. Describes concerns about medical information being leaked, improperly distributed, or eavesdropped through technical means, resulting in potential damage to patients.

Betts, Mitch. "Critics Blast Medical Records Privacy Bill." *Computerworld*, vol. 29, December 4, 1995, p. 69. Describes critics' objections to Senator Robert F. Bennett's Medical Records Confidentiality Act because it makes several exceptions to privacy protection, as in not requiring consent in cases of life-threatening situations, legal investigations, and some kinds of public-health research.

———. "Health Reform Raises Privacy Issues; Bill Would Standardize Rules, Access for Health Care Professionals' Use of Electronic Patient Records." *Computerworld*, vol. 28, April 11, 1994, p. 55. Describes the proposed Fair Health Information Practices Act, which would require both the original collector and each recipient of medical information to agree to keep it confidential; the proposal is supported both by an industry group and the ACLU.

Billings, Paul R. et al. "Discrimination as a Consequence of Genetic Testing." *American Journal of Human Genetics* 50, 1992, np. Discusses the potential for discrimination opened up by the availability of a growing number of genetic tests.

Blodgett, Mindy. "Tighter Control of Medical Records Urged." *Computerworld*, vol. 31, March 10, 1997, p. 8. Describes a National Research Council report that recommends strong data security and privacy regulations for medical data; suggests that the universal health database and health ID numbers required by the Kennedy/Kassebaum health reform bill raise privacy concerns.

Brahams, Diana. "Right of Access to Medical Records." *The Lancet,* vol. 344, September 10, 1994, p. 743. Reviews a case involving a mental patient that demonstrates how British law allows denying an individual access to his or her medical records if it is likely to cause serious harm.

Campbell, Paulette Walker. "Bill Aims to Balance Researchers' Needs with Privacy of Medical Records." *The Chronicle of Higher Education,* vol. 44, March 27, 1998, p. A38. Surveys current legislative proposals to enact federal protection for patient privacy while considering the needs of medical researchers.

———. "Federal Report Faults System for Protecting Patients' Rights in Clinical Research." *The Chronicle of Higher Education,* vol. 44, June 12, 1998, p. A34. Describes a report by the inspector general of the Department of Health and Human Services that finds that Institutional Review Boards that are supposed to monitor medical research are often overworked and undertrained, leaving patients' rights at risk.

Carey, Mary Agnes. "Privacy of Medical Records Under Hill Microscope." *Congressional Quarterly Weekly Report,* vol. 55, November 1, 1997, p. 2682ff. Reports that Congress appears poised to implement new medical privacy rules in keeping with the 1996 legislation, but critics point out that administration proposals would place no restriction on police accessing medical records without a subpoena.

Carman, Dawn Murto. "Balancing Patient Confidentiality and Release of Information." *Bulletin of the American Society for Information Science,* vol. 23, February–March 1997, p. 16ff. Describes the need for medical professionals to be aware of the legal requirements that in some circumstances require protecting privacy and that in others, disclosure of information.

Clever, Linda Hawes. "Obtain Informed Consent Before Publishing Information About Patients." *The Journal of the American Medical Association,* vol. 278, August 27, 1997, p. 628ff. Urges authors of medical studies to obtain informed consent from patients if material in medical studies or papers might reveal their identity; discusses example cases and guidelines.

"Clinton Push on Internet Privacy." (Associated Press) *San Francisco Chronicle,* July 31, 1998, p. A6. Describes the administration's proposed "Electronic Bill of Rights" with its provision for strengthening privacy and protecting kids online; also notes that the administration is withdrawing its proposed universal health ID numbers, which have been criticized by privacy advocates.

Cool, Lisa Collier. "Shrink and Tell: Is Your Confidentiality Being Compromised?" *American Health for Women,* vol. 15, December 1996, p. 16ff. Discusses requirement by HMOs that patients divulge confidential mental

health matters before receiving treatment; such disclosure can have negative career consequences.

Danitz, Tiffany. "Deceit, Denial and the Fate of Privacy." *Insight on the News*,
vol. 14, August 24, 1998, p. 14ff. Discusses the (recently withdrawn)
Clinton administration proposal for a "uniform health identifier" number
that would be used to coordinate national health care policies and systems.
The article places the proposal in the context of other major tracking
systems that will gather information involving welfare programs, immigration, and airline travel. It also warns that the result of such efforts may
be the creation of a huge database without safeguards against misuse by
insurers, government agencies, or law enforcers.

Detmer, Don E., and Elaine B. Steen. "Congress Set to Act on Protection of
Medical Records," *Issues in Science and Technology*, vol. 14, Fall 1997, p. 35.
Points out the likelihood of new health privacy legislation in the late 1990s
because of mandated studies on privacy, data integrity, and security. If
Congress does not act by August 1999, the secretary of the Department of
Health is required to work with the National Committee for Vital and
Health Statistics (NCVHS) to create health data protection standards.

Detmer, Don E., and Elaine B. Steen. "Shoring Up Protection of Personal
Health Data." *Issues in Science and Technology*, vol. 12, Summer 1996, p.
73ff. Evaluates proposed bills to improve protection of privacy for individuals' health records.

Donaldson, Molla S., Kathleen N. Lohr, and Roger J. Bulger. "Use, Disclosure, and Privacy." Two-part article: *The Journal of the American Medical
Association*, vol. 271, May 4, 1994, p. 1308 and vol. 271, May 11, 1994, p.
1392. Explores the implications of large regional health database organizations (HDOs) and the need to develop standards to protect privacy.

Dreyfus, Rochelle Cooper, and Dorothy Nelkin. "The Jurisprudence of
Genetics." *Vanderbilt Law Review 45*, 1992. Surveys the various legal issues
involving genetics, including privacy and misuse of genetic information.

Editorial. "Can Government Guard Our Medical Histories?" *San Francisco
Chronicle*, July 21, 1998, p. A16. Criticizes the Clinton administration's
proposed "unique health identifier" numbers as dangerous to privacy,
particularly given the lack of strong privacy laws.

Elvin, John. "America's Private Parts Available to Prying Eyes." *Insight on the
News*, vol. 13, May 26, 1997, p. 16ff. Warns that Americans are unaware
of the lack of legal protection for their medical records and the vulnerability of the system to snooping and abuse.

Finkelstein, Katherine Eban. "The Computer Cure: Privacy Isn't Always the
Best Medicine." *The New Republic*, vol. 219, September 14, 1998, p. 28ff.
Argues that a national medical records database is worth having despite

privacy concerns because it enables "smart" computer programs to identify drug interactions and other potentially life-threatening situations.

"Flawed U.S. Proposals on Patients' Privacy." *The Lancet*, vol. 350, September 20, 1997, p. 823. Summarizes Clinton administration proposals for new patient privacy guidelines but criticizes them for not placing any restrictions on law enforcement use of medical records.

Forbes, Steve. "Malpractice Bill." *Forbes*, vol. 160, October 6, 1997, p. 27. Objects to administration proposal that would give police access to medical records without patient consent or a court review.

Frawley, Kathleen. "Confidentiality in the Computer Age." *RN*, vol. 57, July 1994, p. 59. Points out that new information technology that can make health care more effective and efficient also opens up new avenues for abuse and thus requirements for regulation; describes changes in hospital procedures and recommends ways to prevent snooping or misuse of data.

———. "Testimony on Health Information Confidentiality." *Bulletin of the American Society for Information Science*, vol. 23, February–March 1997, p. 22. Frawley, director of the American Health Information Management Association, urges that the laws governing access to patients' medical information be standardized.

Freudenheim, Milt. "Privacy a Concern as Medical Industry Turns to Internet." *New York Times*, August 12, 1998. np. Available online. URL: http://www.nytimes.com/. Describes ways both doctors and patients can save time and money by using health insurers' web sites; but the growing amount of patient information that can be accessed via the Internet raises privacy concerns.

Garnett, Leah R. "An Open Book." *Harvard Health Letter*, vol. 20, September 1995, p. 1ff. Discusses ways in which an individual's medical information can be accessed with illustrative anecdotes; explains the operation of the national Medical Information Bureau (MIB) and suggests ways to protect privacy through law and individual action.

Genesen, Leigh, Helen M. Sharp, and Mark C. Genesen. "Faxing Medical Records: Another Threat to Confidentiality in Medicine." *The Journal of the American Medical Association*, vol. 271, May 11, 1994, p. 1401. Gives examples of how mistakes can cause sensitive information to go astray in faxing, causing potential harm to patients.

Gorman, Christine. "Who's Looking at Your Files? Prying Eyes Find Computerized Health Records an Increasingly Tempting Target." *Time*, vol. 147, May 6, 1996, p. 60ff. Describes cases of abuse of medical records by the press, government agencies, and insurance companies; warns that increasing computerization and the placing of medical records on the Internet makes future abuse more likely.

Gostin, Lawrence O. "Health Information Privacy." *Cornell Law Review 45*, 1995, np. Urges a balance between protection of privacy and the need to gather information for research and for evaluation of health care policies.

Gostin, Lawrence O., Zita Lazzarini, Verla S. Neslund, and Michael T. Osterholm. "The Public Health Information Infrastructure: A National Review of the Law on Health Information Privacy." *The Journal of the American Medical Association*, vol. 275, June 26, 1996, p. 1921ff. Reviews state medical privacy laws and concludes they are inadequate; urges requiring more justification for permissible access and tough penalties for divulging medical information without permission.

Hawkins, Dana. "A Bloody Mess at One Federal Lab: Officials May Have Secretly Checked Staff for Syphilis, Pregnancy, and Sickle Cell." U.S. News & World Report, vol. 122, June 23, 1997, p.26ff. Reports that the Lawrence Berkeley Laboratory tested employees for diseases and pregnancy without their consent, raising both privacy and race issues; while the employees' lawsuit was dismissed at first, they are appealing.

———. "Court Declares Right to Genetic Privacy." *U.S. News & World Report*, vol. 124, February 16, 1998, p. 4. Follows up on an earlier report by reporting that the U.S. Court of Appeals has ruled that performing genetic testing without consent violates the Fourth Amendment privacy rights and that testing blacks and Hispanics to a greater extent than whites also violated the Civil Rights Act of 1964.

Joint Commission on Accreditation of Healthcare Organizations and the National Committee for Quality Assurance (NCQA). "Protecting Personal Health Information: A Framework for Meeting the Challenges in a Managed Care Environment." November, 1998. Recommends standards for consent, accountability, patient education, and use of technology to promote privacy and data security.

Korn, David. "Dangerous Intersections." *Issues in Science and Technology*, vol. 13, Fall 1996, p. 55ff. Argues that while researchers must take the potential "psychosocial risk" of genetic tests to survey participants seriously, proposed legislation may be more likely to hamper promising research than to allow research to go forward under stronger privacy guidelines.

Leary, Warrant. "Panel Cites Lack of Security on Medical Records." *New York Times*, March 6, 1997, np. Available online. URL: http://www.nytimes.com/. Reports findings from a National Research Council panel that there are serious problems with security and privacy of medical data, and that while industry could take immediate steps to improve the situation, there was little incentive for them to do so.

Lee, Philip R., and James Scanlon. "The Data Standardization Remedy in Kassebaum-Kennedy." *Public Health Reports*, vol. 112, March–April 1997, p. 114ff. Describes the provisions of the Health Insurance Portability and

Accountability Act of 1996 that provide for standardization of many health care transactions as well as increased data security and privacy protection.

Lindberg, Donald A. B., and Betsy L. Humphreys. "Medical Informatics." *The Journal of the American Medical Association*, vol. 275, June 19, 1996, p. 1821ff, and later article with same title: vol. 277, June 18, 1997, p. 1870ff. Describes data format and software standards that make it easy to share medical records, even making them accessible via the Internet. While these developments promote efficiency and help enable new ways of delivering care such as "telemedicine," new standards are needed to safeguard both technical accuracy and individual privacy.

"Maintaining Confidentiality." *The Lancet*, vol. 346, November 4, 1995, p. 1173. Describes how interlinked computer records and slipshod hospital security practices can cause disclosure of sensitive or confidential information about patients; describes issues such as the conflict between privacy and the desire to protect unwitting partners from AIDS.

Markoff, John. "Patient Files Turn Up in Used Computer." *New York Times*, April 4, 1997. np. Available online. URL: http://www.nytimes.com/. Uses the story of the discovery of pharmacy files on a bargain-priced used computer to illustrate the danger of inadvertently distributing data that can be stored on any one of hundreds of personal computers in an organization.

Marshall, Elliot. "Clinton Backs Broad Genetic Safeguards." *Science*, vol. 277, July 18, 1997, p. 308ff. Summarizes White House proposals that are being developed to prohibit insurers from denying coverage on the basis of genetic test results and to protect the confidentiality of genetic data.

Marwick, Charles. "Increasing Use of Computerized Recordkeeping Leads to Legislative Proposals for Medical Privacy." *The Journal of the American Medical Association*, vol. 276, July 24, 1996, p. 270ff. Discusses proposed laws that would require informed consent for the collection of medical information and for any later use for a different purpose; some privacy advocates say the laws do not go far enough.

———. "Medical Records Privacy: A Patient Rights Issue." *The Journal of the American Medical Association*, vol. 276, December 18, 1996, p. 1861ff. Asserts a patient's "nonnegotiable" right to keep medical information private and argues that privacy can be good for both business and medicine by making patients confident enough to seek early care.

McMenamin, Brigid. "It Can't Happen Here." *Forbes*, vol. 157, May 20, 1996, p. 252ff. Reports on a Maryland health reform that will cause records from all medical visits to be entered into a state-run database. While the state says it will delete names and encrypt Social Security numbers, critics worry that poor security and the voracious demand for information by insurers and others will compromise privacy.

Melton, L. Joseph III. "The Threat to Medical Records Research." *The New England Journal of Medicine*, vol. 337, November 13, 1997, p. 1466ff. Argues that tight new privacy restrictions can deny key data to medical researchers; proposes use of review boards to allow access to records while protecting patients' interests.

Mitchell, Peter. "Confidentiality at Risk in the Electronic Age." *The Lancet*, vol. 349, May 31, 1997, p. 1608. Warns that transmission of medical records is vulnerable to electronic eavesdropping, and that government encryption schemes, while protecting information from private snoops, may allow the government itself to abuse the information.

Mitka, Mike. "Do-It-Yourself Report on Patient Privacy." *The Journal of the American Medical Association*, vol. 280, December 9, 1998, p. 1897. Discusses the privacy recommendations of a report issued by two private groups, the Joint Commission on Accreditation of Healthcare Organizations and the National Committee for Quality Assurance (NCQA).

Natowitcz, Marvin R., et. al. "Genetic Discrimination and the Law." *American Journal of Genetics* 50, 1992, np. Surveys the laws bearing on discriminatory use of genetic information.

O'Harrow, Robert, Jr. "Under Fire, U.S. Amends Plan to Collect Health Care Data." *The Washington Post*, April 1, 1999, p. A05. Reports that a previously announced plan by the Health Care Financing Administration to collect large amounts of data on home health care patients is being scaled back in response to privacy concerns.

Orentlicher, David, and Bob Barr. "Is a 'Unique Health Identifier' for Every American a Good Idea?" *Insight on the News*, vol. 14, August 24, 1998, p. 24ff. Debates the proposed health ID number: Orentlicher believes it would improve medical care and even save lives by detecting harmful drug side effects and interactions; Barr warns of massive invasion of privacy and potential ammunition for government meddlers.

"The Privacy Conundrum: Medical Records." *The Economist*, vol. 335, April 29, 1995, p. 92ff. The American Health Information Management Association raises concerns about improper access to medical records; suggests technical solutions such as improved access control, encryption, and "sanitizer" programs that remove personal identification before forwarding records to researchers.

"Privacy of Health Data Needs Stronger Protection in Emerging Systems." *Public Health Reports*, vol. 109, September–October 1994, p. 718ff. Advocates of health care reform need a growing amount of information stored in HDOs (Health Database Organizations) in order to create and administer national systems, but lack of privacy protection may breed a lack of public confidence and acceptance.

Annotated Bibliography

Raab, Marian. "Genetic Shakeup: In Today's Workplace, Your DNA May Be Used Against You." *Working Woman*, vol. 23, October 1998, p. 14. Points out the lack of regulation against use of genetic test results to discriminate in employment or insurance; notes that Congress has made little progress on the issue thus far.

Samuels, Bruce, and Sydney Wolfe. "How to Obtain Your Medical Records." *Consumers' Research Magazine*, vol. 77, May 1994, p. 18ff. Suggests that patients can become better informed about their health by asking for a copy of their medical records; explains the typical organization of information in a medical record and how to obtain a copy; surveys medical records access by state.

Sandroff, Ronni. "Not-So-Private Practice: The Truth About Who's Reading Your Medical Records." *American Health for Women*, vol. 16, July–August 1997, p. 38ff. Introduces the growing risk of misuses of medical records brought about by computerization and discusses possible legislation. (Related article gives five recommended ways to guard privacy.)

Scart, Maggie. "Keeping Secrets." *New York Times Magazine*, June 16, 1996. p. 38. Suggests that legislation will be needed to protect confidentiality of patient records that are being merged into large databases for managed care.

Schwartz, Paul. "The Protection of Privacy in Health Care Reform." *Vanderbilt Law Review 48*, 1995, np. Urges that while accurate information is necessary for rational health care reform, protection of privacy is equally important for patients to have confidence in the system.

Skolnick, Andrew A. "Opposition to Law Officers Having Unfettered Access to Medical Records." *The Journal of the American Medical Association*, vol. 279, January 28, 1998, p. 257ff. Discusses U.S. Department of Health and Human Services (DHHS) Secretary Donna Shalala's recommendation that law enforcement and intelligence officers have access to medical information needed for their investigations without seeking the patient's permission or obtaining a subpoena. Privacy advocates and medical organizations such as the American Psychiatric Association oppose this proposal. Other privacy legislation and proposals are also discussed.

Snider, Dixie E. "Patient Consent for Publication and the Health of the Public." *The Journal of the American Medical Association*, vol. 278, no. 8, August 27, 1997, p. 624(3). Argues that procedures for removing information about patients' identities and for obtaining informed consent can be too strict in some cases and can prevent timely warnings about serious disease outbreaks.

Spragins, Ellyn E., and Mary Hager. "Naked Before the World: Will Your Medical Secrets Be Safe in a New National Databank?" *Newsweek*, vol. 129, June 30, 1997, p. 84. Warns that while a new database to be shared by health care providers and insurers may improve care and save money, it may also make it easier to abuse individuals' medical records.

Stetson, Douglas M. "Achieving Effective Medical Information Security: Understanding the Culture." *Bulletin of the American Society for Information Science*, vol. 23, February–March 1997, p. 17ff. Suggests how the variety of institutional privacy concerns can be met in implementing secure medical data systems.

Sullivan, Gayle H. "Protecting Patient's Privacy." *RN*, vol. 60, June 1997, p. 55ff. Summarizes for nurses the conditions under which medical information must be divulged (such as reporting cases of abuse) as well as the general confidentiality of information about a patient's diagnosis and treatment.

Thomson, B. "Time for Reassessment of Use of All Medical Information by U.K. Insurers." *The Lancet*, October 10, 1998, p. 1216. Argues that the attempts to prohibit use of genetic-based information by insurers is likely to fail because it is hard to define what information is really genetic-based; suggests looking instead at the fundamental question of what is a private responsibility and thus insurable and what must be covered by the government.

"Trading Trust for Blood Money." *The Lancet*, vol. 346, September 30, 1995, p. 855. Discusses proposed changes in the British blood bank system that may make it more likely that confidential medical information gathered from donors might be misused.

Veatch, Robert M. "Consent, Confidentiality, and Research." *The New England Journal of Medicine*, vol. 336, March 20, 1997, p. 869ff. Describes a study that shows that many patients who received genetic testing were not asked for consent for use of the information in research studies and that doctors who did the tests may not have been fully aware of the purposes of the study.

"Why Your Health Privacy Is Threatened." *Consumers' Research*, vol. 80, April 1997, p. 24ff. As health care organizations strive to control costs, they are creating large centralized databases of electronic medical records that are distributed to an ever-widening array of providers. The article warns that there are no adequate regulations or safeguards against misuse of information.

"Who's Reading Your Medical Records?" *Consumer Reports*, vol. 59, October 1994, p. 628ff. Describes how information previously shared only with one's doctor now routinely finds its way to insurers, employers, and drug companies.

Woodward, Beverly R. "The Computer-Based Patient Record and Confidentiality." *The New England Journal of Medicine*, vol. 333, November 23, 1995, p. 1419ff. Introduces the arguments for increased computerization of health records (efficiency, better medical research) and against (misuse

170

of records to discriminate, leading to serious consequences for insurance and employment).

Zoll, Milton. "Medical Records Bureau Agrees to Open Files." *Nation's Business*, vol. 84, April 1996, p. 67. Reports that the national Medical Information Bureau has agreed to the Federal Trade Commission's request to allow individuals who may have been harmed by adverse information to review their records.

INTERNET DOCUMENTS

Electronic Privacy Information Center. "Medical Privacy Public Opinion Polls: Public Attitudes and Interesting Facts." Available online. URL: http://www.epic.org/privacy/medical/polls.html. Downloaded on January 7, 1999. Summarizes polls on medical privacy conducted by Louis Harris in 1993 and the American Civil Liberties Union in 1994.

———. "Medical Record Privacy." Available online. URL: http://www.epic.org/privacy/medical/. Downloaded on January 8, 1999. Provides news summaries, links, and documents relating to medical privacy issues.

Archive of Postings to INFO-POLICY-NOTES. Available online. URL: http://lists.essential.org/info-policy-notes/. Downloaded on July 4, 1999. Collects postings to medical policy lists; includes medical privacy issues.

Privacy Rights Clearinghouse. "How Private Is My Medical Information?" (Fact Sheet #8). URL: http://www.privacyrights.org/fs/fs8-med.htm. Updated in November 1998. Summarizes who has access to individual medical records, how they can be used (or abused), ways to prevent misuse, and how to obtain one's own records.

WORKPLACE PRIVACY

BOOKS

Decker, Kurt H. *A Manager's Guide to Employee Privacy: Laws, Policies, and Procedures*. New York: John Wiley & Sons, 1989. Explains what managers must do in order to protect employees' privacy and to prevent liability. Covers all procedures from initial interviewing to workplace evaluation, use of medical records, and dealing with issues outside the workplace that may pose problems.

Electronic Mail Association. *Access to and Use and Disclosure of Electronic Mail Sent on Company Computer Systems: A Tool Kit for Formulating Your Company's Policy*. Arlington, Va.: Electronic Mail Association, n.d. Provides resources for establishing an e-mail access, use, and privacy policy for a business.

Hubbartt, William S. *The New Battle over Workplace Privacy: How Far Can Management Go? What Rights Do Employees Have? Safe Practices to Minimize Conflict, Confusion, and Litigation.* New York: AMACOM, 1998. Discusses ways to balance the needs of employers to protect their interests and further workplace efficiency with the legal obligation to avoid infringing on employees' privacy rights. Includes discussions of workplace testing and monitoring, employee records, e-mail surveillance, and other issues.

Jussim, Daniel. *Drug Tests and Polygraphs: Essential Tools or Violations of Privacy?* New York: Messner, 1988. Describes how drug and polygraph (lie detector) tests are increasingly used by employers, but raise important legal issues.

Smith, H. Jeff. *Managing Privacy: Informaton Technology and Corporate America.* Chapel Hill, N.C.: University of North Carolina Press, 1994. Discusses cases of privacy violations in the business world, and recommends reforms.

ARTICLES AND PAPERS

Barsook, Bruce, and Terry Roemer. "Workplace E-Mail Raises Privacy Issues." *American City & County,* vol. 113, September 1998, p. 10. Notes that about 40 percent of e-mail messages at work are personal in nature, but most employees don't realize that employers in most cases have the right to read them. Proposes a sensible policy for employee use of e-mail.

Bohling, Brinton. "Workplace Video Surveillance." *Monthly Labor Review,* vol. 120, July 1997, p. 41ff. Summarizes the legality of workplace surveillance cameras: the First Circuit Court of Appeals ruled them legal if not concealed because workers have no "expectation of privacy" in the workplace. But the National Labor Relations Board said that any use of hidden cameras should be negotiated with the union.

Brandt, John R. "What Price Privacy?" *Industry Week,* vol. 247, May 4, 1998, p. 4. Explores a paradox: as consumers people want their privacy, but businesspeople need to collect detailed information about their consumers if they are to serve them effectively.

Brown, William S. "The Boss Is Watching as Workplace Surveillance Grows." *Knight-Ridder/Tribune News Service,* August 6, 1997, p. 806K6073. Gives statistics that describe the growing extent of workplace surveillance and monitoring, including drug tests. Recommends that such activity be restricted to matters of legitimate business interest and with informed consent.

———. "Workplace Privacy Becomes a Thing of the Past." *Knight-Ridder/Tribune News Service,* April 3, 1997, p. 403K3990. Describes the ease with which employers can use commonly available information such as

Social Security numbers to uncover many details of employees' lives, the ability to monitor workers' activities and speech, and the struggle to draw a line between "due diligence" and unnecessary snooping and control.

Doyle, Rodger. "Privacy in the Workplace." *Scientific American.* Available online. URL: http://www.sciam.com/1999/0199 issue/0199 numbers.html. Downloaded on December 14, 1998. Survey and overview of intrusions on workers' privacy including video monitoring, drug and "honesty" tests, and monitoring of phone conversations and e-mail.

"E-Mail Privacy: Fact or Fallacy?" *Inc.*, vol. 18, July 1996, p. 100. Interview with privacy law expert Lee Gesmer, who tells employers that there are few restrictions on corporate monitoring of employees' e-mail. Gesmer does recommend notifying employees that their e-mail is not to be considered private.

Fader, Shirley Sloan. "Privacy at Work: What You Need to Know." *Family Circle*, vol. 111, March 10, 1998, p. 130ff. Describes the kind of employee testing and monitoring typically used by businesses, and suggests legislation to strengthen workers' privacy.

Fimrite, Peter. "Paws Off Our E-Mail, S.F. Dog Lovers Warn." *San Francisco Chronicle*, December 22, 1998, p. A1, A16. Reports a controversy over dog walking on federal parkland becomes a privacy issue when a government employee allegedly joins an e-mail list to spy on pro-canine activists.

Fost, Dan. "Former Employee Sees Himself as a Freedom Fighter in E-Mail Battle with Intel." *San Francisco Chronicle*, December 28, 1998, p. D1, D3. Presents the story of dissident Intel employee Ken Hamidi, who is accused by his employer of sending unsolicited "spam" messages to the company's mailing list. The employee asserts that he is simply exercising his freedom of speech in sending critical missives.

Garber, Joseph R. "The Right to Goof Off." *Forbes*, vol. 160, October 20, 1997, p. 297. Argues that workplace monitoring is essential to worker productivity and accountability, and that "civil liberties extremists" are going too far.

"Get the Message?" *Managing Office Technology*, vol. 40, September 1995, p. 14. Describes a case where employees who were disciplined for including off-color personal remarks in e-mail unsuccessfully sued on privacy grounds; courts have given employers rather broad rights to control the use of e-mail.

Glassberg, Bonnie C., William J. Kettinger, and John E. Logan. "Electronic Communication: An Ounce of Policy Is Worth a Pound of Cure." *Business Horizons*, vol. 39, July–August 1996, p. 74ff. Warns of the complexities of the new communications medium of e-mail and the potential for misunderstanding messages, as well as the need for a consistent corporate policy on proper use of e-mail and the need to educate employees about it.

Hawkins, Dana. "Who's Watching Now?" *U.S. News & World Report*, vol. 123, September 15, 1997, p. 56ff. Reports that liability concerns and rising health care costs have led employers to monitor employees' movements, conversations, and even e-mail. Also describes "midnight raids" where an employer sends a team of experts to obtain every last bit of data from the office of an employee suspected of misdeeds.

Jaffe, Brian. "Why We Need a Bill of Rights for User Privacy." *PC Week*, vol. 15, July 27, 1998, p. 72. Notes that many corporate computer users don't realize that anything on their desktop PC can be accessed by administrators and support personnel. Training and policies must be designed to respect privacy and to protect sensitive data.

Koch, Kathy. "Drug Testing." *CQ Researcher*, November 20, 1998, p. 1001. Describes the growing use of drug testing in the private sector and the conflict between fighting drugs and protecting privacy.

McClean, Ed. "Privacy Big Issue for Mailers." *Advertising Age*, vol. 65, July 4, 1994, p. 14. Gives examples of how it is important for marketers to have a privacy policy, and to refrain from collecting irrelevant information.

McGee, Marianne Kolbasuk. "E-mail Study Shows Few Constraints." *Information Week*, December 9, 1996, pp. 103–105. Reports that there are few restrictions on the ability of employers to monitor their workers' e-mail.

Peyser, Marc, and Steve Rhodes. "When E-Mail Is Oops-Mail." *Newsweek*, vol. 126, October 16, 1995, p. 82. Warns employees that employers can and do read their private e-mail—and it's probably legal.

Quittel, Fran. "Surf on Your Own Time: At Work You Never Know Who Might Be Watching." *Bay Area Computer Currents*, August 18–September 7, 1998, pp. 107, 109. Describes the growing monitoring of workers' web access by employers and gives examples of the software products being used for the purpose.

Radcliff, Deborah. "Who's Listening In?" *Industry Week*, vol. 247, May 18, 1998, p. 12. Executives who plan strategy over cell phones may not realize that a competitor might be listening in—and the results can be quite expensive. The article recommends use of a digital cellular phone and an encryption device.

Richards, Steven. "Privacy Rights Can Survive War on Insurance Fraud." *National Underwriter*, September 9, 1996, pp. 52, 59. Argues that the goal of preventing insurance fraud can be achieved in a way that respects privacy rights.

Rigdon, Joan Indiana. "Management: Curbing Digital Dillydallying on the Job." *Wall Street Journal*, November 25, 1996, p. B1. Reports on employer efforts to curb nonwork-related use of the web and other computer facilities.

Samuels, Patrice Duggan. "Increasingly, Companies Deny Employees Privacy Rights in E-mail." *New York Times*, May 11, 1996. Available online.

174

URL: http://www.nytimes.com/. Reports that many companies are now making explicit policies that e-mail sent on company equipment is not to be considered private; policies may be driven by fear of liability.

Sipe, Jeffrey R. "Does Legal Eavesdropping Violate Employees' Rights?" *Insight on the News*, vol. 12, March 25, 1996, p. 44. Argues that existing laws have too few restrictions on employers' right to eavesdrop on or monitor employees, and that attempts to provide stronger protection for workers' privacy have so far failed in Congress.

Smolove, Jill. "My Boss, Big Brother: A New Illinois Law Permits Employers to Listen in on Workers' Phones. So Watch What You Say." *Time*, vol. 147, January 22, 1996, p. 56. Discusses a controversial Illinois law that would allow employers to eavesdrop on employees for just about any business-related reason; the AFL-CIO will challenge the law in court.

United States Chamber of Commerce. "Employee E-Mail: Is It Really Private?" *Nation's Business*, vol. 84, March 1996, p. 10. Notes that while employers actually have the right to monitor most employee e-mail, employees often mistakenly believe e-mail they send on company computers is private; suggests that employers fully notify employees that their e-mail is not private and is subject to review.

Van Name, Mark L., and Bill Catchings. "Set Your E-Mail Privacy Policies Now." *PC Week*, vol. 13, October 7, 1996, p. N8. Now that new software makes it practical to automatically monitor e-mail, companies must establish well-considered privacy policies rather than letting individual managers follow their own judgment.

"When Email Zaps Back." *San Francisco Chronicle*. December 6, 1998, p. 8. Explains how carelessly written e-mail can come back to haunt its author—using none other than Bill Gates as an example; also includes a summary of e-mail privacy issues.

INTERNET DOCUMENTS

Johnson, David R. "Access Rights—All Power to the Sysop?" Available online. URL: http://www.eff.org/pub/Legal/access_rights_johnson.article. Posted on January 12, 1994. Argues that the network system operator (sysop) is the key person for enforcing—or abusing—policies that restrain unacceptable use of the system.

Privacy Rights Clearinghouse. "Employee Monitoring: Is There Privacy in the Workplace?" (Fact Sheet #7). Available online. URL: http://www. privacyrights.org/fs/fs7-work.htm. Updated on August 1997. Explains when and how employers are allowed to monitor employee phone calls, conversations, e-mail, and computer activity.

OTHER MEDIA

Privacy and American Business. "Practitioner's Privacy Policy Workshop Recorded Live: 'How To Write or Update Company Privacy Policy in Online, Internet, and Offline Arenas'." La Crescenta, CA: n.d. Audio Archives Int'l Inc. Recording of a workshop presenting background, issues, and guidelines for developing corporate privacy policies.

PRIVACY AND GOVERNMENT AGENCIES

Bollinger, William A. "Information Access Policies in the 1990s: National and International Concerns" in *Proceedings of the National Online Meeting* (New York, May 1–3, 1990). Medford, N.J.: Learned Information, Inc., 1990, pp. 51–55. Gives a perspective on the development of information policies in the 1990s.

Connolly, Frank, Steven W. Gilbert, and Peter Lyman. *A Bill of Rights for Electronic Citizens.* Washington, D.C.: Office of Technology Assessment, 1990. Proposes standards for protecting the rights of individuals in the online world.

Foerstal, Herbert. *Surveillance in the Stacks: The FBI's Library Awareness Program.* New York: Greenwood Press, 1991. Describes the controversial FBI program that enlists the aid of librarians in identifying suspected terrorists.

Haywood, Trevor. "Electronic Information: The Withering of Public Access" in *New Horizons for the Information Profession.* Los Angeles and London: Taylor Graham, 1988, pp. 195–206. Argues that the ability of the public to obtain electronic information is failing to keep up with the expanding collection of it by government agencies.

Informing the Nation: Federal Information Dissemination in an Electronic Age. Washington, D.C.: Office of Technology Assessment, 1988. Describes the policies and procedures in place for distribution of information between government agencies and with the public.

Jabine, Thomas, and Virginia A. de Wolf, eds. Panel on Confidentiality, National Research Council. *Private Lives and Public Policies: Confidentiality and Accessibility of Government Statistics.* Washington, D.C.: National Academy Press, 1993. Discusses privacy issues involving collection of statistical data by government agencies, and recommends appropriate practices.

McWhirter, Darien A. *Search, Seizure, and Privacy.* (Exploring the Constitution series). Phoenix, Ariz.: Onyx Press, 1994. Gives an overview of constitutional issues relating to search and seizure of evidence; written for high school and college undergraduates. Many of these underlying issues apply to government surveillance or use of information.

Annotated Bibliography

ARTICLES AND PAPERS

"Bugging the Castle: Civil Liberties." *The Economist*, vol. 339, June 29, 1996, p. 52ff. Reports on the likely passage of legislation that would give the British security agency MI5 broad new powers to eavesdrop and read mail of persons suspected of criminal behavior.

Curtis, Gregory. "Total Exposure." *Texas Monthly*, vol. 25, September 1997, p. 7ff. Argues against the decision of the Texas legislature to outlaw access to drivers' license records on the Internet. Argues that the information is already theoretically public, and can have legitimate uses such as identifying a stalker.

Graves, Jacqueline M. "Is Big Brother Backing Down?" *Fortune*, vol. 131, March 20, 1995, p. 15ff. Describes the IRS's proposed Compliance 2000 program, which would create a huge database from commercial and other sources and use it to catch tax cheats; privacy advocates such as Marc Rotenberg, director of the Electronic Privacy Information Center, say that the proposal violates the Privacy Act of 1974's restrictions on the scope of government data-gathering.

Heilemann, John. "Did the Feds Break the Law?" *The New Yorker*, vol. 72, July 8, 1996, p. 31ff. Describes the lawsuit filed by Marc Rotenberg of the Electronic Privacy Information Center (EPIC) that contends that the White House violated the rights of ex-White House employees by obtaining their FBI files.

Huber, Peter. "Wiretapper Can't Cope, Seeks Help." *Forbes*, vol. 162, August 24, 1998, p. 264. Suggests that the deregulation and diversity in the telecommunications industry, as well as new encryption technology, makes old-style FBI wiretapping obsolete—and that this is not a bad thing in the long run.

Kimery, Anthony L. "Federal Protection System Could Double as Spy Scam." *Insight on the News*, vol. 11, October 2, 1995, p. 10ff. Argues that the new federal Deposit Tracking System to be used against organized crime and to protect national security could easily become a means for covert spying on ordinary citizens because it lacks any controls or accountability for the information it gathers.

Markhoff, John. "FBI Seeks Access to Mobile Phone Locations." *New York Times*, July 17, 1998. np. Available online. URL: http://www.nytimes.com/. Reports on the FBI's request to phone companies to have equipment that give the exact location of all mobile phone users; privacy advocates say the technology is too intrusive and not adequately supervised by courts, while phone companies say it would be very costly.

Meyer, Michael. "Keeping the Cybercops Out of Cyberspace." *Newsweek*, vol. 123, March 14, 1994, p. 38ff. Reviews controversy over proposed expanded federal wiretapping and the Clipper Chip.

Mitchell, Russ. "Is the FBI Reading Your E-mail?" *U.S. News & World Report,* vol. 123, October 13, 1997, p. 49. Reports on a bill that would allow the FBI and other government agencies to obtain users' encryption keys with a court order; privacy advocates oppose the scheme as dangerous and counterproductive.

Paul, Ron. "Privacy Rights' Days May Be (Federally) Numbered." *Insight on the News,* vol. 14, August 17, 1998, p. 28. Warns that major legislative initiatives in immigration, welfare, and health reform would in effect turn the Social Security number into a national ID, making it easier for the government to track individuals and to invade their privacy.

Pear, Robert. "Web Site on Social Security Benefits to Be Revived." *New York Times,* September 4, 1997. np. Available online. URL: http://www.nytimes.com/. Reports on the second attempt by the Social Security Administration to provide online access to benefits information: the new site will not have earnings history information and will require an e-mail verification code.

Robins, Natalie. "The FBI's Invasion of Libraries." *The Nation,* April 9, 1988, p. 499. Reports on controversial FBI programs to obtain information about library users as part of an antiterrorism effort.

Rodriguez, Paul M. "Alarmed Chairmen Express Concern About Big Brother." *Insight on the News,* vol. 12, August 19, 1996, p. 12ff. Interviews chairmen of congressional committees who became alarmed about possible White House misuse of FBI files and have expanded their concern to the misuse of government databases, files, and reports in general; they urge that other government files get the same restrictions that are currently used for tax returns at the IRS.

Shattuck, John. "The Right to Know: Public Access to Federal Information in the 1980s." *Government Information Quarterly* 5, no. 4 (1988): pp. 369–375. Provides a summary of freedom to access government records activity during the 1980s.

Shill, Harold B. "A Basis for Increasing Public Access to Federal Electronic Information." *Government Information Quarterly* 6, no. 2 (1989) pp. 135–141. Suggests procedures for improving the ability of the public to access electronic information stored by the federal government.

Sipe, Jeffrey R. "Social Security Information: Privacy Issues Continue to Prompt Debate Across the Country." *Insight on the News,* vol. 13, December 1, 1997, p. 40. Reports that many businesses have unnecessary requirements for customers' Social Security numbers, and these numbers can be used to learn a lot about an individual's finances. Looks at contradictory legislative proposals including one that would outlaw the sale of Social Security numbers and one that would expand their use for certain government purposes such as voter registration.

Sussman, Vic. "The Road Worriers: Can Electronic Tolls Be a Tool for Big Brother?" *U.S. News & World Report*, vol. 119, October 2, 1995, p. 78(1). Describes how electronic toll systems can speed drivers through bridges and turnpikes, but can also collect information about drivers' activities. Anonymous toll systems that store no personal data offer an alternative.

Taylor, Brian J. "The Screening of America: Crime, Cops, and Cameras." *Reason*, vol. 29, May 1997, p. 44ff. Surveys the debate over widespread police surveillance of public places: privacy advocates decry instrusiveness, while proponents argue that people should not expect privacy in a public place.

Timberg, Craig. "Virginia Lists Sex Offenders on Internet." *Washington Post*, December 31, 1998, p. A01. Reports on Virginia's listing of the names and addresses of more than 4,600 violent sex offenders on a state web site. Civil libertarians worry that false information in the database could damage the reputations of innocent people, while offenders could be attacked by vigilantes or lose their jobs or homes, destroying their prospects for rehabilitation.

United States General Accounting Office. *Computers and Power: How the Government Obtains, Verifies, Uses and Protects Personal Data*. Briefing to the Chairman, Subcommittee of Telecommunications and Finance, Committee on Energy and Commerce, House of Representatives, August 3, 1990. Describes government privacy practices at the beginning of the 1990s.

———. *National Crime Information Center: Legislation Needed to Deter Misuse of Criminal Justice Information*, GAO/T–GGD–93–41. Washington, D.C., U.S. Government Printing Office, July 1993. Argues for stronger protections against misuse of information gathered by law enforcement agencies and courts.

United States Senate, Appropriations Committee, Subcommittee on Treasury and General Government. *Overview of Internal Revenue Service Employees Misuse of Taxpayers' Files*, Hearings on April 15, 1997, One Hundred Fifth Congress, First Session. Washington, D.C.: Government Printing Office, 1997. Gives overview of public hearings on abuses of taxpayers by IRS personnel.

INTERNET DOCUMENTS

Banisar, Dave. "EPIC Analysis of New Justice Department Draft Guidelines on Searching and Seizing Computers." Available online. URL: http://www.eff.org/pub/Legal/doj_search_seize_ epic.analysis. Posted on January 20, 1995. Analyzes the Department of Justice guidelines that are intended to reduce the unnecessary seizure of computer components and to protect the privacy rights of users who are not targets of an investigation.

Godwin, Michael. "The Feds and the Net: Closing the Culture Gap." Available online. URL: http://www.eff.org/pub/Legal/feds_on_the_net_godwin.article. Downloaded on December 26, 1998. Uses three cases from the early 1990s to suggest that government prosecutors often lack understanding of computer culture, leading them to ignore traditional constitutional protections for defendants. [Originally published in *Internet World*, May 1994.]

Johnson, David R. "Law Enforcement and the Architecture of Cyberspace—Should the Cops on the Beat Design the Electronic Street." Available online. URL: http://www.eff.org/pub/Legal/cops_net_architecture_johnson.article. Posted on February 2, 1994. Attacks the federal Clipper Chip proposal as an attempt to force people to communicate only through government-approved means, leading to overcentralized, clumsy system designs.

Lemmos, Robert. "Crypto Shift Hurts E-Commerce?: Arms-Control Agreement Limits Encryption, Threatens E-Commerce, Industry Says." ZD Net. Available online. URL: http://www.zdnet.com/. Posted December 3, 1998. Reports that the industry group Americans for Computer Privacy is concerned that the new agreement limiting exports to relatively weak encryption threatens the consumer trust that is essential to the growth of electronic commerce.

Pressman, Aaron. "U.S. Gets Its Way on Crypto Controls: Clinton Crypto Czar Says Foreign Countries Agreeing to Export Controls." Reuters/ZD Net. Available online. URL: http://www.zdnet.com/. Posted December 3, 1998. Reports that the Clinton administration has persuaded many foreign countries to go along with tighter cryptology controls that are opposed by most privacy advocates.

Privacy Rights Clearinghouse. "From Cradle to Grave: Government Records and Your Privacy" (Fact Sheet #11). Available online. URL: http://www.privacyrights.org/fs/fs11-pub.htm. Updated in December 1998. Provides a guide to the information that the government collects about citizens and how individuals can protect or correct such information.

Reynolds, Dennis J., ed. "Citizen Rights and Access to Electronic Information." Available online. URL: http://www.eff.org/pub/Legal/elec_rights_ala.papers. Downloaded on December 26, 1998. Online text version of booklet distributed by American Library Association in June 1991; consists of a collection of essays that describe various aspects of people's rights to access information created by government agencies.

"Virginia Lists Sex Offenders on Web Site." Associated Press Online. Document ID ED19981229760000018. Available online. URL:

http://www.nytimes.com/aponline/. Posted December 30, 1998. Reports that the state of Virginia has created a web site with the names, addresses, and photos of convicted violent sex offenders. The American Civil Liberties Union has protested this as an invasion of privacy, a "scarlet letter," and an invitation to vigilantism.

ENCRYPTION, SURVEILLANCE, AND DATA PROTECTION

BOOKS

Bacard, Andre. *The Computer Privacy Handbook: A Practical Guide to E-Mail Encryption, Data Protection, and PGP Privacy Software.* Berkeley, Calif.: Peachpit Press, 1995. Explains procedures and use of software for protecting e-mail and other data.

Banisar, David, and Marc Rotenberg, eds. *1998 Cryptography and Privacy Sourcebook.* Washington, D.C.: Electronic Privacy Information Center, 1998. Collects primary source documents on the topics of cryptography, key escrow, congressional legislation, court decisions, and international policies.

Diffie, Whitfield, and Susan Landau. *Privacy on the Line: The Politics of Wiretapping and Encryption.* Cambridge, Mass.: MIT Press, 1998. Surveys the development of encryption and wiretapping technologies and explores their impact on public policy. (Diffie is a coinventor of public-key cryptography.)

Electronic Frontier Foundation. Gilmore, John, ed. *Cracking DES: Secrets of Encryption Research, Wiretap Politics & Chip Design.* Sebastapol, Calif.: O'Reilly, 1998. Describes in technical detail how computer code-crackers built a relatively inexpensive computer system that "cracked" the government's supposedly secure 56–bit DES code; explores the politics of encryption that prevents stronger legal and encryption standards.

Feghhi, Jalal, Peter Williams, and Jalil Feghhi. *Digital Certificates: Applied Internet Security.* Reading, Mass.: Addison-Wesley, 1998. Describes the design and implementation of digital certificates that use cryptography to authenticate and secure transactions.

Garfinkel, Simson. *PGP: Pretty Good Privacy.* Sebastapol, Calif.: O'Reilly, 1995. Surveys the development of computer cryptography and introduces the freeware PGP encryption program.

Guisnel, Jean. *Cyberwars: Espionage on the Internet.* New York: Plenum, 1997. Describes the fascinating and threatening exploits of hackers and spies who ply their trade in the online world.

Hoffman, Lance J. *Building in Big Brother: The Cryptographic Policy Debate.* New York: Springer-Verlag, 1995. Provides a wide-ranging discussion of the controversy caused by the federal Clipper Chip proposal, pitting privacy against law enforcement and national security issues.

International Workshop on Practice and Theory in Public Key Cryptography. Public Key Cryptography. First International Workshop on Practice and Theory in Public Key Cryptography, Pkc '98, Pacifico Yokohama, Japan, February. New York: Springer, 1998. Collects proceedings of an international conference on the rapidly developing field of public-key cryptography and its applications to many aspects of commerce.

Kahn, David. *The Codebreakers: The Comprehensive History of Secret Communication from Ancient Times to the Internet.* Rev. ed. New York: Scribner, 1996. Describes the wide variety of codes, cyphers, and other systems for secret messages used throughout history; includes coverage of recent developments in computer cryptography and the Internet.

Landau, Susan, Stephen Kent, Clinton Brooks, et. al. *Codes, Keys and Conflicts: Issues in U.S. Crypto Policy.* ACM Press, 1994.

Loshin, Peter. *Personal Encryption Clearly Explained.* San Diego, Calif.: AP Professional, 1998. Introduces encryption concepts and then explains hands-on procedures for using encryption for security.

Neumann, Peter. *Computer-Related Risks.* Reading, Mass.: Addison-Wesley, 1995. Introduces the study of the risks and unforseen consequences of complex computer systems, including threats to privacy.

Sands, Trent. *Reborn in the USA: Personal Privacy Through a New Identity.* Port Townsend, Wash.: Loompanics, 1998. Discusses techniques for creating a new identity to protect privacy—many of which can led to legal problems.

Schwartau, Winn. *Information Warfare: Chaos on the Electronic Superhighway.* New York: Thunder's Mouth Press, 1994. Describes how a growing number of specialists can invade privacy, steal secrets, or damage computer systems and suggests that they pose a serious threat to the future of the information superhighway.

Shimomura, Tsutomu, and John Markhoff. *Take-down: The Pursuit and Capture of Kevin Mitnick, America's Most Wanted Computer Outlaw—By the Man Who Did It.* New York: Hyperion, 1996. Recounts the story of the hunt for and capture of Kevin Mitnick, a famous computer "cracker" who invaded computer systems and stole confidential files.

Stoll, Clifford. *The Cuckoo's Egg: Tracking a Spy Through the Maze of Computer Espionage.* New York: Doubleday, 1989. Provides one of the earliest accounts of the threat of espionage to the Internet.

United States Congress, Office of Technology Assessment. *Defending Secrets, Sharing Data: New Locks and Keys for Electronic Information. OTA–CIT–310.* Washington, D.C.: Government Printing Office, 1987. Summarizes new encryption technology from a government viewpoint.

Annotated Bibliography

United States Congress. Office of Technology Assessment. *Information Security and Privacy in Network Environments. OTA–TCT–606.* Washington, D.C.: Government Printing Office, 1994. Evaluates the security and privacy of computer networks.

Van Der Lubbe, Jan C. A. *Basic Methods of Cryptography.* New York: Cambridge University Press, 1998. Describes the basic application of cryptography in a variety of information systems including banking, medical, and telecommunications.

Wayner, Peter. *Digital Cash: Commerce on the Net.* 2nd ed. Boston: AP Professional, 1997. Provides a detailed overview of various systems for digital cash that can allow for secure online transactions.

PERIODICALS

2600 Magazine. P.O. Box 752, Middle Island, NY 11953. E-mail: 2600@well.com. URL: http://www.2600.com/. Insider's magazine about hacking and security.

Gray Areas. Netta Gilboa, ed. P.O. Box 808, Broomall, PA 19008–0808. Outspoken, controversial publication that looks at privacy, drug testing, prison issues, and other subject areas.

Privacy 2001. Jim Ross, ed. 504 Shaw Road, Suite 222, Sterling, VA 20166. (703) 318–8600. Focuses on technical aspects of privacy and data protection.

Security Insider Report. Winn Schwartau, ed. Interpact Press, Inc. 11511 Pine St. N. Seminole, FL 34642. E-mail: Winn@infowar.com. News, reports, and reviews on information security and privacy, hacking, and "information warfare."

ARTICLES AND PAPERS

Agre, Philip E. and Christine A. Harbs. "Social Choice About Privacy: Intelligent Vehicle-Highway Systems in the United States." *Information Technology and People,* vol. 7, 1994, np. Describes issues raised by the emerging technology of "smart highway" and driver-tracking systems.

Amiel, Barbara. "A Duty to Defy Foolish Regulations." *Maclean's,* vol. 109, August 12, 1996, p. 9. Argues that the Canadian census has failed to protect the confidentiality of people's information, and that both the need for much of the information requested and the idea of a duty to provide it are questionable.

Andrews, Edmund. "U.S. Restrictions on Exports Aid German Software Maker," *New York Times,* April 7, 1997, p. D1. Describes how restrictions on encryption technology in products can hurt American companies in global competition.

Balderston, Jim. "Commerce Department Eases Cryptographic Export Rules." *InfoWorld*, vol. 19, June 2, 1997, p. 15. Reports on government decisions to allow strong 128–bit PGP and VeriFone "secure electronic transaction" software to be exported.

Canon, Maggie. "Yank the Clipper." *MacUser*, vol. 10, June 1994, p. 23. Urges rejection of the federal Clipper Chip proposal because there is no public accountability for its security, serious potential for abuse by the government, and a competitive disadvantage for American companies that might be forced to use it.

Canter, Sheryl. "E-mail Encryption." *PC Magazine*, vol. 16, April 8, 1997, p. 243ff. Reviews the features and methods of operation of six software packages that can be used to encrypt e-mail on networks.

Cassidy, Peter. "New Crypto Controls: Big Step or Big Lie?" *Wired*, March 1997, p. 108. Evaluates (and criticizes) the alleged benefits of proposed new federal controls on cryptography.

Clausing, Jeri. "Administration Announces New Concessions on Encryption Policy." *New York Times*, September 16, 1998. np. Available online. URL: http://www.nytimes.com/. Reports on relaxation of policy to allow U.S. companies to export more powerful encryption software to other nations.

———. "New Encryption Legislation Billed as a Compromise." *New York Times*, May 13, 1998. np. Available online. URL: http://www.nytimes.com/. Describes a compromise "E-Privacy Act" that would strengthen data protection while allowing law enforcers to improve their ability to crack codes; privacy advocates expressed concern about this accommodation to law enforcement.

———. "Want More Online Privacy? Join the Crowd." *New York Times*, August 22, 1998. np. Available online. URL: http://www.nytimes.com/. Describes "anonymizer" services that use software to hide Internet users' identity while they surf, protecting them from information gatherers.

Daniel, Caroline. "Not Citizens but Data Subjects: In the Hi-Tech Information Age Everything from Our Weekly Shopping to Our Intimate Conversations Can Be Someone Else's Business. What Price Privacy?" *New Statesman*, vol. 126, June 13, 1997, p. 23ff. Describes the growing use of closed-circuit TV (CCTV) surveillance cameras in Britain; such systems are popular with much of the public because they are believed to reduce crime, but regulation and an overall policy that takes privacy concerns into account is lacking.

Danitz, Tiffany. "Snooping on Passengers Under FAA's Watchful Eye." *Insight on the News*, vol. 13, March 31, 1997, p. 22ff. Discusses a Federal Aviation Agency initiative to create a detailed database from airline passenger information for use in creating "profiles" of likely terrorists. Critics worry that profiles are often used to discriminate against certain ethnic groups, such as people from the Middle East, and that there is no guarantee the information collected by the airlines won't be distributed to other agencies.

Denning, Dorothy, Mike Godwin, William Bayse, Marc Rotenberg, et. al. "To Tap or Not to Tap." *Communications of the ACM*, vol. 36 (3), March 1993, pp. 24–44. Also available online at: http://www.cpsr.org. Presents panel discussion on criteria and safeguards to be used in the tapping of phone or data lines.

Dunn, Ashley. "Of Keys, Decoders and Personal Privacy." *New York Times*, October 1, 1998. np. Available online. URL: http://www.nytimes.com/. Gives historical background on public-key encryption from its beginnings in the 1970s to Pretty Good Privacy and other programs used today.

Fixmer, Rob. "Tiny New Chip Could Pit Protection of Property Against Right of Privacy." *New York Times*, vol. 148, September 29, 1998, p. B14. Reports that Veridicom's new fingerprint-reading chip may become the standard access control and lock device for many applications, but its ability to track individuals' activities may pose a threat to privacy.

Frankel, Marc. "Candid Camera: Corporate Snooping 101." *The New Republic*, vol. 214, May 20, 1996, p. 11ff. Describes a "Surveillance Expo" that displayed a boggling array of cameras, sensors, and eavesdropping gear and gives anecdotes to illustrate instances of snooping.

Fried, John J. "When Millions of People Want Privacy on the Internet, Things Get Complicated." *Knight-Ridder/Tribune News Service*, March 25, 1998, p. 325K4317. Gives an overview of the encryption debate: consumers and businesses want strong encryption, but the government insists it would make the nation vulnerable to criminals, spies, and terrorists.

Froomkin, A. Michael. "The Metaphor Is the Key: Cryptography, the Clipper Chip, and the Constitution." *University of Pennsylvania Law Review*, vol. 143 (1995), pp. 709–897,

Fulkerson, Jennifer. "The Census and Privacy." *American Demographics*, vol. 17, May 1995, p. 48ff. Argues that despite public skepticism, the U.S. Census has generally had a good record of protecting the confidentiality of census records.

Gibbs, Mark, and Michael S. Lasky. "The Defenders." *PC World*, vol. 16, September 1998, p. 140. Surveys and evaluates software to block viruses, filter spam, reject Internet "cookies," block web cache snoops, encrypt e-mail, and otherwise promote privacy and security.

Gillmor, Dan. "Zimmermann Fighting Battle for Privacy." *Knight-Ridder/Tribune News Service*, April 5, 1995, p. 0405K5065. Describes programmer/activist Phillip Zimmermann's creation of a free software tool that people can use to protect their data from private and government snoops.

Hansell, Saul. "Use of Recognition Technology Grows in Everyday Trans-actions." *New York Times*, August 20, 1997. np. Available online. URL: http://www.nytimes.com/. Describes growing use of "biometrics" equipment that scans and recognizes facial features, fingerprints, and other characteristics for identification purposes and related issues of privacy and consent.

Henderson, Rick. "Clipping Encryption." *Reason*, vol. 30, May 1998, p. 7ff. Argues against government plans that would allow encryption to protect sensitive data but would insist on the government being able to obtain a copy of the code key; opponents argue that the proposals would make it too easy for government agencies to violate privacy without the normal requirements for search warrants.

Horwitz, Leslie Anne. "Smart Surveillance Gadgetry Redefines Policing, Lifestyles." *Insight on the News*, vol. 12, July 15, 1996, p. 42ff. Describes sophisticated new surveillance equipment including "smart badges," scanners that can read facial images, and other "biometric" devices. Privacy activists are concerned that the lack of privacy controls makes it likely that data gathered by surveillance devices will spread to people who have no legitimate need for it.

"Intelligent Highway Systems vs. Privacy." *USA Today* (Magazine), vol. 124, December 1995, p. 14. Discusses Intelligent Transportation Systems (ITS) that will be able to track the exact movements of cars, collecting tolls and providing information and rescue services. ITS raises privacy issues because the information might be used to develop "profiles" of drivers' habits for marketing purposes.

Karr, Albert R. "Administration Moves Toward Encryption," *Wall Street Journal*, July 15, 1996, p. B4. Describes changes in Clinton administration encryption policy.

Lacey, Mark. "Florida Couple Say They Recorded Gingrich's Call." *Los Angeles Times*, January 14, 1997, p. A1. Reports an incident that raised public awareness of the vulnerability of cell phones to eavesdropping.

Lange, Larry. "Net Monitoring Tool Fuels Debate Over Privacy." *Electronic Engineering Times*, December 9, 1997, p. 24. Describes technology that allows system administrators new abilities to monitor computer networks but also to invade users' privacy.

Levy, Stephen. "Battle of the Clipper Chip." *New York Times Magazine*, June 12, 1994, p. 44. Describes the controversy over the government-proposed device that would offer encryption but also give the government a "back door" through which it could retrieve secret information.

Lewis, Bob. "The Feds Are Going Too Far with Security; Are You Violating Privacy?" *InfoWorld*, vol. 18, October 14, 1996, p. 64. Opposes a federal proposal to give the FBI the ability to precisely locate and monitor cell phones, voice mail, and computer network access. Argues that there is

Annotated Bibliography

great potential for abuse, and that users are already vulnerable to anyone who buys a $500 scanner.

Li-Ron, Yael. "PGP Products Protect You Against Internet Snoops." *PC World*, vol. 15, March 1997, p. 78ff. Reviews two commercial products: one uses the Pretty Good Privacy program to encrypt e-mail and the other lets web users control the use of "cookie" files used by web sites to track browsers.

Loshin, Pete. "Cryptography Gets Personal." *Byte*, vol. 22, November 1997, p. 121ff. Evaluates PGP (Pretty Good Privacy) and competing software for encrypting computer communications.

Markoff, John. "A Call for Digital Surveillance Is Delayed." *New York Times*, September 14, 1998. np. Available online. URL: http://www.nytimes.com/. Reports that the Federal Communications Commission has given industry an additional 20 months to comply with the Communications Assistance for Law Enforcement Act, which requires improved abilities for law enforcers to monitor digital communications; privacy advocates continue to oppose the measure.

———. "Cellular Industry Rejects U.S. Plan for Surveillance." *New York Times*, September 20, 1996, p. A1. Reports that phone companies are rejecting government proposals for enhancing their wiretapping capabilities.

———. "Compromise Bills Due on Data Encryption." *New York Times*, March 4, 1996, p. D4. Reports on congressional developments involving data encryption.

———. "Electronics Plan Aims to Balance Government Access with Privacy." *New York Times*, April 16, 1993, p. A1. Reports on what would become the Clipper Chip controversy, pitting encryption versus law enforcement and intelligence agencies.

———. "Microsoft Enters Debate Over Online Privacy by Buying Firefly." *New York Times*. np. Available online. URL: http://www.nytimes.com/. Posted on April 10, 1998. Reports on Microsoft's purchase of Firefly, a technology that can create customized recommendations for web users. Privacy advocates fear that while Firefly would have built-in privacy protection, Microsoft's ability to integrate it into its web browser would build large scale data gathering into the very fabric of the Internet.

———. "U.S. Data-Scrambling Code Cracked with Homemade Equipment." *New York Times*, July 17, 1998. np. Available online, URL: http://www.nytimes.com/. Describes how a code-breaking contest led to the cracking of the government-standard 56-bit DES encryption algorithm, raising concerns that the 40-bit standard the government allows for export is too vulnerable; experts say at least 128-bit keys are required.

———. "U.S. Fails in Global Proposal for Internet Eavesdropping." *New York Times*, March 27, 1997, p. A1. Reports that the United States attempt to

187

get other nations to agree to providing "key escrow" access to encrypted files by law enforcement agencies has failed.

McClure, Stuart. "PGP Brings Security to Masses." *InfoWorld*, vol. 20, October 5, 1998, p. 44C. Review of Pretty Good Privacy implementation in security products for networks.

McGee, Jim. "Tension Rises Over Digital Taps." *Washington Post*, October 27, 1996, p. H1. Reports controversy over government moves to gain the ability to tap large numbers of digital phone lines.

Metcalf, Robert M. "New Technologies Provide Better Combinations of Privacy and Anonymity." *InfoWorld*, vol. 16, November 28, 1994, p. 65. Distinguishes between privacy and anonymity and argues that privacy advocates should not so readily support anonymity that prevents accountability for potentially criminal behavior.

Mitchell, Ross E., and Judith Wagner DeCew. "Dynamic Negotiation in the Privacy Wars." *Technology Review*, vol. 97, November–December 1994, p. 70ff. Suggests that the conflict between callers' and recipients' privacy with Caller ID might be solved by a system that allows anonymous calls, but also allows the recipient to require the caller's number be divulged before allowing the call to go through.

"Monitoring Your Movements." *Bulletin of the American Society for Information Science*, vol. 23, February–March 1997, p. 8ff. Discusses new body-reading image devices, databases, and tracking systems that may be a powerful tool for law enforcers but raise privacy concerns.

Munro, Jay. "Psst! Keep a Secret? (Symantec's Norton Your Eyes Only; Pretty Good Privacy's PGP for Windows, Business Edition; AT&T's Secret Agent; and RSA's SecurPC for Windows 95 Data Encryption Software.)" *PC Magazine*, vol. 15, December 17, 1996, p. 45ff. Reviews four products that use encryption to protect e-mail and other data files.

Naughton, John. "Video Eyes Are Everywhere: 'Big Brother' in Britain." *World Press Review*, vol. 42, April 1995, p. 13. [Reprinted from *The Observer*, Nov. 13, 1994]. Describes the controversy about British police setting up cameras in 300 towns to watch for crimes, raising concerns about bias and invasion of privacy.

Nelson, Matthew. "Commerce Department OKs 128-bit export for PGP." *InfoWorld*, vol. 19, November 17, 1997, p. 106. Describes new export rules that will allow a stronger version of the PGP (Pretty Good Privacy) program to be exported for general business use, perhaps suggesting the dismantling of other export restrictions.

Novak, Janet. "No Place to Hide." *Forbes*, vol. 155, April 10, 1995, p. 58. Describes the work of an IRS employee whose job is trying to make sure the IRS doesn't violate privacy laws in its efforts to catch tax cheats or deadbeat parents. The growing linkage of databases at all levels of government can catch many more offenders but may have a chilling Big Brother effect on citizens.

O'Hara, Colleen, and Heather Harreld. "DOD Sinks the Clipper." *Federal Computer Week*, February 17, 1997. [n.p.] Reports on the withdrawal of the Clipper Chip federal encryption proposal.

Pear, Robert. "Social Security Closes Online Site, Citing Risks to Privacy." *New York Times*, April 10, 1997. np. Available online. URL: http://www.nytimes.com/. Reports that the Social Security Administration shut down its online information site because of concerns about the extent of individual earnings information available and the lack of verification that an inquiry was legitimate.

Peschel, Joe. "PGP Mail Brings Strong Encryption to 32-Bit Platforms." *InfoWorld*, vol. 19, March 31, 1997, p. 94. Review of commercial PGP mail encryption program.

Philips, Don. "Big Brother in the Back Seat?: The Advent of the 'Intelligent Highway' Spurs a Debate Over Privacy." *Washington Post*, February 23, 1995. np. Explores privacy issues raised by proposed intelligent highways with their vehicle tracking and information features.

"Pretty Good Ruling." *Computerworld*, vol. 31, June 2, 1997, p. 8. Announces the Commerce Department's decision to allow export of the stronger 128-bit version of the Pretty Good Privacy encryption program to most countries.

Price, Joyce. "New Surveillance Camera Cheers Police, Worries ACLU." *Insight on the News*, vol. 12, September 9, 1996, p. 41. Describes a new kind of camera called a millimeter wave imager that will enable police to peer into people's clothes and possessions for weapons or other contraband, but privacy and gun rights advocates are concerned that it will be used to violate the rights of law-abiding citizens.

Randall, Neil. "Cookie Managers." *PC Magazine*, vol. 16, September 9, 1997, p. 159ff. Reviews a variety of software packages that allow computer users to monitor and control how and when "cookie" information files are used by web sites.

Rothke, Ben. "Of Munitions and Encryption Software." Storage Management Solutions, July 1997. Available online. URL: http://www.msmag.com/articles/current/Munitions.html. Posted July 1997. Describes the treatment of encryption software as "munitions" under treaty and export control law.

"Scrambled Faxes That Free You from Standing Guard." *Business Week*, no. 3379, July 4, 1994, p. 84E. Discusses Kryptofax, a product that encodes faxes so they cannot be read by office snoops or industrial spies.

Smith, Gina. "The Good Spies." *Popular Science*, vol. 247, December 1995, p. 28. Software companies like Microsoft have new installation programs that keep track of every detail of a user's system configuration. This can make troubleshooting and product support much easier, but unscrupulous companies might market the information they collect from product installation and registration.

Sullivan, Eamonn. "Making Business Secure." *PC Week*, vol. 14, October 27, 1997, p. 72. Reviews a Pretty Good Privacy (PGP) encryption and security product for business PC environments.

Sussman, Vic. "The Road Worriers: Can Electronic Tolls Be a Tool for Big Brother?" *U.S. News & World Report*, vol. 119, October 2, 1995, p. 78. Plans for automatic toll collection on some highways in eastern states raise privacy concerns if they collect personal information about drivers. There are systems, however, that can make toll collection anonymous.

Tacy, Chris. "What Cookies Do and What They Don't." *New York Times*, September 10, 1997. np. Available online. URL: http://www.nytimes.com/. Attempts to demystify "cookie" files, explaining that they generally record only information that the provider in a sense "already knows," and that privacy concerns have been overstated.

Taylor, Brian J. "The Price of Fighting Crime with Hidden Cameras." *Knight-Ridder/Tribune News Service*, April 23, 1997, p. 423K0756. Proponents of surveillance cameras in public places point to a decrease in crime, but opponents cite privacy and civil liberties concerns and argue that cameras just push crime into another neighborhood that lacks the cameras.

———. "The Screening of America: Crime, Cops, and Cameras." *Reason*, vol. 29, May 1997, p. 44ff. Describes the growing use of police surveillance cameras in public places in the United States and the debate over whether they amount to an invasion of privacy.

Walt, Vivianne. "Shelves of Snooping Aids Make Privacy Hard to Buy." *New York Times*, May 20, 1998. np. Available online. URL: http://www.nytimes.com/. Describes the widely available tapping and recording devices that make it easy for anyone to be a spy and invade others' privacy.

Wagner, David. "An Officious Big Brother Builds Wiretap Authority." *Insight on the News*, vol. 13, June 23, 1997, p. 19ff. Argues that the scope of government wiretapping has increased dramatically in the Clinton administration and that export controls on cryptography are unlikely to affect criminals who can use widely available programs.

Wayner, Peter. "Computer Privacy: Your Shield? Or a Threat to National Security?" *New York Times*, September 24, 1997. np. Available online. URL: http://www.nytimes.com/. Gives background on the encryption debate that pits the ability of ordinary citizens to keep their information secret against fears by security agencies that it will make it harder to catch spies or criminals.

Annotated Bibliography

Williams, Robert H. "Economic Spying by Foes, Friends Gains Momentum." *SIGNAL*, July 1992, p. 56–57. Describes the increase in high-tech information espionage.

Woolley, Scott. "Banned in Washington." *Forbes*, vol. 159, April 21, 1997, p. 162ff. Describes how Philip Zimmermann, creator of Pretty Good Privacy (PGP), has overcome government legal challenges and is building a successful company to market the product.

INTERNET DOCUMENTS

Brickell, Ernest F., Dorothy Denning, Stephen Kent, David Maher, and Walter Tuchman. "SKIPJACK Review: Interim Report, The SKIPJACK Algorithm." Available online. URL: http://www.cpsr.org/program/clipper/skipjack-interim-review.html. Posted on July 28, 1993. Evaluates the security of a popular encryption algorithm.

Delaney, Donald P., Dorothy E. Denning, John Kaye, and Alan R. McDonald. "Wiretap Laws and Procedures: What Happens When the U.S. Government Taps a Line." Available online. URL: http://www.cpsr.org/cpsr/privacy/wiretap/wiretap.procedure.html. Posted on September 23, 1993. Describes the detailed legal procedures involved in government wiretapping.

Electronic Privacy Information Center, the Electronic Frontier Foundation, and the American Civil Liberties Union. "[Comments] In the Matter of Communications Assistance for Law Enforcement Act." December 14, 1998. Available online. URL: http://www.epic.org/privacy/wiretap/calea/comments_12_98.html. Joint statement of three civil liberties organizations opposing a proposal that would require phone companies to give assistance to federal law enforcement agencies to improve their ability to tap or monitor communications.

Freeh, Louis H. "Speech Before the International Cryptography Institute." Available online, URL: http://www.fbi.gov/press/dirspch/94-96 archives/crypto.htm. Posted September 21, 1995. Comments on cryptography issues by the director of the FBI.

Froomkin, A. Michael. "Anonymity and Its Enmities." *Journal of Online Law*, June 1995. Available online. URL: http://warthog.cc.wm.edu/law/publications/jol/froomkin.html. Discusses the legal aspects of the ability of computer users to use encryption and anonymous e-mailers to create anonymous identities.

Kapor, Mitch, and Mike Godwin. "Civil Liberties Implications of Computer Searches and Seizures: Some Proposed Guidelines for Magistrates Who Issue Search Warrants." Available online. URL: http://www.eff.org/pub/Legal/search_and_seizure_guidelines.eff. Downloaded on December 26, 1998. Proposed guidelines for issuing search warrants for computer equip-

191

ment and data. Guidelines should take into account the nature of online communication, First Amendment rights for conferencing system users, property rights of innocent businesses, and other considerations.

Morley, Mark. "The Supreme Court and Electronic Surveillance: A Study of Originalism, the Fourth Amendment, and the Powers of Law Enforcement." Available online. URL: http://www.eff.org/pub/Legal/ surveillance_supreme_court.paper. Posted December 21, 1993. Discusses the tension between executive (law enforcement) and legislative (civil rights) agendas in the response to new communications technologies, particularly due to recent developments that have put cryptography in the hands of ordinary citizens, and the attempts of the Supreme Court to resolve such issues.

Moukheiber, Zina Moukheiber. "OECD Adopts Guidelines for Cryptography Policy." URL: http://www.oecd.org/news_and_events/release/nw97-24a.htm. Posted March 27, 1997. Cryptography policy guidelines adopted by member nations of the Organization for Economic Cooperation and Development.

Pressman, Aaron. "U.S. Effort on Encryption 'Back Doors' Ends in Failure." Reuters/ZDNet. Available online. URL: http://www.zdnet.com/zdnn. Posted June 30, 1998. Summarizes the failed and controversial efforts of federal authorities to convince industries to buy into an encryption system that would allow government agencies "backdoor access" to encrypted data.

Privacy Rights Clearinghouse. "Wiretapping/Eavesdropping" (Fact Sheet #9). Available online. URL: http://www.privacyrights.org/fs/fs9-wrtp.htm. Updated on August 1997. Describes the various types of wiretapping and eavesdropping, who can authorize them, the applicable laws, and what one can do if one suspects an unauthorized wiretap.

Riddle, Mike. "Sysop Liability for Enroute (and/or Encrypted) Mail." Available online. URL: http://www.eff.org/pub/Legal/mail_liability.article. Posted November 4, 1994. [Originally published in FIDONEWS—Vol. 10 No. 45 (November 7, 1993)]. Discusses potential liability for system operators (sysops) for transmitting e-mail passing through the system to another destination, or encrypted e-mail, under the Electronic Communications Privacy Act of 1986.

Silverglate, Harvey A., and Thomas C. Viles. "Constitutional, Legal, and Ethical Considerations for Dealing with Electronic Files in the Age of Cyberspace." Available online. URL: http://www.eff.org/pub/Legal/ search_and_seizure_speech. Posted on May 16–17, 1991. Reviews cases in the early 1990s where seizure of computer equipment and files for investigation of computer crimes caused serious damage to businesses and online communities. Urges development of new guidelines and limits on such searches and seizures in keeping with constitutional principles.

CHAPTER 8

ORGANIZATIONS AND AGENCIES

There are many organizations that are devoted in whole or in part to privacy issues. The following entries include consumer advocacy and education groups, trade organizations, professional and technical organizations, and government agencies. In keeping with the widespread use of the Internet and e-mail, the web site (URL) address and e-mail address are given first when available, followed by phone number and postal address.

American Civil Liberties Union (ACLU)
URL: http://www.aclu.org
E-mail: aclu@aclu.org
Phone: (212) 549-2500
125 Broad Street, 18th Floor
New York, NY 10004-2400

Originally founded in 1920, the ACLU conducts extensive litigation on constitutional issues including privacy and free speech.

American Health Information Management Association
URL: http://www.ahima.org
E-mail: info@ahima.org
Phone: (800) 335-5535

919 North Michigan Avenue
Chicago, IL 60611-1683

An industry/professional organization; offers a "white paper" on patient privacy.

Americans for Computer Privacy
URL: http://www.computerprivacy. org/
E-mail: webmaster@computer privacy.org
Phone: (202) 625-1256

An industry coalition working to strengthen privacy protection and to abolish regulations that limit the use of encryption.

Association for Computing Machinery
URL: http://www.acm.org
E-mail: sigs@acm.org (general information)
Phone: (212) 869-7440
One Astor Plaza
1515 Broadway
New York, NY 10036

Premier organization for computer scientists and professionals. Has many educational and technical publications (some online) including those dealing with security and privacy issues.

Bankcard Holders of America
Phone: (540) 389-5445
524 Branch Drive
Salem, VA 24153

Consumer organization promoting rights of credit card users. Offers Debt Zapper, a program that analyzes a consumer's debt situation and suggests ways to reduce the debt. See Debt Zapper news online at URL: http://www.infl.com/zapper/news/.

Center for Democracy and Technology
URL: http://www.cdt.org/
E-mail (info): info@cdt.org
E-mail (general): ask@cdt.org
Phone: (202) 637-9800
1001 G Street Northwest
Suite 700E
Washington, DC 20001

A nonprofit public-interest organization that promotes technology policies and legislation that maximize constitutional principles of free speech and individual privacy.

Center for Media Education
URL: http://www.cme.org/cme/
E-mail: cme@cme.org
Phone: (202) 628-2620
1511 K Street, Northwest
Suite 518
Washington, DC 20005

A national nonprofit organization dedicated to improving the quality of electronic media, especially on the behalf of children and families. Provides guides, reports, and other information on children's and consumer privacy.

Coalition on New Office Technology
Office Technology Education Project
650 Beacon Street, 5th Floor
Boston, MA 02215

Organizes workers and advocates for workplace issues such as privacy and safety.

Communications Workers of America
URL: http://www3.cwa-union.org/home/index.html
E-mail: cwaweb@earthlink.net
Phone: (202) 434-1100
501 3rd Street, Northwest
Washington, DC 20001-2797

Calls itself "The union for the information age." Involved in a variety of workplace issues including worker monitoring and privacy.

Computer Emergency Response Team (CERT)
URL: http://www.cert.org/

E-mail: cert@cert.org
Phone: (412) 268-7090
CERT Coordination Center
Software Engineering Institute
Carnegie Mellon University
Pittsburgh, PA 15213-3890

An organization that attempts to respond quickly to disruptions of computer networks such as those caused by hacker attacks. Issues technical advisories on newly discovered vulnerabilities of computer operating systems.

Computer Professionals for Social Responsibility
URL: http://cpsr.org/cpsr
E-mail: cpsr-info@cpsr.org
Phone: (415) 322-3778
P.O. Box 717
Palo Alto, CA 94301

CPSR sponsors an annual conference, maintains numerous mailing lists on computer-related issues and a large Internet site of information. It also publishes a quarterly newsletter. CPSR sponsors working groups on civil liberties, working in the computer industry and other topics.

Computer Security Institute
URL: http://www.gocsi.com/
E-mail: csi@mfi.com
Phone: (415) 905-2626
600 Harrison Street
San Francisco, CA 94107

An organization for training computer security professionals, dealing with encryption, secure transaction systems, and other issues.

Computing Technology Industry Association (CompTIA)

URL: http://www.comptia.org/
E-mail: info@comptia.org
Phone: (630) 268-1818
450 East 22nd Street
Suite 230
Lombard, IL 60148-6158

A major computer industry association; certifies computer professionals and becomes involved in policy issues.

Consumer Action
URL: http://www.consumer-action.org/
E-mail: webmaster@consumer-action.org
Phone: (415) 777-9635
717 Market Street
Suite 310
San Francisco, CA 94103

A nonprofit consumer advocacy group founded in 1971. Advocates and lobbies for consumer rights, offers multilingual educational material through its National Consumer Resources Center. Its Credit and Finance Project provides links to agencies that can resolve personal credit problems.

Consumer Project on Technology
URL: http://www.cptech.org/
Phone: (202) 387-8030
P.O. Box 19367
Washington, DC 20036

CPT was created by Ralph Nader in the spring of 1995 to focus on a variety of issues, including telecommunications regulation; pricing of ISDN services; fair use under the copyright law; issues relating to the pricing, ownership, and development of pharmaceutical drugs; and impact of technology on personal privacy. Subscribe to its "notes" by sending e-mail to LISTPROC@ESSENTIAL. ORG and putting the following line in the message body: "sub info-pol-icy-notes (followed by your name)."

Direct Marketing Association
URL: http://www.the-dma.org/
E-mail: webmaster@the-dma.org
Phone: (212) 768-7277
1120 Avenue of the Americas
New York, NY 10036-6700

Organization for the promoting of direct marketing. Also runs the Telephone Preference Service (P.O. Box 9014, Farmingdale, NY 11735-9014) that consumers can use to prevent telemarketing calls.

Electronic Frontier Foundation (EFF)
URL: http://www.eff.org
E-mail: ask@eff.org
Phone: (415) 436-9333
1550 Bryant Street
Suite 725
San Francisco, CA 94103-4832

Organization formed in 1990 to maintain and enhance intellectual freedom, privacy, and other values of civil liberties and democracy in networked communications. Publishes newsletters, Internet guidebooks, and other documents; provides mailing lists and other online forums; and hosts a large electronic document archive.

Electronic Messaging Association
URL: http://www.ema.org/
E-mail: info@ema.org
Phone: (703) 524-5550
1655 North Fort Myer Drive

Suite 500
Arlington, VA 22209

An organization for development of electronic communications technology and policy; addresses e-mail privacy issues. Has a "privacy tool kit" available to businesses that seek to develop an e-mail policy.

Electronic Privacy Information Center (EPIC)
URL: http://www.epic.org
E-mail: info@epic.org
Phone: (202) 544-9240
666 Pennsylvania Avenue, Southeast
Suite 301
Washington, DC 20003

EPIC was established in 1994 to focus public attention on emerging privacy issues relating to the National Information Infrastructure, such as the Clipper Chip, the Digital Telephony proposal, medical records privacy, and the sale of consumer data. EPIC conducts litigation, sponsors conferences, produces reports, publishes the *EPIC Alert* and leads campaigns on privacy issues.

Equifax
URL: http://www.equifax.com/
Phone: 1-800-997-2493 (to order copy of credit report)
Equifax Information Service Center
P.O. Box 740241
Atlanta, GA 30374-0241

One of the three major credit bureaus. Can order credit reports at web site.

Experian
URL: http://www.experian.com/
Phone: 1-888-EXPERIAN
(to order credit report)
Experian National Consumer Assistance Center
P.O. Box 2104
Allen, TX 75013-2104

One of the three major credit bureaus. Can order credit reports at web site or remove name from mailing lists.

Federal Bureau of Investigation (FBI)
Phone: (202) 324-5520
FBI
Freedom of Information Privacy Section
935 Pennsylvania Avenue, Northwest
Washington, DC 20535

Citizens can find out if the FBI has records about them by writing to this address. Include complete name, address, place of birth, and notarized signature.

Federal Communications Commission
URL: http://www.fcc.gov/
E-mail: fccinfo@fcc.gov
Phone: 1-888-CALL-FCC
(general info)
1919 M Street Northwest
Washington, DC 20554

The principal federal regulatory agency for all interstate communications by wire, cable, radio, etc.

Federal Trade Commission
URL: http://www.ftc.gov/
Phone: (202) 326-2222
Public Reference Branch

Room 130, FTC
Washington, DC 20580

Federal regulatory agency that regulates many aspects of commerce, including regulations dealing with privacy and information disclosure.

Federation of American Scientists
Project on Government Secrecy
URL: http://www.fas.org/sgp/
Phone: (202) 675-1012
307 Massachusetts Avenue, Northeast
Washington, DC 20002

"Works to challenge excessive government secrecy and to promote public oversight."

Global Internet Liberty Campaign
URL: http://www.gilc.org/
E-mail: info@gilc.org

International coalition of 40 privacy, free speech, and human rights groups dedicated to fighting international threats to privacy and to free speech on the Internet.

Information Systems Security Association
URL: http://www.issa-intl.org/
E-mail: MbrMktg@NaSPA.Net
Phone: (414) 768-8000
Technical Enterprises, Inc.
7044 South 13th Street
Oak Creek, WI 53154

Trade and professional group involved in computer security and privacy issues.

Institute of Electrical and Electronics Engineers (IEEE)
Technical Committee on Security and Privacy

URL: http://www.ieee.org/
E-mail: application request
@ieee.org (for membership
application)
Phone: 800-678-4333
345 East 47th Street
New York, NY 10017

Emphasizes technical issues on computer security and privacy. Offers its newsletter, Cipher, by e-mail to cipher-request@itd.nrl.navy.mil with subject line "subscribe." The IEEE conducts an annual Symposium on Security and Privacy.

International Association for Cryptologic Research
URL: http://www.iacr.org
E-mail: webmaster@iacr.org
IACR General Secretariat
Santa Rosa Administrative Center
University of California—Santa Barbara
Santa Barbara, CA 93106-6120

International organization to further the study and development of cryptography.

International Computer Security Association (ICSA)
URL: http://www.ncsa.com/ncsamain.htm
Phone: (717) 258-1816, ext. 205
110 South Courthouse Avenue
Carlisle, PA 17013

Trade group that promotes security and encryption technology.

Internet Privacy Coalition
URL: http://www.privacy.org/ipc
E-mail: ipc@privacy.org

Coalition of cryptographers, public interest groups, and businesses encouraging the widespread use of cryptography and relaxation of export controls on cryptography. Organizes Golden Key Campaign. Subscribe to *IPC Alert* newsletter by sending e-mail to ipc-announce@privacy.org and put "subscribe ipc-announce" in message body.

Internet Service Providers' Consortium
URL: http://www.ispc.org/
Phone: (310) 827-8466
Deborah Howard, Executive Director
646A Venice Boulevard
Venice, CA 90291

Trade group for Internet service providers; lobbies against legislation that would hamper use of the Internet.

Internet Society
URL: http://www.isoc.org/
E-mail: isoc@isoc.org
Phone: (703) 648-9888
12020 Sunrise Valley Drive
Suite 210
Reston, VA 20191-3429

A wide-ranging professional organization devoted to shaping the future of the Internet. Deals with issues such as privacy and free expression that are important to keeping the Internet viable and growing.

Medical Information Bureau
URL: http://www.mib.com/
Phone: (617) 426-3660
MIB, Inc.
P.O. Box 105
Essex Station
Boston, MA 02112

Central clearinghouse for medical records information; designed primarily to fight insurance fraud. Attempts to deal with privacy concerns that arise in its distribution of medical records.

National Coalition for Patient Rights
URL: http://www.nationalcpr.org
E-mail: ncpr@nationalcpr.org
Phone: (781) 861-0635
405 Waltham Street
Suite 218
Lexington, MA 02173

Patients' rights organization; has privacy and the abuse of medical records by government or private companies as one of its main concerns.

National Employee Rights Institute
URL: http://www.workdoctor.com/ home/legal.html
Phone: (800) 469-6374
414 Walnut Street, No. 911
Cincinnati, OH 45202

Addresses workplace issues, including privacy.

Organization for Economic Cooperation and Development
URL: http://www.oecd.org/
E-mail: webmaster@oecd.org
Phone: +33 (0)1.45.24.82.00
2, rue André-Pascal
75775 Paris Cedex 16
FRANCE

Organization of 29 nations in Europe and Asia (and the United States and Mexico). It promotes development of the market economy. Includes policies and proposals relating to privacy, data security, and electronic commerce.

PGP Users' Mailing List
URL: http://pgp.rivertown.net/ charter.html

To subscribe send e-mail to: pgp-users-subscribe@joshua.rivertown.net
Internet mailing list covering all aspects of using the Pretty Good Privacy encryption program.

Privacy International
URL: http://www.privacy international.org
E-mail: pi@privacy.org
666 Pennsylvania Avenue, Southeast
Suite 301
Washington, DC 20003

International organization that monitors both government and private surveillance and threats to privacy.

Privacy Rights Clearinghouse
URL: http://www.privacyrights. org
E-mail: prc@privacyrights.org
Phone: (619) 298-3396
1717 Kettner Avenue
Suite 105
San Diego, CA 92101

Produces useful fact sheets and an annual report, and maintains a toll-free hot line to provide advice to consumers about their rights.

Private Citizen
URL: http://www.private-citizen. com
E-mail: pci@private-citizen.com
Phone: 1-800-CUT-JUNK

Gives consumers help for fighting junk mail, junk calls, including a *How to Sue a Telemarketer* book.

RISKS Digest
URL: http://catless.ncl.ac.uk/ Risks/15.30.html

To receive current postings, use web browser or news reader to access newsgroup: comp.risks

A Usenet newsgroup devoted to exploring the hidden risks and consequences that can arise from the computer systems upon which so much of our society now depends. Moderated by the ACM Committee on Computers and Public Policy.

Society for Electronic Access (SEA)
URL: http://www.sea.org/
Phone: (212) 592-3801
The Society for Electronic Access
P.O. Box 7081
New York, NY 10116-7081

Focuses on educating people about the potential uses of online technology and on promoting basic civil rights (including privacy) in cyberspace.

Software and Information Industry Association
Public Policy and Government Relations Council
URL: http://www.infoindustry.org/
E-mail: pubpol@infoindustry.org
Phone: (202) 986-0280
1625 Massachusetts Avenue
Suite 700
Washington, DC 20036

Trade group for the computer industry; involved in policy and legislative issues.

State Public Interest Groups (PIRGs)
URL: http://www.pirg.org/

The State Public Interest Research Groups (PIRGs) are nonprofit, nonpartisan consumer and environmental watchdog groups. Advocates for better consumer privacy laws, preventing identity theft, and correcting credit reports. Fact sheets and reports available on web. See also U.S. Public Interest Group.

Telecommunications Policy Roundtable
For information: contact Center for Media Education (q.v.)

To subscribe to mailing list, send e-mail to: listproc@cni.org. Put: "SUBSCRIBE ROUNDTABLE <firstname> <lastname>" in message body.
Phone: (202) 628-2620

A coalition of more than 100 organizations organized in 1993 to discuss federal telecommunications policy. This "umbrella group" includes several privacy-related organizations such as the Electronic Frontier Foundation.

Trans Union
URL: http://www.tuc.com/
Phone: (312) 258–1717
555 West Adams Street
Chicago, IL 60661

For credit report requests:
Trans Union Corporation
Consumer Disclosure Center
P.O. Box 390
Springfield, PA 19064-0390

One of the three major credit bureaus. Can order credit reports on the web site as well as see information about privacy rights and policies and "opting out" of mailing lists.

TRUSTe
URL: http://www.etrust.org/

Organization seeking to create policies and mechanisms for safe commerce on the Internet, including protection of privacy.

U.S. Department of Health and Human Services
URL: http://www.dhhs.gov
Phone: (202) 690-5896
200 Independence Avenue, Southwest
Washington, DC 20201

Has a number of policies and efforts relating to patient privacy; see web site for search forms.

U.S. Privacy Council
E-mail: privtime@access.digex.net.
Phone: (202) 829-3660
P.O. Box 15060
Washington, DC 20003

A coalition of U.S. privacy groups and individuals founded in 1991 to deal with privacy issues in the United States. USPC works in Washington monitoring legislation and the activities of government agencies. Interests include National ID cards, credit reporting, Caller ID, and international issues.

U.S. Public Interest Research Group
URL: http://www.igc.apc.org/ pirg/uspirg/index.htm
Phone: (202) 546-9707
218 D Street, Southeast
Washington, DC 20003-1900

The national public interest group; watchdog for environment and consumer rights. Has become more involved with privacy interests. See also State Public Interest Groups.

World Wide Web Consortium
URL: http://www.w3.org/
E-mail: kotok@w3.org
Phone: (617) 253-2613
U.S. Office:
Massachusetts Institute of Technology
Laboratory for Computer Science
545 Technology Square
Cambridge, MA 02139

International industry consortium for development of protocols and other standards to "lead the Web to its full potential." Includes a section for privacy, and is developing the Platform for Privacy Preferences, a way to have web sites uniformly disclose privacy practices and to allow users (or their software) to negotiate with them. See URL: http://www.w3. org/P3P/.

APPENDICES

APPENDIX A

U.S. SUPREME COURT RULING: *KATZ V. UNITED STATES*, 1967

KATZ v. UNITED STATES
CERTIORARI TO THE UNITED STATES
COURT OF APPEALS FOR THE NINTH
CIRCUIT. No. 35.

Argued October 17, 1967.
Decided December 18, 1967.

Petitioner was convicted under an indictment charging him with transmitting wagering information by telephone across state lines in violation of 18 U.S.C. 1084. Evidence of petitioner's end of the conversations, overheard by FBI agents who had attached an electronic listening and recording device to the outside of the telephone booth from which the calls were made, was introduced at the trial. The Court of Appeals affirmed the conviction, finding that there was no Fourth Amendment violation since there was "no physical entrance into the area occupied by" petitioner. Held:

1. The Government's eavesdropping activities violated the privacy upon which petitioner justifiably relied while using the telephone booth and thus constituted a "search and seizure" within the meaning of the Fourth Amendment. Pp. 350–353.

(a) The Fourth Amendment governs not only the seizure of tangible items but extends as well to the recording of oral statements. Silverman v. United States, 365 U.S. 505, 511. P. 353.

(b) Because the Fourth Amendment protects people rather than places, its reach cannot turn on the presence or absence of a physical intrusion into any given enclosure. The "trespass" doctrine of Olmstead v. United States, 277 U.S. 438, and Goldman v. United States, 316 U.S. 129, is no longer controlling. Pp. 351, 353.

Appendix A

---

2. Although the surveillance in this case may have been so narrowly circumscribed that it could constitutionally have been authorized in advance, it was not in fact conducted pursuant to the warrant procedure which is a constitutional precondition of such electronic surveillance. Pp. 354–359.

369 F.2d 130, reversed.

Burton Marks and Harvey A. Schneider argued the cause and filed briefs for petitioner. [389 U.S. 347, 348]

John S. Martin, Jr., argued the cause for the United States. With him on the brief were Acting Solicitor General Spritzer, Assistant Attorney General Vinson and Beatrice Rosenberg.

MR. JUSTICE STEWART delivered the opinion of the Court.

The petitioner was convicted in the District Court for the Southern District of California under an eight-count indictment charging him with transmitting wagering information by telephone from Los Angeles to Miami and Boston, in violation of a federal statute. At trial the Government was permitted, over the petitioner's objection, to introduce evidence of the petitioner's end of telephone conversations, overheard by FBI agents who had attached an electronic listening and recording device to the outside of the public telephone booth from which he had placed his calls. In affirming his conviction, the Court of Appeals rejected the contention that the recordings had been obtained in violation of the Fourth Amendment, [389 U.S. 347, 349] because "[t]here was no physical entrance into the area occupied by [the petitioner]." We granted certiorari in order to consider the constitutional questions thus presented.

The petitioner has phrased those questions as follows:

"A. Whether a public telephone booth is a constitutionally protected area so that evidence obtained by attaching an electronic listening recording device to the top of such a booth is obtained in violation of the right to privacy of the user of the booth. [389 U.S. 347, 350]

"B. Whether physical penetration of a constitutionally protected area is necessary before a search and seizure can be said to be violative of the Fourth Amendment to the United States Constitution."

We decline to adopt this formulation of the issues. In the first place, the correct solution of Fourth Amendment problems is not necessarily promoted by incantation of the phrase "constitutionally protected area." Secondly, the Fourth Amendment cannot be translated into a general constitutional "right to privacy." That Amendment protects individual privacy against certain kinds of governmental intrusion, but its protections go further, and often have nothing to do with privacy at all. Other provisions of the Constitution protect personal privacy from other forms of governmental invasion. But the protection of a person's general right to privacy—his right to be let alone by other people—is, like the [389 U.S. 347, 351] protection of his property and of his very life, left largely to the law of the individual States.

Because of the misleading way the issues have been formulated, the parties have attached great significance to the characterization of the telephone booth from which the petitioner placed his calls. The petitioner has strenuously argued that the booth was a "constitutionally protected area." The Government has maintained with equal vigor that it was not. But this effort to decide whether or not a given "area," viewed in the abstract, is "constitutionally protected" deflects attention from the problem presented by this case. For the Fourth Amendment protects people, not places. What a person knowingly exposes to the public, even in his own home or office, is not a subject of Fourth Amendment protection. See Lewis v. United States, 385 U.S. 206, 210; United States v. Lee, 274 U.S. 559, 563. But what he seeks to preserve as private, even in an area accessible to the public, may be constitutionally protected. [389 U.S. 347, 352] See Rios v. United States, 364 U.S. 253; Ex parte Jackson, 96 U.S. 727, 733.

The Government stresses the fact that the telephone booth from which the petitioner made his calls was constructed partly of glass, so that he was as visible after he entered it as he would have been if he had remained outside. But what he sought to exclude when he entered the booth was not the intruding eye—it was the uninvited ear. He did not shed his right to do so simply because he made his calls from a place where he might be seen. No less than an individual in a business office, in a friend's apartment, or in a taxicab, a person in a telephone booth may rely upon the protection of the Fourth Amendment. One who occupies it, shuts the door behind him, and pays the toll that permits him to place a call is surely entitled to assume that the words he utters into the mouthpiece will not be broadcast to the world. To read the Constitution more narrowly is to ignore the vital role that the public telephone has come to play in private communication.

The Government contends, however, that the activities of its agents in this case should not be tested by Fourth Amendment requirements, for the surveillance technique they employed involved no physical penetration of the telephone booth from which the petitioner placed his calls. It is true that the absence of such penetration was at one time thought to foreclose further Fourth Amendment inquiry, Olmstead v. United States, 277 U.S. 438, 457, 464, 466; Goldman v. United States, 316 U.S. 129, 134–136, for that Amendment was thought to limit only searches and seizures of tangible [389 U.S. 347, 353] property. But "[t]he premise that property interests control the right of the Government to search and seize has been discredited." Warden v. Hayden, 387 U.S. 294, 304. Thus, although a closely divided Court supposed in Olmstead that surveillance without any trespass and without the seizure of any material object fell outside the ambit of the Constitution, we have since departed from the narrow view on which that decision rested. Indeed, we have expressly held that the Fourth Amendment governs not only the seizure of tangible items, but extends as well to the recording of oral statements, overheard without any "technical trespass under . . . local property law." Silverman v. United States, 365 U.S. 505, 511. Once this much is acknowledged, and once it is recognized that the Fourth Amendment protects people—and not simply "areas"—against unreasonable searches and seizures, it becomes clear that the reach of that Amendment cannot turn upon the presence or absence of a physical intrusion into any given enclosure.

We conclude that the underpinnings of Olmstead and Goldman have been so eroded by our subsequent decisions that the "trespass" doctrine there enunciated can no longer be regarded as controlling. The Government's activities in electronically listening to and recording the petitioner's words violated the privacy upon which he justifiably relied while using the telephone booth and thus constituted a "search and seizure" within the meaning of the Fourth Amendment. The fact that the electronic device employed to achieve that end did not happen to penetrate the wall of the booth can have no constitutional significance. [389 U.S. 347, 354]

The question remaining for decision, then, is whether the search and seizure conducted in this case complied with constitutional standards. In that regard, the Government's position is that its agents acted in an entirely defensible manner: They did not begin their electronic surveillance until investigation of the petitioner's activities had established a strong probability that he was using the telephone in question to transmit gambling information to persons in other States, in violation of federal law. Moreover, the surveillance was limited, both in scope and in duration, to the specific purpose of establishing the contents of the petitioner's unlawful telephonic communications. The agents confined their surveillance to the brief periods during which he used the telephone booth, and they took great care to overhear only the conversations of the petitioner himself.

Accepting this account of the Government's actions as accurate, it is clear that this surveillance was so narrowly circumscribed that a duly authorized magistrate, properly notified of the need for such investigation, specifically informed of the basis on which it was to proceed, and clearly apprised of the precise intrusion it would entail, could constitutionally have authorized, with appropriate safeguards, the very limited search and seizure that the Government asserts in fact took place. Only last Term was sustained the validity of [389 U.S. 347, 355] such an authorization, holding that, under sufficiently "precise and discriminate circumstances," a federal court may empower government agents to employ a concealed electronic device "for the narrow and particularized purpose of ascertaining the truth of the . . . allegations" of a "detailed factual affidavit alleging the commission of a specific criminal offense." Osborn v. United States, 385 U.S. 323, 329–330. Discussing that holding, the Court in Berger v. New York, 388 U.S. 41, said that "the order authorizing the use of the electronic device" in Osborn "afforded similar protections to those . . . of conventional warrants authorizing the seizure of tangible evidence." Through those protections, "no greater invasion of privacy was permitted than was necessary under the circumstances." Id., at 57. Here, too, a similar [389 U.S. 347, 356] judicial order could have accommodated "the legitimate needs of law enforcement" by authorizing the carefully limited use of electronic surveillance.

The Government urges that, because its agents relied upon the decisions in Olmstead and Goldman, and because they did no more here than they might properly have done with prior judicial sanction, we should retroactively validate their conduct. That we cannot do. It is apparent that the agents in this case acted with restraint. Yet the inescapable fact is that this restraint was imposed by the agents themselves, not by a judicial officer. They were not required, before commencing the search, to present their estimate of probable cause for detached scrutiny by a neutral magistrate. They were not compelled, during the conduct of the search itself, to observe precise limits established in advance by a specific court order. Nor were they directed, after the search had been completed, to notify the authorizing magistrate in detail of all that had been seized. In the absence of such safeguards, this Court has never sustained a search upon the sole ground that officers reasonably expected to find evidence of a particular crime and voluntarily confined their activities to the least intrusive [389 U.S. 347, 357] means consistent with that end. Searches conducted without warrants have been held unlawful "notwithstanding facts unquestionably showing probable cause," Agnello v. United States, 269 U.S. 20, 33, for the Constitution requires "that the deliberate, impartial judgment of a judicial officer . . . be interposed between the citizen and the police. . . ." Wong Sun v. United States, 371 U.S. 471, 481–482. "Over and again this Court has emphasized that the mandate of the [Fourth] Amendment requires adherence to judicial processes," United States v. Jeffers, 342 U.S. 48, 51, and that searches conducted outside the judicial process, without prior approval by judge or magistrate, are per se unreasonable under the Fourth Amendment—subject only to a few specifically established and well-delineated exceptions.

It is difficult to imagine how any of those exceptions could ever apply to the sort of search and seizure involved in this case. Even electronic surveillance substantially contemporaneous with an individual's arrest could hardly be deemed an "incident" of that arrest. [389 U.S. 347, 358] Nor could the use of electronic surveillance without prior authorization be justified on grounds of "hot pursuit." And, of course, the very nature of electronic surveillance precludes its use pursuant to the suspect's consent.

The Government does not question these basic principles. Rather, it urges the creation of a new exception to cover this case. It argues that surveillance of a telephone booth should be exempted from the usual requirement of advance authorization by a magistrate upon a showing of probable cause. We cannot agree. Omission of such authorization "bypasses the safeguards provided by an objective predetermination of probable cause, and substitutes instead the far less reliable procedure of an after-the-event justification for the . . . search, too likely to be subtly influenced by the familiar shortcomings of hindsight judgment." Beck v. Ohio, 379 U.S. 89, 96.

And bypassing a neutral predetermination of the scope of a search leaves individuals secure from Fourth Amendment [389 U.S. 347, 359] violations "only in the discretion of the police." Id., at 97.

These considerations do not vanish when the search in question is transferred from the setting of a home, an office, or a hotel room to that of a telephone booth. Wherever a man may be, he is entitled to know that he will remain free from unreasonable searches and seizures. The government agents here ignored "the procedure of antecedent justification . . . that is central to the Fourth Amendment," a procedure that we hold to be a constitutional precondition of the kind of electronic surveillance involved in this case. Because the surveillance here failed to meet that condition, and because it led to the petitioner's conviction, the judgment must be reversed.
It is so ordered.

MR. JUSTICE MARSHALL took no part in the consideration or decision of this case.

[All Footnotes and Footnote references have been omitted.]

APPENDIX B

FREEDOM OF INFORMATION ACT (5 USC 552)

-CITE-
5 USC Sec. 552
-EXPCITE-
TITLE 5—GOVERNMENT ORGANIZATION AND EMPLOYEES
PART I—THE AGENCIES GENERALLY
CHAPTER 5—ADMINISTRATIVE PROCEDURE
SUBCHAPTER II—ADMINISTRATIVE PROCEDURE
-HEAD-
Sec. 552. Public information; agency rules, opinions, orders, records, and proceedings
-STATUTE-

(a) Each agency shall make available to the public information as follows:

(1) Each agency shall separately state and currently publish in the Federal Register for the guidance of the public—

(A) descriptions of its central and field organization and the established places at which, the employees (and in the case of a uniformed service, the members) from whom, and the methods whereby, the public may obtain information, make submittals or requests, or obtain decisions;

(B) statements of the general course and method by which its functions are channeled and determined, including the nature and requirements of all formal and informal procedures available;

(C) rules of procedure, descriptions of forms available or the places at which forms may be obtained, and instructions as to the scope and contents of all papers, reports, or examinations;

(D) substantive rules of general applicability adopted as authorized by law, and statements of general policy or interpretations of general applicability formulated and adopted by the agency; and

(E) each amendment, revision, or repeal of the foregoing.

Except to the extent that a person has actual and timely notice of the terms thereof, a person may not in any manner be required to resort to, or be adversely affected by, a matter required to be published in the Federal Register and not so published. For the purpose of this paragraph, matter reasonably available to the class of persons affected thereby is deemed published in the Federal Register when incorporated by reference therein with the approval of the Director of the Federal Register.

(2) Each agency, in accordance with published rules, shall make available for public inspection and copying—

(A) final opinions, including concurring and dissenting opinions, as well as orders, made in the adjudication of cases;

(B) those statements of policy and interpretations which have been adopted by the agency and are not published in the Federal Register;

(C) administrative staff manuals and instructions to staff that affect a member of the public;

(D) copies of all records, regardless of form or format, which have been released to any person under paragraph (3) and which, because of the nature of their subject matter, the agency determines have become or are likely to become the subject of subsequent requests for substantially the same records; and

(E) a general index of the records referred to under subparagraph (D); unless the materials are promptly published and copies offered for sale. For records created on or after November 1, 1996, within one year after such date, each agency shall make such records available, including by computer telecommunications or, if computer telecommunications means have not been established by the agency, by other electronic means. To the extent required to prevent a clearly unwarranted invasion of personal privacy, an agency may delete identifying details when it makes available or publishes an opinion, statement of policy, interpretation, staff manual, instruction, or copies of records referred to in subparagraph (D). However, in each case the justification for the deletion shall be explained fully in writing, and the extent of such deletion shall be indicated on the portion of the record which is made available or published, unless including that indication would harm an interest protected by the exemption in subsection (b) under which the deletion is made. If technically feasible, the extent of the deletion shall be indicated at the place in the record where the deletion was made. Each agency shall also maintain and make available for public inspection and copying current indexes providing identifying information for the public as to any matter issued, adopted, or promulgated after July 4, 1967, and required by this paragraph to be made available or published. Each agency shall promptly publish, quarterly or more frequently, and distribute (by sale or otherwise) copies of each index or supplements thereto unless it determines by order published in the Federal Register that the publication would be unnecessary and impracticable, in which case the agency shall nonetheless provide copies of such index on request at a cost not to exceed the direct cost of duplication. Each agency shall make the index referred to in subparagraph

(E) available by computer telecommunications by December 31, 1999. A final order, opinion, statement of policy, interpretation, or staff manual or instruction that affects a member of the public may be relied on, used, or cited as precedent by an agency against a party other than an agency only if—

(i) it has been indexed and either made available or published as provided by this paragraph; or

(ii) the party has actual and timely notice of the terms thereof.

(3) (A) Except with respect to the records made available under paragraphs (1) and (2) of this subsection, each agency, upon any request for records which (i) reasonably describes such records and (ii) is made in accordance with published rules stating the time, place, fees (if any), and procedures to be followed, shall make the records promptly available to any person.

(B) In making any record available to a person under this paragraph, an agency shall provide the record in any form or format requested by the person if the record is readily reproducible by the agency in that form or format. Each agency shall make reasonable efforts to maintain its records in forms or formats that are reproducible for purposes of this section.

(C) In responding under this paragraph to a request for records, an agency shall make reasonable efforts to search for the records in electronic form or format, except when such efforts would significantly interfere with the operation of the agency's automated information system.

(D) For purposes of this paragraph, the term "search" means to review, manually or by automated means, agency records for the purpose of locating those records which are responsive to a request.

(4) (A) (i) In order to carry out the provisions of this section, each agency shall promulgate regulations, pursuant to notice and receipt of public comment, specifying the schedule of fees applicable to the processing of requests under this section and establishing procedures and guidelines for determining when such fees should be waived or reduced. Such schedule shall conform to the guidelines which shall be promulgated, pursuant to notice and receipt of public comment, by the Director of the Office of Management and Budget and which shall provide for a uniform schedule of fees for all agencies.

(ii) Such agency regulations shall provide that—

(I) fees shall be limited to reasonable standard charges for document search, duplication, and review, when records are requested for commercial use;

(II) fees shall be limited to reasonable standard charges for document duplication when records are not sought for commercial use and the request is made by an educational or noncommercial scientific institution, whose purpose is scholarly or scientific research; or a representative of the news media; and

(III) for any request not described in (I) or (II), fees shall be limited to reasonable standard charges for document search and duplication.

(iii) Documents shall be furnished without any charge or at a charge reduced below the fees established under clause (ii) if disclosure of the information is in the public interest because it is likely to contribute significantly to public understanding of the operations or activities of the government and is not primarily in the commercial interest of the requester.

(iv) Fee schedules shall provide for the recovery of only the direct costs of search, duplication, or review. Review costs shall include only the direct costs incurred during the initial examination of a document for the purposes of determining whether the documents must be disclosed under this section and for the purposes of withholding any portions exempt from disclosure under this section. Review costs may not include any costs incurred in resolving issues of law or policy that may be raised in the course of processing a request under this section. No fee may be charged by any agency under this section—

(I) if the costs of routine collection and processing of the fee are likely to equal or exceed the amount of the fee; or

(II) for any request described in clause (ii) (II) or (III) of this subparagraph for the first two hours of search time or for the first one hundred pages of duplication.

(v) No agency may require advance payment of any fee unless the requester has previously failed to pay fees in a timely fashion, or the agency has determined that the fee will exceed $250.

(vi) Nothing in this subparagraph shall supersede fees chargeable under a statute specifically providing for setting the level of fees for particular types of records.

(vii) In any action by a requester regarding the waiver of fees under this section, the court shall determine the matter de novo: Provided, That the court's review of the matter shall be limited to the record before the agency.

(B) On complaint, the district court of the United States in the district in which the complainant resides, or has his principal place of business, or in which the agency records are situated, or in the District of Columbia, has jurisdiction to enjoin the agency from withholding agency records and to order the production of any agency records improperly withheld from the complainant. In such a case the court shall determine the matter de novo, and may examine the contents of such agency records in camera to determine whether such records or any part thereof shall be withheld under any of the exemptions set forth in subsection (b) of this section, and the burden is on the agency to sustain its action. In addition to any other matters to which a court accords substantial weight, a court shall accord substantial weight to an affidavit of an agency concerning the agency's determination as to technical feasibility under paragraph (2) (C) and subsection (b) and reproducibility under paragraph (3) (B).

(C) Notwithstanding any other provision of law, the defendant shall serve an answer or otherwise plead to any complaint made under this subsection within thirty days after service upon the defendant of the pleading in which such complaint is made, unless the court otherwise directs for good cause shown.

(D) Repealed. Pub. L. 98-620, title IV, Sec. 402(2), Nov. 8, 1984, 98 Stat. 3357.)

(E) The court may assess against the United States reasonable attorney fees and other litigation costs reasonably incurred in any case under this section in which the complainant has substantially prevailed.

(F) Whenever the court orders the production of any agency records improperly withheld from the complainant and assesses against the United States reasonable attorney fees and other litigation costs, and the court additionally issues a written finding that the circumstances surrounding the withholding raise questions whether agency personnel acted arbitrarily or capriciously with respect to the withholding, the Special Counsel shall promptly initiate a proceeding to determine whether disciplinary action is warranted against the officer or employee who was primarily responsible for the withholding. The Special Counsel, after investigation and consideration of the evidence submitted, shall submit his findings and recommendations to the administrative authority of the agency concerned and shall send copies of the findings and recommendations to the officer or employee or his representative. The administrative authority shall take the corrective action that the Special Counsel recommends.

(G) In the event of noncompliance with the order of the court, the district court may punish for contempt the responsible employee, and in the case of a uniformed service, the responsible member.

(5) Each agency having more than one member shall maintain and make available for public inspection a record of the final votes of each member in every agency proceeding.

(6) (A) Each agency, upon any request for records made under paragraph (1), (2), or (3) of this subsection, shall—

(i) determine within 20 days (excepting Saturdays, Sundays, and legal public holidays) after the receipt of any such request whether to comply with such request and shall immediately notify the person making such request of such determination and the reasons therefor, and of the right of such person to appeal to the head of the agency any adverse determination; and

(ii) make a determination with respect to any appeal within twenty days (excepting Saturdays, Sundays, and legal public holidays) after the receipt of such appeal. If on appeal the denial of the request for records is in whole or in part upheld, the agency shall notify the person making such request of the provisions for judicial review of that determination under paragraph (4) of this subsection.

(B) (i) In unusual circumstances as specified in this subparagraph, the time limits prescribed in either clause (i) or clause (ii) of subparagraph (A) may be extended by written notice to the person making such request setting forth the unusual circumstances for such extension and the date on which a determination is expected to be dispatched. No such notice shall specify a date that would result in an extension for more than ten working days, except as provided in clause (ii) of this subparagraph.

(ii) With respect to a request for which a written notice under clause (i) extends the time limits prescribed under clause (i) of subparagraph (A), the agency shall notify the person making the request if the request cannot be processed within the time limit specified in that clause and shall provide the person an opportunity to limit the scope of the request so that it may be processed within that time limit or an opportunity to arrange with the agency an alternative time frame for processing the request or a modified request. Refusal by the person to reasonably modify the request or arrange such an alternative time frame shall be considered as a factor in determining whether exceptional circumstances exist for purposes of subparagraph (C).

(iii) As used in this subparagraph, "unusual circumstances" means, but only to the extent reasonably necessary to the proper processing of the particular requests—

(I) the need to search for and collect the requested records from field facilities or other establishments that are separate from the office processing the request;

(II) the need to search for, collect, and appropriately examine a voluminous amount of separate and distinct records which are demanded in a single request; or

(III) the need for consultation, which shall be conducted with all practicable speed, with another agency having a substantial interest in the determination of the request or among two or more components of the agency having substantial subject-matter interest therein.

(iv) Each agency may promulgate regulations, pursuant to notice and receipt of public comment, providing for the aggregation of certain requests by the same requestor, or by a group of requestors acting in concert, if the agency reasonably believes that such requests actually constitute a single request, which would otherwise satisfy the unusual circumstances specified in this subparagraph, and the requests involve clearly related matters. Multiple requests involving unrelated matters shall not be aggregated.

(C) (i) Any person making a request to any agency for records under paragraph (1), (2), or (3) of this subsection shall be deemed to have exhausted his administrative remedies with respect to such request if the agency fails to comply with the applicable time limit provisions of this paragraph. If the Government can show exceptional circumstances exist and that the agency is exercising due diligence in responding to the request, the court may retain jurisdiction and allow the agency additional time to complete its review of the records. Upon any determination by an agency to comply with a request for records, the records shall be made promptly available to such person making such request. Any notification of denial of any request for records under this subsection shall set forth the names and titles or positions of each person responsible for the denial of such request.

(ii) For purposes of this subparagraph, the term "exceptional circumstances" does not include a delay that results from a predictable agency workload of requests under this section, unless the agency demonstrates reasonable progress in reducing its backlog of pending requests.

(iii) Refusal by a person to reasonably modify the scope of a request or arrange an alternative time frame for processing a request (or a modified request) under clause (ii) after being given an opportunity to do so by the agency to whom the person made the request shall be considered as a factor in determining whether exceptional circumstances exist for purposes of this subparagraph.

(D) (i) Each agency may promulgate regulations, pursuant to notice and receipt of public comment, providing for multitrack processing of requests for records based on the amount of work or time (or both) involved in processing requests.

(ii) Regulations under this subparagraph may provide a person making a request that does not qualify for the fastest multitrack processing an opportunity to limit the scope of the request in order to qualify for faster processing.

(iii) This subparagraph shall not be considered to affect the requirement under subparagraph (C) to exercise due diligence.

(E) (i) Each agency shall promulgate regulations, pursuant to notice and receipt of public comment, providing for expedited processing of requests for records—

(I) in cases in which the person requesting the records demonstrates a compelling need; and

(II) in other cases determined by the agency.

(ii) Notwithstanding clause (i), regulations under this subparagraph must ensure—

(I) that a determination of whether to provide expedited processing shall be made, and notice of the determination shall be provided to the person making the request, within 10 days after the date of the request; and

(II) expeditious consideration of administrative appeals of such determinations of whether to provide expedited processing.

(iii) An agency shall process as soon as practicable any request for records to which the agency has granted expedited processing under this subparagraph. Agency action to deny or affirm denial of a request for expedited processing pursuant to this subparagraph, and failure by an agency to respond in a timely manner to such a request shall be subject to judicial review under paragraph (4), except that the judicial review shall be based on the record before the agency at the time of the determination.

(iv) A district court of the United States shall not have jurisdiction to review an agency denial of expedited processing of a request for records after the agency has provided a complete response to the request.

(v) For purposes of this subparagraph, the term "compelling need" means—

(I) that a failure to obtain requested records on an expedited basis under this paragraph could reasonably be expected to pose an imminent threat to the life or physical safety of an individual; or

(II) with respect to a request made by a person primarily engaged in disseminating *information*, urgency to inform the public concerning actual or alleged Federal Government activity.

(vi) A demonstration of a compelling need by a person making a request for expedited processing shall be made by a statement certified by such person to be true and correct to the best of such person's knowledge and belief.

(F) In denying a request for records, in whole or in part, an agency shall make a reasonable effort to estimate the volume of any requested matter the provision of which is denied, and shall provide any such estimate to the person making the request, unless providing such estimate would harm an interest protected by the exemption in subsection (b) pursuant to which the denial is made.

(b) This section does not apply to matters that are—

(1) (A) specifically authorized under criteria established by an Executive order to be kept secret in the interest of national defense or foreign policy and (B) are in fact properly classified pursuant to such Executive order;

(2) related solely to the internal personnel rules and practices of an agency;

(3) specifically exempted from disclosure by statute (other than section 552b of this title), provided that such statute (A) requires that the matters be withheld from the public in such a manner as to leave no discretion on the issue, or (B) establishes particular criteria for withholding or refers to particular types of matters to be withheld;

(4) trade secrets and commercial or financial information obtained from a person and privileged or confidential;

(5) inter-agency or intra-agency memorandums or letters which would not be available by law to a party other than an agency in litigation with the agency;

(6) personnel and medical files and similar files the disclosure of which would constitute a clearly unwarranted invasion of personal privacy;

(7) records or information compiled for law enforcement purposes, but only to the extent that the production of such law enforcement records or information (A) could reasonably be expected to interfere with enforcement proceedings, (B) would deprive a person of a right to a fair trial or an impartial adjudication, (C) could reasonably be expected to constitute an unwarranted invasion of personal privacy, (D) could reasonably be expected to disclose the identity of a confidential source, including a State, local, or foreign agency or authority or any private institution which furnished information on a confidential basis, and, in the case of a record or information compiled by criminal law enforcement authority in the course of a criminal investigation or by an agency conducting a lawful national security intelligence investigation, information furnished by a confidential source, (E) would disclose techniques and procedures for law enforcement investigations or prosecutions, or would disclose guidelines for law enforcement investigations or prosecutions if such disclosure could reasonably be expected to risk circumvention of the law, or (F) could reasonably be expected to endanger the life or physical safety of any individual;

(8) contained in or related to examination, operating, or condition reports prepared by, on behalf of, or for the use of an agency responsible for the regulation or supervision of financial institutions; or

(9) geological and geophysical information and data, including maps, concerning wells.

Any reasonably segregable portion of a record shall be provided to any person requesting such record after deletion of the portions which are exempt under this subsection. The amount of information deleted shall be indicated on the released portion of the record, unless including that indication would harm an interest protected by the exemption in this subsection under which the deletion is made. If technically feasible, the amount of the information deleted shall be indicated at the place in the record where such deletion is made.

(c) (1) Whenever a request is made which involves access to records described in subsection (b) (7) (A) and—

(A) the investigation or proceeding involves a possible violation of criminal law; and

(B) there is reason to believe that (i) the subject of the investigation or proceeding is not aware of its pendency, and (ii) disclosure of the existence of the records could reasonably be expected to interfere with enforcement proceedings, the agency may, during only such time as that circumstance continues, treat the records as not subject to the requirements of this section.

(2) Whenever informant records maintained by a criminal law enforcement agency under an informant's name or personal identifier are requested by a third party according to the informant's name or personal identifier, the agency may treat the records as not subject to the requirements of this section unless the informant's status as an informant has been officially confirmed.

(3) Whenever a request is made which involves access to records maintained by the Federal Bureau of Investigation pertaining to foreign intelligence or counterintelligence, or international terrorism, and the existence of the records is classified information as provided in subsection (b) (1), the Bureau may, as long as the existence of the records remains classified information, treat the records as not subject to the requirements of this section.

(d) This section does not authorize withholding of information or limit the availability of records to the public, except as specifically stated in this section. This section is not authority to withhold information from Congress.

(e) (1) On or before February 1 of each year, each agency shall submit to the Attorney General of the United States a report which shall cover the preceding fiscal year and which shall include—

(A) the number of determinations made by the agency not to comply with requests for records made to such agency under subsection (a) and the reasons for each such determination;

(B) (i) the number of appeals made by persons under subsection (a) (6), the result of such appeals, and the reason for the action upon each appeal that results in a denial of information; and

(ii) a complete list of all statutes that the agency relies upon to authorize the agency to withhold information under subsection (b) (3), a description of whether a court has upheld the decision of the agency to withhold information under each such statute, and a concise description of the scope of any information withheld;

(C) the number of requests for records pending before the agency as of September 30 of the preceding year, and the median number of days that such requests had been pending before the agency as of that date;

(D) the number of requests for records received by the agency and the number of requests which the agency processed;

(E) the median number of days taken by the agency to process different types of requests;

(F) the total amount of fees collected by the agency for processing requests; and

(G) the number of full-time staff of the agency devoted to processing requests for records under this section, and the total amount expended by the agency for processing such requests.

(2) Each agency shall make each such report available to the public including by computer telecommunications, or if computer telecommunications means have not been established by the agency, by other electronic means.

(3) The Attorney General of the United States shall make each report which has been made available by electronic means available at a single electronic access point. The Attorney General of the United States shall notify the Chairman and ranking minority member of the Committee on Government Reform and Oversight of the House of Representatives and the Chairman and ranking minority member of the Committees on Governmental Affairs and the Judiciary of the Senate, no later than April 1 of the year in which each such report is issued, that such reports are available by electronic means.

(4) The Attorney General of the United States, in consultation with the Director of the Office of Management and Budget, shall develop reporting and performance guidelines in connection with reports required by this subsection by October 1, 1997, and may establish additional requirements for such reports as the Attorney General determines may be useful.

(5) The Attorney General of the United States shall submit an annual report on or before April 1 of each calendar year which shall include for the prior calendar year a listing of the number of cases arising under this section, the exemption involved in each case, the disposition of such case, and the cost, fees, and penalties assessed under subparagraphs (E), (F), and (G) of subsection (a) (4). Such report shall also include a description of the efforts undertaken by the Department of Justice to encourage agency compliance with this section.

(f) For purposes of this section, the term—

(1) "agency" as defined in section 551(1) of this title includes any executive department, military department, Government corporation, Government controlled corporation, or other establishment in the executive branch of the Government (including the Executive Office of the President), or any independent regulatory agency; and

(2) "record" and any other term used in this section in reference to information includes any information that would be an agency record subject to the requirements of this section when maintained by an agency in any format, including an electronic format.

(g) The head of each agency shall prepare and make publicly available upon request, reference material or a guide for requesting records or information from the agency, subject to the exemptions in subsection (b), including—

(1) an index of all major information systems of the agency;

(2) a description of major information and record locator systems maintained by the agency; and

(3) a handbook for obtaining various types and categories of public *information* from the agency pursuant to chapter 35 of title 44, and under this section.

-SOURCE-

(Pub. L. 89–554, Sept. 6, 1966, 80 Stat. 383; Pub. L. 90–23, Sec. 1, June 5, 1967, 81 Stat. 54; Pub. L. 93–502, Sec. 1–3, Nov. 21, 1974, 88 Stat. 1561–1564; Pub. L. 94–409, Sec. 5(b), Sept. 13, 1976, 90 Stat. 1247; Pub. L. 95–454, title IX, Sec. 906(a)(10), Oct. 13, 1978, 92 Stat. 1225; Pub. L. 98–620, title IV, Sec. 402(2), Nov. 8, 1984, 98 Stat. 3357; Pub. L. 99–570, title I, Sec. 1802, 1803, Oct. 27, 1986, 100 Stat. 3207–48, 3207–49; Pub. L. 104–231, Sec. 3–11, Oct. 2, 1996, 110 Stat. 3049–3054.)

APPENDIX C

PRIVACY ACT OF 1974

-CITE-
5 USC Sec. 552a
-EXPCITE-
TITLE 5—GOVERNMENT ORGANIZATION AND EMPLOYEES
PART I—THE AGENCIES GENERALLY
CHAPTER 5—ADMINISTRATIVE PROCEDURE
SUBCHAPTER II—ADMINISTRATIVE PROCEDURE
-HEAD-
Sec. 552a. Records maintained on individuals
-STATUTE-

(a) Definitions.—For purposes of this section—

(1) the term "agency" means agency as defined in section 552(e) (FOOTNOTE 1) of this title;

(FOOTNOTE 1) See References in Text note below.

(2) the term "individual" means a citizen of the United States or an alien lawfully admitted for permanent residence;

(3) the term "maintain" includes maintain, collect, use, or disseminate;

(4) the term "record" means any item, collection, or grouping of information about an individual that is maintained by an agency, including, but not limited to, his education, financial transactions, medical history, and criminal or employment history and that contains his name, or the identifying number, symbol, or other identifying particular assigned to the individual, such as a finger or voice print or a photograph;

(5) the term "system of records" means a group of any records under the control of any agency from which information is retrieved by the name of the individual or by some identifying number, symbol, or other identifying particular assigned to the individual;

(6) the term "statistical record" means a record in a system of records maintained for statistical research or reporting purposes only and not used in whole or in part in making any determination about an identifiable individual, except as provided by section 8 of title 13;

(7) the term "routine use" means, with respect to the disclosure of a record, the use of such record for a purpose which is compatible with the purpose for which it was collected;

(8) the term "matching program"—

(A) means any computerized comparison of—

(i) two or more automated systems of records or a system of records with non-Federal records for the purpose of—

(I) establishing or verifying the eligibility of, or continuing compliance with statutory and regulatory requirements by, applicants for, recipients or beneficiaries of, participants in, or providers of services with respect to, cash or in-kind assistance or payments under Federal benefit programs, or

(II) recouping payments or delinquent debts under such Federal benefit programs, or

(ii) two or more automated Federal personnel or payroll systems of records or a system of Federal personnel or payroll records with non-Federal records,

(B) but does not include—

(i) matches performed to produce aggregate statistical data without any personal identifiers;

(ii) matches performed to support any research or statistical project, the specific data of which may not be used to make decisions concerning the rights, benefits, or privileges of specific individuals;

(iii) matches performed, by an agency (or component thereof) which performs as its principal function any activity pertaining to the enforcement of criminal laws, subsequent to the initiation of a specific criminal or civil law enforcement investigation of a named person or persons for the purpose of gathering evidence against such person or persons;

(iv) matches of tax information (I) pursuant to section 6103(d) of the Internal Revenue Code of 1986, (II) for purposes of tax administration as defined in section 6103(b)(4) of such Code, (III) for the purpose of intercepting a tax refund due an individual under authority granted by section 404(e), 464, or 1137 of the Social Security Act; or (IV) for the purpose of intercepting a tax refund due an individual under any other tax refund intercept program authorized by statute which has been determined by the Director of the Office of Management and Budget to contain verification, notice, and hearing requirements that are substantially similar to the procedures in section 1137 of the Social Security Act;

(v) matches—

(I) using records predominantly relating to Federal personnel, that are performed for routine administrative purposes (subject to guidance provided by the Director of the Office of Management and Budget pursuant to subsection (v)); or

(II) conducted by an agency using only records from systems of records maintained by that agency; if the purpose of the match is not to take any adverse financial, personnel, disciplinary, or other adverse action against Federal personnel;

(vi) matches performed for foreign counterintelligence purposes or to produce background checks for security clearances of Federal personnel or Federal contractor personnel; or

(vii) matches performed incident to a levy described in section 6103(k)(8) of the Internal Revenue Code of 1986;

(9) the term "recipient agency" means any agency, or contractor thereof, receiving records contained in a system of records from a source agency for use in a matching program;

(10) the term "non-Federal agency" means any State or local government, or agency thereof, which receives records contained in a system of records from a source agency for use in a matching program;

(11) the term "source agency" means any agency which discloses records contained in a system of records to be used in a matching program, or any State or local government, or agency thereof, which discloses records to be used in a matching program;

(12) the term "Federal benefit program" means any program administered or funded by the Federal Government, or by any agent or State on behalf of the Federal Government, providing cash or in-kind assistance in the form of payments, grants, loans, or loan guarantees to individuals; and

(13) the term "Federal personnel" means officers and employees of the Government of the United States, members of the uniformed services (including members of the Reserve Components), individuals entitled to receive immediate or deferred retirement benefits under any retirement program of the Government of the United States (including survivor benefits).

(b) Conditions of Disclosure.—No agency shall disclose any record which is contained in a system of records by any means of communication to any person, or to another agency, except pursuant to a written request by, or with the prior written consent of, the individual to whom the record pertains, unless disclosure of the record would be—

(1) to those officers and employees of the agency which maintains the record who have a need for the record in the performance of their duties;

(2) required under section 552 of this title;

(3) for a routine use as defined in subsection (a)(7) of this section and described under subsection (e)(4)(D) of this section;

(4) to the Bureau of the Census for purposes of planning or carrying out a census or survey or related activity pursuant to the provisions of title 13;

(5) to a recipient who has provided the agency with advance adequate written assurance that the record will be used solely as a statistical research or reporting record, and the record is to be transferred in a form that is not individually identifiable;

(6) to the National Archives and Records Administration as a record which has sufficient historical or other value to warrant its continued preservation by the United States Government, or for evaluation by the Archivist of the United States or the designee of the Archivist to determine whether the record has such value;

(7) to another agency or to an instrumentality of any governmental jurisdiction within or under the control of the United States for a civil or criminal law enforcement activity if the activity is authorized by law, and if the head of the agency or instrumentality has made a written request to the agency which maintains the record specifying the particular portion desired and the law enforcement activity for which the record is sought;

(8) to a person pursuant to a showing of compelling circumstances affecting the health or safety of an individual if upon such disclosure notification is transmitted to the last known address of such individual;

(9) to either House of Congress, or, to the extent of matter within its jurisdiction, any committee or subcommittee thereof, any joint committee of Congress or subcommittee of any such joint committee;

(10) to the Comptroller General, or any of his authorized representatives, in the course of the performance of the duties of the General Accounting Office;

(11) pursuant to the order of a court of competent jurisdiction; or

(12) to a consumer reporting agency in accordance with section 3711(e) of title 31.

(c) Accounting of Certain Disclosures.—Each agency, with respect to each system of records under its control, shall—

(1) except for disclosures made under subsections (b)(1) or (b)(2) of this section, keep an accurate accounting of—

(A) the date, nature, and purpose of each disclosure of a record to any person or to another agency made under subsection (b) of this section; and

(B) the name and address of the person or agency to whom the disclosure is made;

(2) retain the accounting made under paragraph (1) of this subsection for at least five years or the life of the record, whichever is longer, after the disclosure for which the accounting is made;

(3) except for disclosures made under subsection (b)(7) of this section, make the accounting made under paragraph (1) of this subsection available to the individual named in the record at his request; and

(4) inform any person or other agency about any correction or notation of dispute made by the agency in accordance with subsection (d) of this section of any record that has been disclosed to the person or agency if an accounting of the disclosure was made.

(d) Access to Records.—Each agency that maintains a system of records shall—

(1) upon request by any individual to gain access to his record or to any information pertaining to him which is contained in the system, permit him and upon his request, a person of his own choosing to accompany him, to review the record and have a copy made of all or any portion thereof in a form comprehensible to him, except that the agency may require the individual to furnish a written statement authorizing discussion of that individual's record in the accompanying person's presence;

(2) permit the individual to request amendment of a record pertaining to him and—

(A) not later than 10 days (excluding Saturdays, Sundays, and legal public holidays) after the date of receipt of such request, acknowledge in writing such receipt; and

(B) promptly, either—

(i) make any correction of any portion thereof which the individual believes is not accurate, relevant, timely, or complete; or

(ii) inform the individual of its refusal to amend the record in accordance with his request, the reason for the refusal, the procedures established by the agency for the individual to request a review of that refusal by the head of the agency or an officer designated by the head of the agency, and the name and business address of that official;

(3) permit the individual who disagrees with the refusal of the agency to amend his record to request a review of such refusal, and not later than 30 days (excluding Saturdays, Sundays, and legal public holidays) from the date on which the individual requests such review, complete such review and make a final determination unless, for good cause shown, the head of the agency extends such 30-day period; and if, after his review, the reviewing official also refuses to amend the record in accordance with the request, permit the individual to file with the agency a concise statement setting forth the reasons for his disagreement with the refusal of the agency, and notify the individual of the provisions for judicial review of the reviewing official's determination under subsection (g)(1)(A) of this section;

(4) in any disclosure, containing information about which the individual has filed a statement of disagreement, occurring after the filing of the

statement under paragraph (3) of this subsection, clearly note any portion of the record which is disputed and provide copies of the statement and, if the agency deems it appropriate, copies of a concise statement of the reasons of the agency for not making the amendments requested, to persons or other agencies to whom the disputed record has been disclosed; and

(5) nothing in this section shall allow an individual access to any information compiled in reasonable anticipation of a civil action or proceeding.

(e) Agency Requirements.—Each agency that maintains a system of records shall—

(1) maintain in its records only such information about an individual as is relevant and necessary to accomplish a purpose of the agency required to be accomplished by statute or by executive order of the President;

(2) collect information to the greatest extent practicable directly from the subject individual when the information may result in adverse determinations about an individual's rights, benefits, and privileges under Federal programs;

(3) inform each individual whom it asks to supply information, on the form which it uses to collect the information or on a separate form that can be retained by the individual—

(A) the authority (whether granted by statute, or by executive order of the President) which authorizes the solicitation of the information and whether disclosure of such information is mandatory or voluntary;

(B) the principal purpose or purposes for which the information is intended to be used;

(C) the routine uses which may be made of the information, as published pursuant to paragraph (4)(D) of this subsection; and

(D) the effects on him, if any, of not providing all or any part of the requested information;

(4) subject to the provisions of paragraph (11) of this subsection, publish in the Federal Register upon establishment or revision a notice of the existence and character of the system of records, which notice shall include—

(A) the name and location of the system;

(B) the categories of individuals on whom records are maintained in the system;

(C) the categories of records maintained in the system;

(D) each routine use of the records contained in the system, including the categories of users and the purpose of such use;

(E) the policies and practices of the agency regarding storage, retrievability, access controls, retention, and disposal of the records;

(F) the title and business address of the agency official who is responsible for the system of records;

(G) the agency procedures whereby an individual can be notified at his request if the system of records contains a record pertaining to him;

(H) the agency procedures whereby an individual can be notified at his request how he can gain access to any record pertaining to him contained in the system of records, and how he can contest its content; and

(I) the categories of sources of records in the system;

(5) maintain all records which are used by the agency in making any determination about any individual with such accuracy, relevance, timeliness, and completeness as is reasonably necessary to assure fairness to the individual in the determination;

(6) prior to disseminating any record about an individual to any person other than an agency, unless the dissemination is made pursuant to subsection (b)(2) of this section, make reasonable efforts to assure that such records are accurate, complete, timely, and relevant for agency purposes;

(7) maintain no record describing how any individual exercises rights guaranteed by the First Amendment unless expressly authorized by statute or by the individual about whom the record is maintained or unless pertinent to and within the scope of an authorized law enforcement activity;

(8) make reasonable efforts to serve notice on an individual when any record on such individual is made available to any person under compulsory legal process when such process becomes a matter of public record;

(9) establish rules of conduct for persons involved in the design, development, operation, or maintenance of any system of records, or in maintaining any record, and instruct each such person with respect to such rules and the requirements of this section, including any other rules and procedures adopted pursuant to this section and the penalties for noncompliance;

(10) establish appropriate administrative, technical, and physical safeguards to insure the security and confidentiality of records and to protect against any anticipated threats or hazards to their security or integrity which could result in substantial harm, embarrassment, inconvenience, or unfairness to any individual on whom information is maintained;

(11) at least 30 days prior to publication of information under paragraph (4)(D) of this subsection, publish in the Federal Register notice of any new use or intended use of the information in the system, and provide an opportunity for interested persons to submit written data, views, or arguments to the agency; and

(12) if such agency is a recipient agency or a source agency in a matching program with a non-Federal agency, with respect to any establishment or revision of a matching program, at least 30 days prior to conducting such program, publish in the Federal Register notice of such establishment or revision.

(f) Agency Rules.—In order to carry out the provisions of this section, each agency that maintains a system of records shall promulgate rules, in accordance with the requirements (including general notice) of section 553 of this title, which shall—

(1) establish procedures whereby an individual can be notified in response to his request if any system of records named by the individual contains a record pertaining to him;

(2) define reasonable times, places, and requirements for identifying an individual who requests his record or information pertaining to him before the agency shall make the record or information available to the individual;

(3) establish procedures for the disclosure to an individual upon his request of his record or information pertaining to him, including special procedure, if deemed necessary, for the disclosure to an individual of medical records, including psychological records, pertaining to him;

(4) establish procedures for reviewing a request from an individual concerning the amendment of any record or information pertaining to the individual, for making a determination on the request, for an appeal within the agency of an initial adverse agency determination, and for whatever additional means may be necessary for each individual to be able to exercise fully his rights under this section; and

(5) establish fees to be charged, if any, to any individual for making copies of his record, excluding the cost of any search for and review of the record.

The Office of the Federal Register shall biennially compile and publish the rules promulgated under this subsection and agency notices published under subsection (e)(4) of this section in a form available to the public at low cost.

(g)(1) Civil Remedies.—Whenever any agency

(A) makes a determination under subsection (d)(3) of this section not to amend an individual's record in accordance with his request, or fails to make such review in conformity with that subsection;

(B) refuses to comply with an individual request under subsection (d)(1) of this section;

(C) fails to maintain any record concerning any individual with such accuracy, relevance, timeliness, and completeness as is necessary to assure fairness in any determination relating to the qualifications, character, rights, or opportunities of, or benefits to the individual that may be made on the basis of such record, and consequently a determination is made which is adverse to the individual; or

(D) fails to comply with any other provision of this section, or any rule promulgated thereunder, in such a way as to have an adverse effect on an individual, the individual may bring a civil action against the agency, and the district courts of the United States shall have jurisdiction in the matters under the provisions of this subsection.

(2)(A) In any suit brought under the provisions of subsection (g)(1)(A) of this section, the court may order the agency to amend the individual's record in accordance with his request or in such other way as the court may direct. In such a case the court shall determine the matter de novo.

(B) The court may assess against the United States reasonable attorney fees and other litigation costs reasonably incurred in any case under this paragraph in which the complainant has substantially prevailed.

(3) (A) In any suit brought under the provisions of subsection (g)(1)(B) of this section, the court may enjoin the agency from withholding the records and order the production to the complainant of any agency records improperly withheld from him. In such a case the court shall determine the matter de novo, and may examine the contents of any agency records in camera to determine whether the records or any portion thereof may be withheld under any of the exemptions set forth in subsection (k) of this section, and the burden is on the agency to sustain its action.

(B) The court may assess against the United States reasonable attorney fees and other litigation costs reasonably incurred in any case under this paragraph in which the complainant has substantially prevailed.

(4) In any suit brought under the provisions of subsection (g)(1)(C) or (D) of this section in which the court determines that the agency acted in a manner which was intentional or willful, the United States shall be liable to the individual in an amount equal to the sum of—

(A) actual damages sustained by the individual as a result of the refusal or failure, but in no case shall a person entitled to recovery receive less than the sum of $1,000; and

(B) the costs of the action together with reasonable attorney fees as determined by the court.

(5) An action to enforce any liability created under this section may be brought in the district court of the United States in the district in which the complainant resides, or has his principal place of business, or in which the agency records are situated, or in the District of Columbia, without regard to the amount in controversy, within two years from the date on which the cause of action arises, except that where an agency has materially and willfully misrepresented any information required under this section to be disclosed to an individual and the information so misrepresented is material to establishment of the liability of the agency to the individual under this section, the action may be brought at any time within two years after discovery by the individual of the misrepresentation. Nothing in this section shall be construed to authorize any civil action by reason of any

injury sustained as the result of a disclosure of a record prior to September 27, 1975.

(h) Rights of Legal Guardians.—For the purposes of this section, the parent of any minor, or the legal guardian of any individual who has been declared to be incompetent due to physical or mental incapacity or age by a court of competent jurisdiction, may act on behalf of the individual.

(i)(1) Criminal Penalties.—Any officer or employee of an agency, who by virtue of his employment or official position, has possession of, or access to, agency records which contain individually identifiable information the disclosure of which is prohibited by this section or by rules or regulations established thereunder, and who knowing that disclosure of the specific material is so prohibited, willfully discloses the material in any manner to any person or agency not entitled to receive it, shall be guilty of a misdemeanor and fined not more than $5,000.

(2) Any officer or employee of any agency who willfully maintains a system of records without meeting the notice requirements of subsection (e)(4) of this section shall be guilty of a misdemeanor and fined not more than $5,000.

(3) Any person who knowingly and willfully requests or obtains any record concerning an individual from an agency under false pretenses shall be guilty of a misdemeanor and fined not more than $5,000.

(j) General Exemptions.—The head of any agency may promulgate rules, in accordance with the requirements (including general notice) of sections 553(b)(1), (2), and (3), (c), and (e) of this title, to exempt any system of records within the agency from any part of this section except subsections (b), (c)(1) and (2), (e)(4)(A) through (F), (e)(6), (7), (9), (10), and (11), and (i) if the system of records is—

(1) maintained by the Central Intelligence Agency; or

(2) maintained by an agency or component thereof which performs as its principal function any activity pertaining to the enforcement of criminal laws, including police efforts to prevent, control, or reduce crime or to apprehend criminals, and the activities of prosecutors, courts, correctional, probation, pardon, or parole authorities, and which consists of (A) information compiled for the purpose of identifying individual criminal offenders and alleged offenders and consisting only of identifying data and notations of arrests, the nature and disposition of criminal charges, sentencing, confinement, release, and parole and probation status; (B) information compiled for the purpose of a criminal investigation, including reports of informants and investigators, and associated with an identifiable individual; or (C) reports identifiable to an individual compiled at any stage of the process of enforcement of the criminal laws from arrest or indictment through release from supervision.

Appexdix C

At the time rules are adopted under this subsection, the agency shall include in the statement required under section 553(c) of this title, the reasons why the system of records is to be exempted from a provision of this section.

(k) Specific Exemptions.—The head of any agency may promulgate rules, in accordance with the requirements (including general notice) of sections 553(b)(1), (2), and (3), (c), and (e) of this title, to exempt any system of records within the agency from subsections (c)(3), (d), (e)(1), (e)(4)(G), (H), and (I) and (f) of this section if the system of records is—

(1) subject to the provisions of section 552(b)(1) of this title;

(2) investigatory material compiled for law enforcement purposes, other than material within the scope of subsection (j)(2) of this section: Provided, however, That if any individual is denied any right, privilege, or benefit that he would otherwise be entitled by Federal law, or for which he would otherwise be eligible, as a result of the maintenance of such material, such material shall be provided to such individual, except to the extent that the disclosure of such material would reveal the identity of a source who furnished information to the Government under an express promise that the identity of the source would be held in confidence, or, prior to the effective date of this section, under an implied promise that the identity of the source would be held in confidence;

(3) maintained in connection with providing protective services to the President of the United States or other individuals pursuant to section 3056 of title 18;

(4) required by statute to be maintained and used solely as statistical records;

(5) investigatory material compiled solely for the purpose of determining suitability, eligibility, or qualifications for Federal civilian employment, military service, Federal contracts, or access to classified information, but only to the extent that the disclosure of such material would reveal the identity of a source who furnished information to the Government under an express promise that the identity of the source would be held in confidence, or, prior to the effective date of this section, under an implied promise that the identity of the source would be held in confidence;

(6) testing or examination material used solely to determine individual qualifications for appointment or promotion in the Federal service the disclosure of which would compromise the objectivity or fairness of the testing or examination process; or

(7) evaluation material used to determine potential for promotion in the armed services, but only to the extent that the disclosure of such material would reveal the identity of a source who furnished information to the Government under an express promise that the identity of the source would

be held in confidence, or, prior to the effective date of this section, under an implied promise that the identity of the source would be held in confidence.

(1) At the time rules are adopted under this subsection, the agency shall include in the statement required under section 553(c) of this title, the reasons why the system of records is to be exempted from a provision of this section.

(1) Archival Records.—Each agency record which is accepted by the Archivist of the United States for storage, processing, and servicing in accordance with section 3103 of title 44 shall, for the purposes of this section, be considered to be maintained by the agency which deposited the record and shall be subject to the provisions of this section. The Archivist of the United States shall not disclose the record except to the agency which maintains the record, or under rules established by that agency which are not inconsistent with the provisions of this section.

(2) Each agency record pertaining to an identifiable individual which was transferred to the National Archives of the United States as a record which has sufficient historical or other value to warrant its continued preservation by the United States Government, prior to the effective date of this section, shall, for the purposes of this section, be considered to be maintained by the National Archives and shall not be subject to the provisions of this section, except that a statement generally describing such records (modeled after the requirements relating to records subject to subsections (e)(4)(A) through (G) of this section) shall be published in the Federal Register.

(3) Each agency record pertaining to an identifiable individual which is transferred to the National Archives of the United States as a record which has sufficient historical or other value to warrant its continued preservation by the United States Government, on or after the effective date of this section, shall, for the purposes of this section, be considered to be maintained by the National Archives and shall be exempt from the requirements of this section except subsections (e)(4)(A) through (G) and (e)(9) of this section.

(m)(1) Government Contractors.—When an agency provides by a contract for the operation by or on behalf of the agency of a system of records to accomplish an agency function, the agency shall, consistent with its authority, cause the requirements of this section to be applied to such system. For purposes of subsection (i) of this section any such contractor and any employee of such contractor, if such contract is agreed to on or after the effective date of this section, shall be considered to be an employee of an agency.

(2) A consumer reporting agency to which a record is disclosed under section 3711(e) of title 31 shall not be considered a contractor for the purposes of this section.

(n) Mailing Lists.—An individual's name and address may not be sold or rented by an agency unless such action is specifically authorized by law. This provision shall not be construed to require the withholding of names and addresses otherwise permitted to be made public.

(o) Matching Agreements.—(1) No record which is contained in a system of records may be disclosed to a recipient agency or non-Federal agency for use in a computer matching program except pursuant to a written agreement between the source agency and the recipient agency or non-Federal agency specifying—

(A) the purpose and legal authority for conducting the program;

(B) the justification for the program and the anticipated results, including a specific estimate of any savings;

(C) a description of the records that will be matched, including each data element that will be used, the approximate number of records that will be matched, and the projected starting and completion dates of the matching program;

(D) procedures for providing individualized notice at the time of application, and notice periodically thereafter as directed by the Data Integrity Board of such agency (subject to guidance provided by the Director of the Office of Management and Budget pursuant to subsection (v)), to—

(i) applicants for and recipients of financial assistance or payments under Federal benefit programs, and

(ii) applicants for and holders of positions as Federal personnel,

that any information provided by such applicants, recipients, holders, and individuals may be subject to verification through matching programs;

(E) procedures for verifying information produced in such matching program as required by subsection (p);

(F) procedures for the retention and timely destruction of identifiable records created by a recipient agency or non-Federal agency in such matching program;

(G) procedures for ensuring the administrative, technical, and physical security of the records matched and the results of such programs;

(H) prohibitions on duplication and redisclosure of records provided by the source agency within or outside the recipient agency or the non-Federal agency, except where required by law or essential to the conduct of the matching program;

(I) procedures governing the use by a recipient agency or non-Federal agency of records provided in a matching program by a source agency, including procedures governing return of the records to the source agency or destruction of records used in such program;

(J) information on assessments that have been made on the accuracy of the records that will be used in such matching program; and

(K) that the Comptroller General may have access to all records of a recipient agency or a non-Federal agency that the Comptroller General deems necessary in order to monitor or verify compliance with the agreement.

(2)(A) A copy of each agreement entered into pursuant to paragraph (1) shall—

(i) be transmitted to the Committee on Governmental Affairs of the Senate and the Committee on Government Operations of the House of Representatives; and

(ii) be available upon request to the public.

(B) No such agreement shall be effective until 30 days after the date on which such a copy is transmitted pursuant to subparagraph (A)(i).

(C) Such an agreement shall remain in effect only for such period, not to exceed 18 months, as the Data Integrity Board of the agency determines is appropriate in light of the purposes, and length of time necessary for the conduct, of the matching program.

(D) Within 3 months prior to the expiration of such an agreement pursuant to subparagraph (C), the Data Integrity Board of the agency may, without additional review, renew the matching agreement for a current, ongoing matching program for not more than one additional year if—

(i) such program will be conducted without any change; and

(ii) each party to the agreement certifies to the Board in writing that the program has been conducted in compliance with the agreement.

(p) Verification and Opportunity to Contest Findings.—(1) In order to protect any individual whose records are used in a matching program, no recipient agency, non-Federal agency, or source agency may suspend, terminate, reduce, or make a final denial of any financial assistance or payment under a Federal benefit program to such individual, or take other adverse action against such individual, as a result of information produced by such matching program, until—

(A)(i) the agency has independently verified the information; or

(ii) the Data Integrity Board of the agency, or in the case of a non-Federal agency the Data Integrity Board of the source agency, determines in accordance with guidance issued by the Director of the Office of Management and Budget that—

(I) the information is limited to identification and amount of benefits paid by the source agency under a Federal benefit program; and

(II) there is a high degree of confidence that the information provided to the recipient agency is accurate;

(B) the individual receives a notice from the agency containing a statement of its findings and informing the individual of the opportunity to contest such findings; and

(C)(i) the expiration of any time period established for the program by statute or regulation for the individual to respond to that notice; or

(ii) in the case of a program for which no such period is established, the end of the 30-day period beginning on the date on which notice under subparagraph (B) is mailed or otherwise provided to the individual.

(2) Independent verification referred to in paragraph (1) requires investigation and confirmation of specific information relating to an individual that is used as a basis for an adverse action against the individual, including where applicable investigation and confirmation of—

(A) the amount of any asset or income involved;

(B) whether such individual actually has or had access to such asset or income for such individual's own use; and

(C) the period or periods when the individual actually had such asset or income.

(3) Notwithstanding paragraph (1), an agency may take any appropriate action otherwise prohibited by such paragraph if the agency determines that the public health or public safety may be adversely affected or significantly threatened during any notice period required by such paragraph.

(q) Sanctions.—(1) Notwithstanding any other provisions of law, no source agency may disclose any record which is contained in a system of records to a recipient agency or non-Federal agency for a matching program if such source agency has reason to believe that the requirements of subsection (p), or any matching agreement entered into pursuant to subsection (o), or both, are not being met by such recipient agency.

(2) No source agency may renew a matching agreement unless—

(A) the recipient agency or non-Federal agency has certified that it has complied with the provisions of that agreement; and

(B) the source agency has no reason to believe that the certification is inaccurate.

(r) Report on New Systems and Matching Programs.—Each agency that proposes to establish or make a significant change in a system of records or a matching program shall provide adequate advance notice of any such proposal (in duplicate) to the Committee on Government Operations of the House of Representatives, the Committee on Governmental Affairs of the Senate, and the Office of Management and Budget in order to permit an evaluation of the probable or potential effect of such proposal on the *privacy* or other rights of individuals.

(s) Biennial Report.—The President shall biennially submit to the Speaker of the House of Representatives and the President pro tempore of the Senate a report—

(1) describing the actions of the Director of the Office of Management and Budget pursuant to section 6 of the Privacy Act of 1974 during the preceding 2 years;

(2) describing the exercise of individual rights of access and amendment under this section during such years;

(3) identifying changes in or additions to systems of records;

(4) containing such other information concerning administration of this section as may be necessary or useful to the Congress in reviewing the effectiveness of this section in carrying out the purposes of the Privacy Act of 1974.

(t)(1) Effect of Other Laws.—No agency shall rely on any exemption contained in section 552 of this title to withhold from an individual any record which is otherwise accessible to such individual under the provisions of this section.

(2) No agency shall rely on any exemption in this section to withhold from an individual any record which is otherwise accessible to such individual under the provisions of section 552 of this title.

(u) Data Integrity Boards.—(1) Every agency conducting or participating in a matching program shall establish a Data Integrity Board to oversee and coordinate among the various components of such agency the agency's implementation of this section.

(2) Each Data Integrity Board shall consist of senior officials designated by the head of the agency, and shall include any senior official designated by the head of the agency as responsible for implementation of this section, and the inspector general of the agency, if any. The inspector general shall not serve as chairman of the Data Integrity Board.

(3) Each Data Integrity Board—

(A) shall review, approve, and maintain all written agreements for receipt or disclosure of agency records for matching programs to ensure compliance with subsection (o), and all relevant statutes, regulations, and guidelines;

(B) shall review all matching programs in which the agency has participated during the year, either as a source agency or recipient agency, determine compliance with applicable laws, regulations, guidelines, and agency agreements, and assess the costs and benefits of such programs;

(C) shall review all recurring matching programs in which the agency has participated during the year, either as a source agency or recipient agency, for continued justification for such disclosures;

(D) shall compile an annual report, which shall be submitted to the head of the agency and the Office of Management and Budget and made available to the public on request, describing the matching activities of the agency, including—

(i) matching programs in which the agency has participated as a source agency or recipient agency;

(ii) matching agreements proposed under subsection (o) that were disapproved by the Board;

(iii) any changes in membership or structure of the Board in the preceding year;

(iv) the reasons for any waiver of the requirement in paragraph (4) of this section for completion and submission of a cost-benefit analysis prior to the approval of a matching program;

(v) any violations of matching agreements that have been alleged or identified and any corrective action taken; and

(vi) any other information required by the Director of the Office of Management and Budget to be included in such report;

(E) shall serve as a clearinghouse for receiving and providing information on the accuracy, completeness, and reliability of records used in matching programs;

(F) shall provide interpretation and guidance to agency components and personnel on the requirements of this section for matching programs;

(G) shall review agency recordkeeping and disposal policies and practices for matching programs to assure compliance with this section; and

(H) may review and report on any agency matching activities that are not matching programs.

(4)(A) Except as provided in subparagraphs (B) and (C), a Data Integrity Board shall not approve any written agreement for a matching program unless the agency has completed and submitted to such Board a cost-benefit analysis of the proposed program and such analysis demonstrates that the program is likely to be cost effective. (FOOTNOTE 2)

(FOOTNOTE 2) So in original. Probably should be "cost-effective."

(B) The Board may waive the requirements of subparagraph (A) of this paragraph if it determines in writing, in accordance with guidelines prescribed by the Director of the Office of Management and Budget, that a cost-benefit analysis is not required.

(C) A cost-benefit analysis shall not be required under subparagraph (A) prior to the initial approval of a written agreement for a matching program that is specifically required by statute. Any subsequent written agreement for such a program shall not be approved by the Data Integrity Board unless the agency has submitted a cost-benefit analysis of the program as conducted under the preceding approval of such agreement.

(5)(A) If a matching agreement is disapproved by a Data Integrity Board, any party to such agreement may appeal the disapproval to the Director of the

Office of Management and Budget. Timely notice of the filing of such an appeal shall be provided by the Director of the Office of Management and Budget to the Committee on Governmental Affairs of the Senate and the Committee on Government Operations of the House of Representatives.

(B) The Director of the Office of Management and Budget may approve a matching agreement notwithstanding the disapproval of a Data Integrity Board if the Director determines that—

(i) the matching program will be consistent with all applicable legal, regulatory, and policy requirements;

(ii) there is adequate evidence that the matching agreement will be cost-effective; and

(iii) the matching program is in the public interest.

(C) The decision of the Director to approve a matching agreement shall not take effect until 30 days after it is reported to committees described in subparagraph (A).

(D) If the Data Integrity Board and the Director of the Office of Management and Budget disapprove a matching program proposed by the inspector general of an agency, the inspector general may report the disapproval to the head of the agency and to the Congress.

(6) The Director of the Office of Management and Budget shall, annually during the first 3 years after the date of enactment of this subsection and biennially thereafter, consolidate in a report to the Congress the information contained in the reports from the various Data Integrity Boards under paragraph (3)(D). Such report shall include detailed information about costs and benefits of matching programs that are conducted during the period covered by such consolidated report, and shall identify each waiver granted by a Data Integrity Board of the requirement for completion and submission of a cost-benefit analysis and the reasons for granting the waiver.

(7) In the reports required by paragraphs (3)(D) and (6), agency matching activities that are not matching programs may be reported on an aggregate basis, if and to the extent necessary to protect ongoing law enforcement or counterintelligence investigations.

(v) Office of Management and Budget Responsibilities.—The Director of the Office of Management and Budget shall—

(1) develop and, after notice and opportunity for public comment, pre-scribe guidelines and regulations for the use of agencies in implementing the provisions of this section; and

(2) provide continuing assistance to and oversight of the implementation of this section by agencies.

[Footnotes omitted]

APPENDIX D

FAIR CREDIT REPORTING ACT

-CITE-
15 USC Sec. 1681
-EXPCITE-
TITLE 15—COMMERCE AND TRADE
CHAPTER 41—CONSUMER CREDIT PROTECTION
SUBCHAPTER III—CREDIT REPORTING AGENCIES
-HEAD-
Sec. 1681. Congressional findings and statement of purpose
-STATUTE-

(a) Accuracy and fairness of credit reporting
The Congress makes the following findings:

(1) The banking system is dependent upon fair and accurate credit reporting. Inaccurate credit reports directly impair the efficiency of the banking system, and unfair credit reporting methods undermine the public confidence which is essential to the continued functioning of the banking system.

(2) An elaborate mechanism has been developed for investigating and evaluating the credit worthiness, (FOOTNOTE 1) credit standing, credit capacity, character, and general reputation of consumers.

(FOOTNOTE 1) So in original. Probably should be "creditworthiness,".

(3) Consumer reporting agencies have assumed a vital role in assembling and evaluating consumer credit and other information on consumers.

(4) There is a need to insure that consumer reporting agencies exercise their grave responsibilities with fairness, impartiality, and a respect for the consumer's right to privacy.

(b) Reasonable procedures
It is the purpose of this subchapter to require that consumer reporting agencies adopt reasonable procedures for meeting the needs of commerce for consumer credit, personnel, insurance, and other information in a manner

which is fair and equitable to the consumer, with regard to the confidentiality, accuracy, relevancy, and proper utilization of such information in accordance with the requirements of this subchapter.
-SOURCE-
(Pub. L. 90–321, title VI, Sec. 602, as added Pub. L. 91–508, title VI, Sec. 601, Oct. 26, 1970, 84 Stat. 1128.)
-MISC1-

EFFECTIVE DATE

Section 504(d) of Pub. L. 90–321, as added by Pub. L. 91–508, title VI, Sec. 602, Oct. 26, 1970, 84 Stat. 1136, provided that: "Title VI (enacting this subchapter) takes effect upon the expiration of one hundred and eighty days following the date of its enactment (Oct. 26, 1970)."

SHORT TITLE

This subchapter known as the "Fair Credit Reporting Act", see Short Title note set out under section 1601 of this title.
-CITE-
15 USC Sec. 1681a
-EXPCITE-
TITLE 15—COMMERCE AND TRADE
CHAPTER 41—CONSUMER CREDIT PROTECTION
SUBCHAPTER III—CREDIT REPORTING AGENCIES
-HEAD-
Sec. 1681a. Definitions; rules of construction
-STATUTE-

(a) Definitions and rules of construction set forth in this section are applicable for the purposes of this subchapter.

(b) The term "person" means any individual, partnership, corporation, trust, estate, cooperative, association, government or governmental subdivision or agency, or other entity.

(c) The term "consumer" means an individual.

(d) Consumer Report.—

    (1) In general.—The term "consumer report" means any written, oral, or other communication of any information by a consumer reporting agency bearing on a consumer's credit worthiness, (FOOTNOTE 1) credit standing, credit capacity, character, general reputation, personal characteristics,

or mode of living which is used or expected to be used or collected in whole or in part for the purpose of serving as a factor in establishing the consumer's eligibility for—

(FOOTNOTE 1) So in original. Probably should be "creditworthiness,".

(A) credit or insurance to be used primarily for personal, family, or household purposes;

(B) employment purposes; or

(C) any other purpose authorized under section 1681b of this title.

(2) Exclusions.—The term "consumer report" does not include—

(A) any—

(i) report containing information solely as to transactions or experiences between the consumer and the person making the report;

(ii) communication of that information among persons related by common ownership or affiliated by corporate control; or

(iii) any communication of other information among persons related by common ownership or affiliated by corporate control, if it is clearly and conspicuously disclosed to the consumer that the information may be communicated among such persons and the consumer is given the opportunity, before the time that the information is initially communicated, to direct that such information not be communicated among such persons;

(B) any authorization or approval of a specific extension of credit directly or indirectly by the issuer of a credit card or similar device;

(C) any report in which a person who has been requested by a third party to make a specific extension of credit directly or indirectly to a consumer conveys his or her decision with respect to such request, if the third party advises the consumer of the name and address of the person to whom the request was made, and such person makes the disclosures to the consumer required under section 1681m of this title; or

(D) a communication described in subsection (o) of this section.

(e) The term "investigative consumer report" means a consumer report or portion thereof in which information on a consumer's character, general reputation, personal characteristics, or mode of living is obtained through personal interviews with neighbors, friends, or associates of the consumer reported on or with others with whom he is acquainted or who may have knowledge concerning any such items of information. However, such information shall not include specific factual information on a consumer's credit record obtained directly from a creditor of the consumer or from a consumer reporting agency when such information was obtained directly from a creditor of the consumer or from the consumer.

(f) The term "consumer reporting agency" means any person which, for monetary fees, dues, or on a cooperative nonprofit basis, regularly engages in whole or in part in the practice of assembling or evaluating consumer credit information or other information on consumers for the purpose of furnishing consumer reports to third parties, and which uses any means or facility of interstate commerce for the purpose of preparing or furnishing consumer reports.

(g) The term "file", when used in connection with information on any consumer, means all of the information on that consumer recorded and retained by a consumer reporting agency regardless of how the information is stored.

(h) The term "employment purposes" when used in connection with a consumer report means a report used for the purpose of evaluating a consumer for employment, promotion, reassignment or retention as an employee.

> (i) The term "medical information" means information or records obtained, with the consent of the individual to whom it relates, from licensed physicians or medical practitioners, hospitals, clinics, or other medical or medically related facilities.

(j) Definitions Relating to Child Support Obligations.—

> (1) Overdue support.—The term "overdue support" has the meaning given to such term in section 666(e) of title 42.

> (2) State or local child support enforcement agency.—The term "State or local child support enforcement agency" means a State or local agency which administers a State or local program for establishing and enforcing child support obligations.

(k) Adverse Action.—

> (1) Actions included.—The term "adverse action"—
>
> (A) has the same meaning as in section 1691(d)(6) of this title; and
>
> (B) means—
>
> > (i) a denial or cancellation of, an increase in any charge for, or a reduction or other adverse or unfavorable change in the terms of coverage or amount of, any insurance, existing or applied for, in connection with the underwriting of insurance;
> >
> > (ii) a denial of employment or any other decision for employment purposes that adversely affects any current or prospective employee;
> >
> > (iii) a denial or cancellation of, an increase in any charge for, or any other adverse or unfavorable change in the terms of, any license or benefit described in section 1681b(a)(3)(D) of this title; and
> >
> > (iv) an action taken or determination that is—
> >
> > > (I) made in connection with an application that was made by, or a transaction that was initiated by, any consumer, or in connection with a review of an account under section 1681b(a)(3)(F)(ii) of this title; and
> > >
> > > (II) adverse to the interests of the consumer.

Appendix D

(2) Applicable findings, decisions, commentary, and orders.—

For purposes of any determination of whether an action is an adverse action under paragraph (1)(A), all appropriate final findings, decisions, commentary, and orders issued under section 1691(d)(6) of this title by the Board of Governors of the Federal Reserve System or any court shall apply.

(1) Firm Offer of Credit or Insurance.—The term "firm offer of credit or insurance" means any offer of credit or insurance to a consumer that will be honored if the consumer is determined, based on information in a consumer report on the consumer, to meet the specific criteria used to select the consumer for the offer, except that the offer may be further conditioned on one or more of the following:

(1) The consumer being determined, based on information in the consumer's application for the credit or insurance, to meet specific criteria bearing on credit worthiness (FOOTNOTE 2) or insurability, as applicable, that are established—

(FOOTNOTE 2) So in original. Probably should be "creditworthiness".

(A) before selection of the consumer for the offer; and

(B) for the purpose of determining whether to extend credit or insurance pursuant to the offer.

(2) Verification—

(A) that the consumer continues to meet the specific criteria used to select the consumer for the offer, by using information in a consumer report on the consumer, information in the consumer's application for the credit or insurance, or other information bearing on the credit worthiness (FOOTNOTE 2) or insurability of the consumer; or

(B) of the information in the consumer's application for the credit or insurance, to determine that the consumer meets the specific criteria bearing on credit worthiness (FOOTNOTE 2) or insurability.

(3) The consumer furnishing any collateral that is a requirement for the extension of the credit or insurance that was—

(A) established before selection of the consumer for the offer of credit or insurance; and

(B) disclosed to the consumer in the offer of credit or insurance.

(m) Credit or Insurance Transaction That Is Not Initiated by the Consumer.—The term "credit or insurance transaction that is not initiated by the consumer" does not include the use of a consumer report by a person with which the consumer has an account or insurance policy, for purposes of—

(1) reviewing the account or insurance policy; or

(2) collecting the account.

(n) State.—The term "State" means any State, the Commonwealth of Puerto Rico, the District of Columbia, and any territory or possession of the United States.

(o) Excluded Communications.—A communication is described in this subsection if it is a communication—

(1) that, but for subsection (d)(2)(E) of this section, would be an investigative consumer report;

(2) that is made to a prospective employer for the purpose of—

(A) procuring an employee for the employer; or

(B) procuring an opportunity for a natural person to work for the employer;

(3) that is made by a person who regularly performs such procurement;

(4) that is not used by any person for any purpose other than a purpose described in subparagraph (A) or (B) of paragraph (2); or

(5) with respect to which—

(A) the consumer who is the subject of the communication—

(i) consents orally or in writing to the nature and scope of the communication, before the collection of any information for the purpose of making the communication;

(ii) consents orally or in writing to the making of the communication to a prospective employer, before the making of the communication; and

(iii) in the case of consent under clause (i) or (ii) given orally, is provided written confirmation of that consent by the person making the communication, not later than 3 business days after the receipt of the consent by that person;

(B) the person who makes the communication does not, for the purpose of making the communication, make any inquiry that if made by a prospective employer of the consumer who is the subject of the communication would violate any applicable Federal or State equal employment opportunity law or regulation; and

(C) the person who makes the communication—

(i) discloses in writing to the consumer who is the subject of the communication, not later than 5 business days after receiving any request from the consumer for such disclosure, the nature and substance of all information in the consumer's file at the time of the request, except that the sources of any information that is acquired solely for use in making the communication and is actually used for no other purpose, need not be disclosed other than under appropriate discovery procedures in any court of competent jurisdiction in which an action is brought; and

(ii) notifies the consumer who is the subject of the communication, in writing, of the consumer's right to request the information described in clause (i).

(p) Consumer Reporting Agency That Compiles and Maintains Files on Consumers on a Nationwide Basis.—The term "consumer reporting agency that compiles and maintains files on consumers on a nationwide basis" means a consumer reporting agency that regularly engages in the practice of assembling or evaluating, and maintaining, for the purpose of furnishing consumer reports to third parties bearing on a consumer's credit worthiness, (FOOTNOTE 3) credit standing, or credit capacity, each of the following regarding consumers residing nationwide:

(FOOTNOTE 3) So in original. Probably should be "creditworthiness,".

(1) Public record information.

(2) Credit account information from persons who furnish that information regularly and in the ordinary course of business.

INDEX

Index

249

Index

Index

Index

Index

Index

Index